Building for Oil

HARVARD-YENCHING INSTITUTE MONOGRAPH SERIES 110

Building for Oil

Daqing and the Formation of the Chinese Socialist State

Hou Li

Published by the Harvard University Asia Center
Distributed by Harvard University Press
Cambridge (Massachusetts) and London 2021

© 2018, 2021 by the President and Fellows of Harvard College
Printed in the United States of America

The Harvard-Yenching Institute, founded in 1928, is an independent foundation dedicated to the advancement of higher education in the humanities and social sciences in Asia. Headquartered on the campus of Harvard University, the Institute provides fellowships for advanced research, training, and graduate studies at Harvard by competitively selected faculty and graduate students from Asia. The Institute also supports a range of academic activities at its fifty partner universities and research institutes across Asia. At Harvard, the Institute promotes East Asian studies through annual contributions to the Harvard-Yenching Library and publication of the *Harvard Journal of Asiatic Studies* and the Harvard-Yenching Institute Monograph Series.

Library of Congress Cataloging-in-Publication Data

Names: Hou, Li, 1973– author.
Title: Building for oil : Daqing and the formation of the Chinese socialist state / Li Hou.
Other titles: Harvard-Yenching Institute monograph series ; 110.
Description: Cambridge, Massachusetts : Published by the Harvard University Asia Center, 2018. | Series: Harvard-Yenching Institute monograph series ; 110 | Includes bibliographical references and index.
Identifiers: LCCN 2017029370 | ISBN 9780674983816 (hardcover : alk. paper) ISBN 9780674260221 (pbk : alk. paper)
Subjects: LCSH: Daqing (Heilongjiang Sheng, China)—History. | Regional planning—China—Daqing (Heilongjiang Sheng)—History. | Industrialization—China—Daqing (Heilongjiang Sheng)—History. | Petroleum industry and trade—China—Daqing (Heilongjiang Sheng)— History. | Petroleum workers—China—Daqing (Heilongjiang Sheng)—Social conditions. | China—Social conditions—1949–

Classification: LCC HT395.C6 H68 2018 | DDC 307.1/2095184—dc23 LC record available at https://lccn.loc.gov/2017029370

Index by Alexander Trotter
First paperback edition 2021
♾ Printed on acid-free paper

Last figure below indicates year of this printing
27 26 25 24 23 22 21

To Peter

Contents

List of Maps and Figures

Maps

Figures

Acknowledgments

Writing a book is often a very solitary pursuit. Fortunately, I never felt that I was entirely on my own. More than ten years have passed since I started this research, which marks a long phase in my life. During this period I have encountered enormous kindness and encouragement, as well as intellectual and spiritual support. One of the distinctive features of this book is that I've interwoven a female urban planner's experiences into the national narrative of planning and construction. I have also woven this work deeply into my life. It has connected me with my parents' generation and helped me sort out the life path I would like to pursue. The process of writing has indeed changed me. It has helped me to become stronger, more confident, more resilient, and a more sensible human being. In completing this book, I have accumulated a debt of gratitude to many more people than the limited number I can mention here.

My first and foremost thanks go to my mentor, Peter Rowe, from the Harvard University Graduate School of Design (GSD), for years of invaluable intellectual guidance, inspiration, and unfailing support. Peter served as the dean of GSD for twelve years, during which he established the doctor of design program and the exchange program with Chinese universities. These programs offered me the opportunity to begin this academic journey, and he has guided me through every step ever since. He has been so supportive and protective that I often feel pampered. But this doesn't mean he hasn't motivated me with appropriate pressure—I love his cynical tone, sarcasm, and distinctive humor. He has also provided me a model of how to gracefully balance life's many demands without straying too far from my true interests and instincts, which I have greatly benefited from. This book is dedicated to him.

I am tremendously grateful to Elizabeth Perry, a brilliant teacher, mentor, and scholar. I rely greatly on her profound scholarship on contemporary China. I am always amazed by her prompt reply whenever I seek guidance from her, either intellectually or logistically. Without her affirmation, I would not have the courage to continuously challenge myself and walk the hard road. I am still not very clear what she saw in me when we first met, but I am trying my best to catch up to what she thinks of me.

The Harvard-Yenching Institute offered generous support for my nine-month stay in Cambridge, from 2014 to 2015, during which I was able to focus on writing and research. There is no better place for writing a book about China than my office on 2 Divinity Ave; right across the hallway are Liz's office and the Harvard-Yenching Library, my sources of positive energy. During my breaks, I often gazed in awe at the portraits, photographs, calligraphy, and, most of all, those brilliant books produced by great souls, reminding us who we are and what we shall treasure. I am very thankful to Li Ruohong, Lindsay Strogatz, Susan Scott, and Elain Witham for accommodating me as part of this vibrant academic community, and to Nobuhiko Abe for bringing beautiful flowers to the library every day, creating a sweet home-like environment. My office mates, Chisako Masuo and Zhang Yuanlin, a promising political scientist and a respected art historian, respectively, brought me intellectual inspiration, laughter, and even babysitting support, beyond sharing office space.

My special thanks go to Nancy Hearst, a remarkable librarian in the Fairbank Center Fung Library and a dedicated editor for young and foreign scholars like me. She helped me first as a librarian and then as an editor. I am fortunate to have met Robert Graham, head of the Harvard Asia Center publications program, who has been so kind and professional, guiding me through the academic publishing labyrinth. Anonymous reviewers invited by the Harvard Asia Center and Routledge provided generous comments and valuable criticism. A few other brave scholars also read my entire manuscript and offered constructive advice: Kristin Stapleton, Richard Legates, and Zhu Jieming. I have presented pieces of this work on occasions too numerous to mention. I hope the many gracious scholars in the States and my colleagues at Tongji University will accept my collective thanks. I particularly benefited from the insightful commentary of June Manning Thomas, Zhao Min, Wu Zhiqiang, Li Jingsheng, and Sun Shiwen.

I have benefited over the years from extended conversations with a circle of scholarly friends and "comrades-in-pen" across different disciplines at Harvard, especially Gareth Doherty, Motokazu Matsutani, Nick Smith, and Meg Rithmire, who have shared their joys and pains in doing field research, writing theses, publishing, and surviving in a more and more brutal academic world. Gary alerted me in Dublin in 2013 that I should not postpone my writing plan any longer. Nick and Meg generously dedicated their precious time to be my pro-bono editors, helping to transform my draft "into English," as Peter put it. The title *Building for Oil* came from Nick.

I must also mention Margaret Crawford, who was on my dissertation committee and was always available to me at Harvard and at Berkeley and was both critical and encouraging. Several other professors at Harvard and MIT deserve mention, too. Chief among these are Roderick MacFarquhar, Alan Altshuler, Antoine Picon, Susan Fainstein, and Diane Davis, whose work and classes provided the foundation for my scholarship and inspired my research. In the academic community at GSD, I was fortunate to make a number of extraordinary friends who made the process illuminating and fun with their sound advice, technical support, and good humor. Special thanks go to Doreen Heng Liu, Har Ye Kan, Jan Jungclaus, Kyung Min Kim, Masayoshi Oka, Peeradorn Kaewlai, Saehoon Kim, Stephen Ramos, Warinporn Yangyuenwong, Guan Chenghe, Lü Yingying, and Zhang Jingyi, among many others. My heartfelt gratitude also goes to Barbara Elfman and Maria Moran for providing encouragement and support during my life as a graduate student and as an inexperienced mother at GSD. The Fairbank Center for Chinese Studies, Frank Tsao Chinese Teacher's Fund, and East-West Culture Development Fund provided the necessary financial support for my research at Harvard and for my two field trips to China.

Many good friends in Boston and Shanghai offered their hands and shoulders during the most difficult moments, bringing warmth to Boston's harsh winters: Chen Jin, Wang Lin, Wang Ying, Yang Xiaowen, Wei Ming, to name just a few. My college classmate Yang Yuxiang read and commented on my first few revised chapters and each version of the outline as well as the proposals. I never thought an investment banker, who left the urban planning profession after our graduation twenty years ago, would be interested in such a book. With a sharp mind and a warm heart, he not only raised sound questions but also convinced me that it was possible to make the book appeal to a broader readership.

My biggest debt, of course, is to my family. The challenges and demands of having a decent academic career and raising two young children at the same time would have been impossible were it not for my family's unfailing support. My mother and Yao Dong often take up more responsibility in the family and endure my intense focus on writing. My son and daughter, Daren and Youdi, are my sources of positive energy and havens from work. They shared my burdens, softened my edges, suffered from my constant absence, physically and emotionally, while growing beautifully without my full attention. My father was the reason that I chose this topic in the first place. He would be very proud if he knew what I have accomplished.

Finally, I would like to thank the people who kindly assisted me during my field research and the participants in my interviews, who provided the substance on which this book was written. When I began this research in 2006, I did not expect to discover and document such an unusual episode in history. Every single one of these conversations was enormously illuminating. Note that most of the names in the book, with the exception of a few public figures, have been changed to protect the privacy of these individuals. I am especially grateful to Zha Binhua and Yang Ruisong, whose story has contributed a concrete part of this book. They opened their doors and their lives to me and made this book more human. And more thanks go to Zhou Ganzhi (1930–2014), Zou Deci, Shi Nan, Qu Changhong, Zhang Bing, Huang Li, Li Jiangyun, Du Lizhu, He Xifeng, Xi Chengjun, Liu Ren, Han Fukui, Han Lianzhong, Wang Changhai, Li Ning, Su Guirong, and Hu Bingyan, among many, many others. Lü Yingying and my graduate students Shen Yun and Wu You helped me with illustrations and maps.

For those helping me see in a way I would never have seen otherwise, I am forever grateful. I know more books will be required to make it worth their love and kindness.

December 31, 2016
Shanghai

Preface

Outside it is cold and raining in Cambridge, Massachusetts, and we are about to plunge into an unusually snowy winter. I am sitting in the reading room of the Harvard-Yenching Library, feeling the weight of history as I examine the calligraphy scrolls hanging on the walls. My unfulfilled roles as a mother and a wife and my preoccupation with my career as an educator and a city planner in a rapidly urbanizing China postponed the writing of this book for some five years. Finally, I can enjoy this precious moment to think about the history of China's urban construction and about the working men and women who inhabited China's northeastern landscape.

Throughout my career, I have often felt that what happens not only on an urban scale but also in those twists and turns in individual lives is heavily influenced by the global structuring and restructuring of capital, production, and national competition for wealth and power. This inescapable fact is especially true in the case of China as it enters the age of modernity. As a planner, I was trained to search for ways to make a better future for society. But being contemporary Chinese means we have to face constant changes and diversions. It is difficult to simply follow one's own life course, not to mention find tangible structures and a vision for all.

I grew up on an oil field in North China, in an area that lies along the plains of the Bohai Gulf, divided from the rest of the Shandong peninsula by the Yellow River. The region is marked by a dynamic, ever-changing earth, exposed by myriad holes drilled in search of oil and natural gas.

The land was created in modern times by rich sediments of the river as it flowed halfway across the country. But because the river frequently flooded the area, it remained largely uninhabited until the late 1950s. The area consists of diverse combinations of saline land, tidal pools, muddy swamps, and green fields. It is vast and flat, and one can easily see far into the horizon. As my mother suffered from neurasthenia and a sleeping disorder—hallmarks for women of her generation who moved from populous southern towns into the middle of nowhere in North China—I spent most of my childhood wandering idly on the prairie. Buzzing sounds from wooden electric poles connecting the production fronts, the repetitive up-and-down movement of iron machines extracting crude oil from deep in the earth, and clusters of single-story mud-and-brick housing compounds characterized the sparse land. Both nature and the oil production field were equally uncultivated. Other than that, my childhood was no different from that of any other country girl. I chased wild rabbits and geese and captured hedgehogs and cockroaches to keep as pets. My friends and I would sometimes ignite dangerous fires and watch them spread across the prairie before coming to a stop as they approached the barren saline land. On our way to school, we fished for tadpoles in the scattered ponds, and when we stomped on the muddy unpaved school playground, the seawater would ooze out from underground. This unique combination of industrial and natural landscape is a concrete part of my childhood memories. In 1979, when the first three-story *loufang* building was erected to serve as a cadre-training center for the oil field, all of the children in our neighborhood crowded around the construction site to catch our first sight of stairs. We felt scared and dizzy as we stood on the top floor for the first time. Before long, we had all moved into similar multistory concrete buildings. The rural-like setting was gradually disappearing, and we became typical urban kids living in standard residential microdistricts (*xiao qu*).

In 1990, immediately after the Chinese central government announced its policy of opening up Shanghai and designated it the "Dragon Head" of the economic reforms, I entered the Department of Urban Planning in Shanghai's Tongji University. Historically, Shanghai has been the most populous and most prosperous place in China—"the capital of modernity" (*mo du*) in the minds of many Chinese. But when I first arrived there, I was shocked by the sight of the dilapidated dusty city, which was not much more urban than the oil field where I had grown up. It did not take long, however, before a profound transformation began to take place. After years of rigorous destruction and construction, the Shanghai I saw when I first arrived no longer existed.

Since the 1990s, urban planning has become an increasingly prominent profession. There have been heavy demands to provide more space for the rapidly growing urban economy and the rising urban population, as well as a surging desire to become larger even faster. With the retreat of economic planning, land-use planning has become an important means for the state to control the distribution of resources, to provide public goods, and to facilitate economic growth. With the strong state presence and assisted by public ownership of urban land, Chinese planners have helped to lift millions out of poverty, building an unprecedented number of new structures for schools, hospitals, transportation, manufacturing, and housing and preparing huge areas of land for new construction, thereby increasing the urban built area sevenfold within only three decades.[1] During this construction fiesta, half of the nation became urban. On the one hand, unlike in other developing countries, there are arguably no large-scale squatter towns. The rigorous growth of the urban population and the economy have been orderly due to extensive planning efforts. On the other hand, China's urban society currently faces many serious challenges. Rural migrant workers and their families do not receive equal treatment as citizens in the cities. Serious corruption afflicts many urban development and planning programs. Large-scale demolitions and relocations of the population have taken a toll on the local residents. Heavy pollution, terrible traffic jams, the lack of access to public services, and the contested use of public spaces are but a few of the numerous problems currently confronting the city. Real estate prices have increased much more rapidly than the value of China's GDP, and Shanghai has become one of the world's most expensive cities, comparable now to New York City or Tokyo. Urban disease has accompanied the excessive growth of the urban districts, both planned and unplanned. Such urban crises are spatially, socially, and politically embedded within the urban structures. Considering all of these challenges, how is it possible for planners not to struggle with their conscience? The present is so overwhelming that the future has become blurred.

In 2003 I was given an award by the Frank Tsao Chinese Teachers' Fund to study at the Harvard University Graduate School of Design.

During my first year, I took courses in urban economics, real estate finance, planning and environmental law—classes that I assumed would be useful when I returned to China. Also, my master's thesis at Tongji University was about land reform and its influence on the spatial patterns of urban development. Since the mid-1990s, the buzz words of Marxism have been replaced by those of neoliberal economics in Chinese academics. The China Scholarship Council was offering full support for overseas doctoral students in the field of urban economics, so I intended to submit an application. Nevertheless, during my first year of study I became more interested in history: first the history of Soviet planning and American company towns, and then the history of China in the twentieth century. I wrote a term paper on the history of building a company town in the area where I had grown up. I found the topic so intriguing that I decided to continue in this direction for my dissertation. It was then that I turned to a study of the original Daqing model that, over a period of fifteen years, had had a profound influence on Chinese oil fields as well as on the entire country. I was often asked why I chose a remote 1960s oil field as the topic of my research when contemporary China was facing so many challenging planning issues.

I took my indulgence in history as an attempt to seek identity and meaning while confronting loss. The purpose was both academic and personal. After all, our knowledge of the past constructs who we are in the present and helps us to proceed better into the future. Contemporary Chinese history is often seen as a radical break with its immediate past. My goal was to build connections. In this sense, I was naturally biased. The three decades covered in the book, from 1949 to 1979, were marked by a series of revolutions and ideological shifts, which began and ended with seemingly unusual historic discontinuities.[2] Millions of Chinese were dislodged from their familiar environment. Their old ways of thinking and living underwent a thorough reshaping. Then events in 1979 completely overturned those of the past. Overnight, many revolutionaries became the counterrevolutionaries they had formerly derided—"capitalist running dogs" who advocated a market economy. How did this come about? What was the contribution of the first three decades of the republic to the subsequent years? Additionally, the overall performance of economic growth during the 1960s and the 1970s was quite substantial despite stagnating urbanization and political turmoil. How was that possible? According to the National Bureau of Statistics, GNP output more than doubled from 1960 to 1979. The manufacturing industry enjoyed an annual growth rate of 5.8 percent, and the energy and chemical industries enjoyed even more rapid growth. Agricultural performance was far greater in the 1960s and the 1970s than it had been in the 1950s. Beginning in the mid-1960s, grain production steadily increased, finally reaching a record high in 1984. How was such growth achieved against the backdrop of the so-called de-urbanization processes? What was occurring at the local level? What had happened to the people of my parents' generation? My father had been an oil engineer dispatched to the northern frontier in the 1960s. Unfortunately I never had an opportunity to engage in in-depth conversations with my father about his experiences during that period.

These questions ultimately led me to this volume. It is about the production of a model "city"—the Daqing Oil Field—that became the industrial landmark of the era. The book focuses on the construction of the Chinese socialist state, the urbanization and industrialization strategies during the early years of the People's Republic, the consumption of land and resources, and the divide between urban and rural areas. It records the continuing restructuring of central-planning mechanisms, beginning as early as the mid-1950s, and the ways in which urban construction was negotiated both nationally and locally. My purpose is to show how communist ideology, political conflicts, urban planning discipline, and popular attitudes were all articulated in the creation of the model city of Daqing, as lived and experienced on a daily basis and as a political entity—a space of control and coercion but also of dissidence and contestation. The book is also the story of food and energy, two key elements that determined life and death in the People's Republic.

Research is a process of constant disorientation and reorientation. I often experienced conflicts with preconceived ideas and things. During the research, I became increasingly attached to the place and the people I was studying. I could feel their hardships, and I was moved by their sacrifices. I became extremely distressed when I read about the ambitious oil production goals imposed by the radical petroleum leaders that affected the people's livelihoods and lives, demanding extreme self-sacrifice, and I was simultaneously moved by the people's devotion and strong belief in modernization. What surprised me most were those I had labeled ultraleftists, who advocated self-sufficiency but who eventually became pioneers in joint ventures with foreign capitalists. Their slogan "Less empty talk, more solid work" did not greatly differ from their political rival's "Practice is the sole criterion for testing the truth." Both high-level cadres and common grass-roots men and women were tough, respected, and stubborn in facing hardships. They made great efforts to obtain oil, food, and proper housing and to conquer, excel, and ultimately survive. I found them equally sentimental when Petroleum Industry Minister Song Zhenming's last wish was to have his cremated ashes spread around the site of the first oil well where he had worked as a pioneer, while at the same time many of Song's former comrades only wanted to leave the barren oil fields for good.

I absorbed as much as I could of such vivid and contradictory memories. A great number of people lost their sanity or even their lives in the face of insurmountable struggles. The tensions of life, the conflicts between collective and individual interests, the distance between the urban and the rural and between the ideal and the reality, exhausted both the people and the land. The stubborn drive to achieve modernization ultimately devalued the meaning of modernity. There remain today many people whose memories are inaccessible. Due to a lack of adequate materials, it is impossible to construct decent biographies, especially of those who are illiterate and who lost so much during those years of harsh battles.

In this book, parallel with each chapter I develop the story of a female planner living in Daqing. Her personal feelings provide texture to the larger narrative that I have sought to build. I am fortunate to have found Zha Binhua—named "Hua" in this book—and grateful for her willingness to allow me to publish her story. I first came to know of her while reading an article published in 1966 in the *Journal of Architecture* (*Jian zhu xue bao*) that describes her transition from a city planner educated in "Western values and methodology" at Tongji University to a local practitioner in Daqing consciously "representing the true interests of the workers and peasants." The article is based on a speech she gave at the National Conference of the Chinese Society of Architecture that preceded the Great Proletarian Cultural Revolution. Needless to say, at the time her speech hurt the feelings of many senior designers and planning professors at Tongji University. I tracked her down through Tongji University's alumni network and slowly began to establish a relationship with her. In many ways, she reminded me of myself. She was passionate in her devotion to building an oil frontier for her motherland, not realizing that she was exposing her loved ones to danger. She was not a true "revolutionary rebel." Or, to be fair, she was, but only for a short period. Then she developed mixed feelings about her job in city planning and struggled between her role as a professional and her role as a mother as she maintained a long-distance relationship with her family during years of hardship. She was both intelligent and emotional. Tears welled up in my eyes when I heard her say that she did not deserve the title of mother; she regretted that she was "too ambitious" in her career to be able to take good care of her young daughters. It was just at that time that I too was forced to leave my daughter at home for months on end in order to complete my dissertation. And while reading her letters and diary I felt the same pain of missing faraway love ones.

The state policies of Hua's generation required strict adherence to containing "urban consumption," and the civil engineering projects in which she and her colleagues participated were very limited. According to her husband, also a Tongji architecture graduate, the most meaningful civil engineering structure they built during this time was a container made of paper that could hold as many eggs as they could smuggle home to their children from the black market. But within a decade, urban construction experienced an extraordinary rise in scale that had been unimaginable in the past. What formerly was strictly controlled is now encouraged as the engine of new growth. Hua's and my parents' generation survived a much more conflict-ridden life. They left a legacy that is not well understood. Energy and food constraints continue to be critical issues in China today, but they also have a greater impact on the outside world.

As Lin Yutang summarizes in his 1936 book *My Country and My People*, "This is the story of the birth of a nation. . . . It was merely a sprawling mass of humanity trying to live out their individual lives, and nobody could question their right to do so. . . . The story of China's rebirth as a modern nation is therefore more tragedy than comedy. . . . Every step in her advance as a modern nation was due to a bitter lesson in disillusionment." After completing this book, I do not feel any less lost; China is facing yet another dramatic turn, economically, socially, and politically. But I do hope that China's future will be less bleak. In the summer of 2014, Xinhua News Agency announced an investigation into Zhou Yongkang, a former member of the Chinese Communist Party's Politburo

Standing Committee, for corruption and abuse of power. Zhou began as an oil man in Shengli Oil Field in North China and was seen as the top leader behind a series of "petroleum scandals." The prosecution of Zhou, possibly the most senior Chinese official to face a criminal trial in decades, exposes Daqing's hidden legacy. The disclosure of the new-generation "Petroleum Group" (Shiyou Bang) might encourage more people to take an interest in the history of China's modern petroleum industry. It is my sincere hope that this book will help readers understand China and also that, to some extent, it will help contemporary Chinese value their own past and think more cautiously about their future.

INTRODUCTION

There is . . . a politics to place construction ranging . . . across material, representational, and symbolic activities which find their
hallmark in the way individuals invest in places and thereby em-
power themselves collectively by virtue of that investment.

—David Harvey

If one approaches Daqing from the Harbin-Daqing Highway, the un-
folding landscape cannot be distinguished from any of the other new
towns sprouting up all over China. It bears many of the same features as
other cities—broad roads, super blocks, majestic squares, and huge
parks—marked by rigid land-use divisions and street patterns and standardized housing. The Daqing municipal government, the universities,
and the large housing quarters built for municipal employees are located
in East Wind (Dongfeng) Village. However, if one passes East Wind
Village and continues heading west, passing a natural landscape of scattered settlements with intense green grass that is perfect for grazing,
sprouting wildflowers, widespread small ponds, thick grids of electrical
wire and polls, paved roads, as well as scattered oil extraction wells, one
realizes that Daqing is actually an oil town, a mixture of pastoral landscape and growing industry, an oil production site that is neither urban
nor rural. Along the highway, some simple and practical low-rise industrial buildings will appear. Steps away from the transportation corridor,
oil production sites stand among abandoned public buildings and villages
of single-story brick or mud houses. Since the mid-1990s in this area,
called Saertu, urban construction has come to an end to provide space for
oil production. As a result, urban construction was transferred to East
Town and West Town as public safety became a serious issue and families who lived in the villages complained about poor accessibility to public
services, such as hospitals, schools, and daily supplies. This decision to

relocate to East Town and West Town preserved the original landscape of the oil town in the 1960s and 1970s, a decaying living museum of the past. Farther to the west, comprising two districts, Ranghulu and Riding-the-Wind (Chengfeng) Village, the area is more urban and organically developed. West Town is the seat of the Daqing Oil Field Management Bureau and the PetroChina Daqing Company.

Today's Daqing might appear similar to other Chinese cities, but it has experienced an exceptional history. The scattered landscape is far more than an industrial phenomenon. The large oil deposits in Daqing were discovered in the Northeast ten years after the establishment of the People's Republic of China (PRC). On September 26, 1959, Daqing succeeded in drilling its first oil production well. This event was crucial to the young PRC as its Soviet "big brother" threatened to cut off its supply of oil following the Sino-Soviet ideological split. The name Daqing (大庆), literally meaning "great celebration" and referring to the celebration of the tenth anniversary of the PRC, is indicative of Daqing's strategic significance to the country.

From 1964 to 1980, the Daqing Oil Field accounted for well over 50 percent of China's annual crude oil production, producing over 68.1 billion yuan in profits and taxes for the state. Beginning in 1966, Daqing led the country as the industrial enterprise with the highest annual financial payments to the state. In the mid-1980s, no less than 3 percent of the total revenue that the state was earning from enterprise profits and taxes was coming from Daqing. But at least 11 percent of the state's foreign currency earnings were derived from Daqing's petroleum exports, in part due to the price of oil.[1] Without Daqing, China's industrialization and drive to modernity would have been seriously weakened.

Daqing was more than just an oil town. It was a symbol and a showcase of the PRC's modern industry and independence. It represented a "Great Leap Forward" in China's state-led industrialization program. There is no other place in China where the physical landscape and the people's everyday lives were more intertwined with state interests and ideological debates. It is the place where the communist utopia and the people's revolutionary spirit sought to conquer reality. As an exemplar of the tenets of Mao Zedong's thought, it saved the country from a depressed economy, and it gave Mao confidence to maintain the country's revolutionary path. Furthermore, Daqing symbolized a rejection of bourgeois society and a challenge to Soviet socialist construction. It was a model that Chinese leaders hoped would propel the entire country to the longed-for industrialized future and to a society built on equality, productivity, and revolutionary progress. The "Daqing Spirit, the Daqing People" represented intense personal commitments in the pursuit of national objectives, a self-sufficient frugal way of life, and unique "urban-rural integrated" land-use patterns, and it served as a model for the entire country for the future decade.[2]

Daqing's urban-rural integrated landscape was thought to embody the ideal communist society as described by Marx because it eliminated the three great gaps: between town and countryside, between workers and peasants, and between mental and manual labor. Daqing was established during an era when both cities and countryside were losing significant amounts of population—an era of de-urbanization after the catastrophic Great Leap Forward and during which the country was facing a serious threat of war. The *gandalei* spirit, manifested by the local-style houses with their walls made of pounded earth, led to a national wave in building frugal housing for workers. Thousands of "socialist new men and women," the model workers of Daqing, became representatives of China's emerging working class. The so-called Petroleum Group, led by General Yu Qiuli, served as an important agent to promote the Daqing model in all fields of endeavor, shaping China's path to industrialization and modernization throughout the 1960s and the 1970s.[3]

Organization of the Book

This book, presented as a straightforward narrative, is organized in chronological order, though every chapter has a thematic focus, so that the time span in some chapters slightly overlaps with those in other chapters. Specifically, chapter 1 introduces the discovery of the Daqing Oil Field, implementation of the PRC's First Five-Year Plan, and the urgent call to shore up a supply of energy. Chapter 2 takes up the massive mobilization and resettling of the population along the frontier, foreshadowing the emerging alternative landscape that later became the model pattern. Chapter 3 begins with earlier debates on planning and construction and then explains how Daqing came to be recognized as an ideal model. Chapter 4 describes how the Daqing model, together with its leaders, appeared on center stage, an event that gave birth to an episode of unusual industrialization and urbanization strategies nationwide. Chapter 5 describes the daily lives of and attempts to educate the new socialist men and women. Chapter 6 reveals how the Daqing model reached its zenith during the Great Proletarian Cultural Revolution (1966–1976), only to fall dramatically thereafter. It also addresses the politics of oil and its influence on China's international relations. The rejection of the legacy of oil production brought an end to the model of "industrialization without urbanization" and paved the way for future economic reforms.

The story of Daqing offers a microcosm of PRC history during a period of thirty years. It covers a wide range of national and international political and economic changes, as well as developments in Chinese urban policies, planning, and city buildings. Parallel to each chapter there is also a story of a female planner, Hua, who lived in Daqing from 1962 to 1975. Her personal account can be read with the larger historical narrative either as a whole or in parts, in which the two accounts serve as supplements to each other.

CHAPTER I

The Discovery of Daqing

China entered the twentieth century in decline. Its territorial
fringes . . . its capital—were occupied. . . . The country's ideology
and institutions . . . were in crisis. . . . Outside half a dozen major
urban centres, the economy remained stubbornly, overwhelmingly,
agrarian. . . . In almost every respect China was ill prepared for
the struggle between industrialized nations destined to shape
the new century.

—Hutchings, *Modern China*

We are not only good at destroying an old world, we are going to
be good at building a whole new world.

—*Mao Zedong, Report to the Party Congress, 1949*

Time begins.

—*Hu Feng, "Time Begins," 1949, in Hu Feng wenji*

Oil has been central to national security, prosperity, and the very nature of industrialization in the modern world. The discovery of the
Daqing Oil Field, along with other important mining resources, helped
the Chinese state to jump-start its extensive industrialization plans,
fertilizing the land to feed its people. Such resources were necessary for
China's transformation from a largely agrarian, rural-based society into
an industrial, urban society. The land in China was by no means barren; however, it took the efforts of generations to achieve its value. The
discovery of oil occurred during the modern transformation of traditional
Chinese society, after multiple failed attempts by various states. Although
the PRC, established in 1949, rejected much of China's past, it accepted
more of its legacy than is generally assumed. Its success in oil drilling is
but one example. During the long period of foreign aggression and national disintegration and the very slowly growing industrial capacity of
the national economy, the newly emerging social elites who turned their

belief in Confucianism into modern science and technology and its accompanying institutions, albeit few in number and young to the industrialized world, were sufficient to produce the success of the Daqing Oil Field. The discovery of Daqing, with its rich oil deposits, was crucial to the new regime, which, after its break with the Soviet Union, the big brother that had provided not only oil but also technological and financial support for the country's heavy industrialization programs, would have faced serious problems of survival. It was a discovery that saved the newborn state from starvation.

The Search for Oil

China is well known for her rich coal resources. However, in the twentieth century, oil, rather than coal, proved to be much a more efficient fuel and was transformed into a source of power for the modern world. Compared to the process of coal mining, the process of oil discovery is scientifically, technologically, and financially much more demanding, testing a country's knowledge, wealth, and power. If we look at world history, it is fair to say that the discovery of rich oil deposits can affect the pace of a country's modernization. But the spatial distribution of oil deposits on earth is so uneven that their discovery is often merely a matter of chance.

This story of the search for oil in modern China is seemingly technical, but it is also political in nature. "A large part of the Chinese Republic consists of rocks of types and ages in which no possibility of commercial oil deposit exists," wrote Standard Oil consulting geologist Frederick G. Clapp in *The Science of Petroleum* in 1938.[1] This is the most often quoted sentence in the official narrative about the development of the Chinese petroleum industry—that "arrogant American geologists" underrated possible oil deposits within Chinese territory and concluded that China was destined to be poor, at least in terms of oil. However, Clapp's next sentence is "Some parts of the country, however, have seepages and other surface indications or structures of suitable types in sedimentary basins," but the introduction of these promising oil-rich basins was intentionally ignored.

OIL, MINING, AND THE AUTHORITIES

The use of kerosene for illumination was introduced into China in the mid-nineteenth century. It soon became the most profitable export to China for foreign oil companies. Such exports were made possible due to China's historic defeat by England in the first Opium War of 1839–1842. After its defeat, China was forced to sign the Treaty of Nanjing and its supplementary articles, opening the country's domestic market to foreign trade. The Treaty of Nanjing provided a legal basis for foreign goods to enter China and facilitated the domestic sale of kerosene. As compared to kerosene, the traditional vegetable oil for lighting was smoky, inefficient, and relatively expensive. The Standard Oil Company extended its business into China not long after it was founded by John Rockefeller in Cleveland, Ohio, in 1870. It quickly stepped up its volume of sales to become the largest American company in China, even as it faced critical challenges at home.[2] Decades later, Texaco Petroleum Company—another American company—and Asiatic Petroleum Company, the Far Eastern branch of the Royal Dutch Shell Company, became the two other most competitive companies to enter the Chinese market.

Toward the end of the nineteenth century, kerosene had become part of everyday Chinese life in both the cities and the countryside.[3] The newly established lifestyle—which involved steadily rising consumption of oil products—and China's large population presented an attractive market for both foreign and domestic merchants. As the value of commercial crude oil was realized, the search for domestic fields within China began.

However, mining was strictly prohibited in late Qing China because the traditional cosmological view regarded the land as a sacred legacy and the mountains as the "dragon veins" of the nation. Hence digging was considered disrespectful to both the ancestors and the gods. Also there were rising concerns about national conflicts of interest when the formerly self-contained country suddenly discovered that it was surrounded by foreign powers drooling for a big share of the Chinese pie. In 1850, the Fujian provincial government authorized officials to closely inspect local mining activities and "mercilessly shoot down any unworthy people secretly digging coal mines so as to put an end to those malpractices of plotting with foreigners."[4]

The ban on mining was finally lifted during the Self-Strengthening Movement, the modernization effort of the declining Qing Court. This attempt to build a modern industry and a royal navy required a substantial supply of fuel. In 1875, the Qing Court designated Cizhou in Zhili (now Hebei province) and Taiwan in Fujian province as testing grounds for state extractions.[5] Thereafter, there were several attempts during the late Qing period to explore for crude-oil fields during the late Qing period. But mining operations by the state were often plagued with corruption and low efficiency, and domestic merchants could not sustain the heavy investments required for extraction and transportation. When foreign assistance was sought, the Qing Court worried about "the selling of the country to foreigners." The lack of financial means, up-to-date technology, and a sufficient management capacity, as well disputes over foreign funding of heavy capital projects and fears of foreign influence, were recurring problems in the shaping of China's petroleum strategy (see figs. 1.1 and 1.2).

Following the collapse of the Qing dynasty in 1911, the newly established republican government, which was not able to control the economy as it wished, announced that all local oil mines would be confiscated by the state. In 1913, the Beijing warlord government began negotiations with Standard Oil of New York, offering exclusive exploration rights in the Yanchang Basin of Shaanxi and in Zhili (Hebei) province, in exchange for a US$15 million political loan to save it from financial crisis.[6] By February 1914, Standard Oil and the Beijing government had completed negotiations and signed a contract for joint exploration. According to the terms of the contract, Standard Oil received exclusive exploration rights in the Yanchang region. If commercially profitable sources of oil were to be found, Standard Oil would receive refining and marketing rights for the petroleum products for the next sixty years. In return, Standard Oil agreed to assist the Beijing government to procure loans in the United States "under the table."[7] However, the contract, especially the failed attempt to secretly receive foreign loans in exchange for national oil resources, became caught up in the successive waves of nationalism that had begun to sweep across China after the first Opium War. It also increased resentment due to the conflicting corporate interests of the British and Japanese companies. As conditions were still primitive, Standard Oil extended the contract for an additional year to determine whether

FIGURE I.I Hauling five-gallon cans of kerosene in the North China countryside, Shanxi province, 1919. Photo courtesy of National Archives of the United States, Washington, DC.

FIGURE I.2 Loading kerosene onto a boat in the central Yangzi region at Xiangtan, Hunan province, 1930. Photo courtesy of National Archives of the United States, Washington, DC.

any oil could be found. For almost three years, Standard geologists carried out investigations in an area of about 50,000 square kilometers and conducted a survey in an area of 100,000 square kilometers, producing a detailed 1:12,000-scale map. Unfortunately, drilling in Yanchang was not successful during the period of the contract. Both Standard Oil and the Beijing government lost confidence in the project as both faced increasing domestic and international pressures. Eventually, in 1917, the contract was abrogated by mutual consent. The drilling machines were abandoned on site because of the exorbitant transportation costs to remove them.

WAR, INDUSTRY, AND RESOURCES

The Japanese invasion of Manchuria in September 1931 marked a turning point with respect to oil exploration in China. The utility of oil products shifted from a source contributing to the people's livelihood to a strategic commodity during the war. By the 1930s, gasoline had replaced kerosene as China's most important petroleum product. Imports of kerosene declined sharply under the republican regime; Chinese urban and rural areas resorted to the use of electricity.[8] At the same time, automobiles powered by gasoline became an important means of transportation. During the six years of the warlord government, from 1921 to 1927, the total length of highways in the country was extended from 1,185 to 29,170 kilometers. Thereafter, the Nationalist (Kuomintang) government that assumed power in 1928 continued to invest heavily in road building. More than 82,000 kilometers of roads were added during the Nanjing decade (1928–1937), most of which were for military purposes.[9] Many Chinese cities destroyed their city walls and shantytowns to make way for more roads. The Nationalist government's efforts to build a national air force also consumed huge amounts of gasoline. But at the time, China's consumption of gasoline was highly dependent on the three global oil companies: Standard, Asiatic, and Texaco. The imported oil was first stored in the coastal treaty ports, including Shanghai, Tianjin, Ningbo, and Guangzhou, and then it was delivered to the hinterlands mostly by ship, the safest and cheapest means of transportation. The Yangzi River became the main transportation corridor for the oil trade.

The Manchurian Incident forced the Nationalist government to place a priority on building up the nation's military capacity. It was under these special circumstances that the National Defense Planning Commission, later renamed the National Resources Commission (NRC), was established to make defense preparations through rigorous efforts to seek oil resources.[10] The establishment of the NRC, led by a prestigious geologist and made up of a group of scientists, specialists, and engineers, was critical in the search for oil. Weng Wenhao, who had received his doctorate from Louvain University in Belgium in 1912, served as secretary-general of the Commission. Over the years the Commission was noted for its non-partisanship and integrity in terms of investing in China's industrial capacity. In the 1930s, Chinese specialists gradually took over the technical positions that formerly had been held by foreigners, an outcome of earlier efforts to modernize education. Disappointed with China's past defeats and government scandals, this group of scientists and engineers shared a belief that the building of heavy industry would be the most effective way to resist Japan and other colonial threats, which was "too important to leave to the politicians."[11]

The NRC put a great deal of emphasis on surveying and exploiting Chinese raw materials.[12] With its consistent planning and investment, the Commission was able to open several state mines and heavy industrial plants. In terms of oil, in 1934, under Vice Commissioner Sun Yueqi, NRC geologists, utilizing the equipment that had been abandoned by Standard Oil, were successful in discovering rich oil deposits in the Yanchang region, allowing two oil wells to enter into production. One year later, the mine was taken over by the Red Army and became an important source of revenue for the Soviet government.

The Japanese army soon seized control of the key cities along the coast as well as the major communication links. As a result, coal-powered trains and ships were no longer considered safe. The importance of road traffic, requiring supplies of gasoline, increased significantly. However, the channels for the shipping of oil were blocked. The oil companies were thus forced to relocate to Burma, leaving the risks of domestic transportation to the buyers. Starting in 1938, construction of the Burma Road cost thousands of lives, and its primitive conditions permitted transport of only the most strategic materials. By 1942 that primitive link was severed as well

FIGURE I.3 Salvaging a 400-ton oil-drilling machine from the Jialing River, near Chongqing, 1937. Photo courtesy of China Petroleum Corp., Limited (Republic of China).

FIGURE I.4 The Yumen Oil Refinery, located in the mountains, with a dormitory at the middle right, year unknown. Photo courtesy of China Petroleum Corp., Limited (Republic of China).

and China was almost completely cut off from outside industrial assistance. For example, imports of gasoline in 1942 dropped to 0.1 percent of the imports in 1936. This was barely sufficient even for military use.[13]

In 1938, the NRC discovered the Yumen Oil Field in Gansu province, the first Chinese field with rich oil deposits capable of industrial production. Located in the most deserted area of the northwest, it was 2,552 kilometers from Chongqing, the wartime capital of republican China. Drilling and production machines had to be conveyed over thousands of miles during periods of serious military threats. Production also lacked a sufficient number of laborers, an unusual problem in populous China. However, because of the war there was a serious shortage of young men. Sun Yueqi was assigned by the NRC to begin production in the Yumen Oil Field as soon as possible. But with the outbreak of the Pacific War in 1941, most imports of oil-production machines from the United States were either blocked in Burma or lost en route. At this crucial moment, China received its most valuable return on past investments in modern knowledge and manpower. Chinese engineers and workers were able to assemble the available machine parts and to quickly begin production in the Yumen field (see figs. 1.3 and 1.4). The mine produced 520,000 tons of crude oil before 1949, contributing some 95 percent of the national output.

Another promising region for oil was Xinjiang, along the Sino-Soviet border in the northwest. In the 1930s and the 1940s Warlord Sheng Shicai worked closely with the Soviet Union to explore oil deposits in the region.[14] An elaborate geological survey was conducted by Soviet geologists, resulting in the discovery of two promising fields, one in Wusu and one in Dushanzi. With Soviet aid, the first modern oil refinery began production in Dushanzi in 1937.[15] But production was halted and all equipment was removed in 1942 when Sheng Shicai suddenly ended the collaboration with the Soviets.

By 1949 only the Yumen Oil Field was sustaining industrial production in China. It had survived China's crisis during the war years, but it hardly met the country's needs for a massive transformation. Nevertheless, the half-century search for oil and the continuous attempts to modernize had provided groups of Chinese oil geologists, engineers, and workers with the necessary knowledge, skills, and experience. The Yumen Oil Field was peacefully transferred to the People's Liberation Army (PLA) without significant sabotage due to the efforts by Sun Yueqi and his colleagues. In fact, most of the geologists and engineers in the NRC remained in Mainland China to work for the new PRC government. After its departure to Taiwan, the NRC left on the mainland more than a hundred heavy industrial enterprises; nearly one thousand manufacturing, mining, and power generation units; thirty-two thousand staff members, and more than 600,000 skilled workers. This legacy and continuity contributed greatly to the post-1949 production successes.

The Weakness of the State Industrialization Plan

By the time Mao Zedong stood atop the Gate of Heavenly Peace (Tiananmen) in Beijing in 1949 to announce the founding of the PRC, the population of China had reached half a billion, with the great majority—nearly 90 percent—living in poverty in the countryside due to the turmoil over the past century. Many Chinese, and the Chinese Communist Party (CCP), believed that socialism, as a new form of production relations and a new way of life, would liberate the forces of production so as to lift the Chinese people out of poverty and restore the nation's rightful position in the modern world.

Eight months before the 1949 event in Tiananmen Square, Mao had warned the CCP in Xibaipo, wartime headquarters of the Party, that unlike in the past, the cities would lead the revolution. Prior to 1949 the Party had tested its governance skills in some of China's poorest, largely rural regions in the nation's interior. However, after 1949 the Party would need to transfer the focus of its work in rural areas to urban areas, and from the regions to the nation. "The period 'from the city to the village' and of the city leading the village has now begun. . . . The centre of gravity of the party's work has shifted from the village to the city. If we do not pay attention . . . we shall be unable to maintain our political power, we shall be unable to stand on our feet, . . . to steadily transform China from an agricultural into an industrial country and build China into a great socialist state. Not only can the Chinese people live without begging alms . . . they will live a better life."[16]

BUILDING THE STATE APPARATUS

An administrative apparatus was established to govern the country after 1949. It was primarily modeled after the Soviet apparatus, but it clearly carried a legacy of the Chinese past. During the early days of the PRC, the structure and functions of the administration were constantly tested and adjusted, until the second half of the 1960s, when they were severely challenged by the Cultural Revolution.

After the founding of the People's Republic, the Central Finance and Economy Commission under the transitional Government Administrative Council (Zheng wu yuan) was the single organ that focused on national economic planning and construction management in the central government, the so-called Economic Cabinet based on the CCP experience in Yan'an from 1937 to 1945. Restoring national economic order, stabilizing currency and market prices, establishing a planned-economy management mechanism, and preparing for the First Five-Year Plan were among the major functions of the Central Finance and Economy Commission. After October 1949, the Commission was expanded to include more than three hundred people, mainly economic leaders from the regional and central governments, famous scholars and scientists, and business representatives. This was a relatively educated group, many of the members of the central leadership coming from urban backgrounds. Chen Yun and Bo Yibo, two prestigious Party leaders with rich experience in economic management dating back to the Yan'an era, were the heads of the Commission. It should also be noted that more than fifteen members of the National Resource Commission of the former Nanjing government were invited to work on the Central Finance and Economy Commission.[17] Sun Yueqi served as vice head of the Commission's Planning Bureau, a key organ in charge of planning and construction. The Division of Basic Construction, under the Planning Bureau, was in charge of state "basic construction" (*jiben jianshe*)—the physical construction of important capital projects. One of Sun's first jobs was to draft the 1951 "Temporary Instructions on Procedures for Basic Construction Work," which established the norms and standards for the construction of state projects.[18] This "democratic" structure of the central leadership soon turned out to be only transitional. Most cadres who formerly had worked for the republican government were under strict scrutiny or suspicion during the "anticorruption, antiwaste, and antibureaucratism" movement in 1952, and they gradually were dismissed from their key positions. As for Sun Yueqi, in June 1952 he "voluntarily" left the Planning Bureau to work at the Kailuan Coal Mine in Hebei province.

The Ministry of the Fuel Industry was one of the earliest ministries to be established after 1949, suggesting its great importance to the nation's development. Under the Ministry there was a Bureau of Power, a Bureau of the Coal Industry, and a Bureau of the Petroleum Industry.[19] In 1955, all three of these bureaus were upgraded to ministries, becoming the Ministry of the Power Industry, the Ministry of the Coal Industry, and the Ministry of the Petroleum Industry.

The first generation of ministers in the People's Republic generally came from peasant backgrounds and had extensive military experience. For example, the first minister of the Ministry of the Petroleum Industry, Li Jukui, a veteran of the Long March, had joined the Communist Revolution in 1928 together with General Peng Dehuai. He was from a destitute family in the Hunan countryside, was basically illiterate, and had no experience working in urban settings. Nevertheless, seats for technical experts were always reserved at the national, provincial, and local levels of the government. These "technical leaders" provided leadership stability due to their longer tenure during the transition of political leaders on the first front. Such "red experts," who had proved their loyalty to the Party based on their solid educational background and their work on the ground, served as the backbone of the country's industrialization projects. In the case of the Ministry of the Petroleum Industry, Vice Minister Li Fanyi had been educated at Columbia University and had served the Nanjing republican government in its communications, construction, and education departments. An important figure in the discovery of the Daqing Oil Field was Kang Shi'en, a typical "red specialist" who had joined the communist army in the 1930s and had majored in geology at prestigious Tsinghua University. Li Jukui served as the first minister of the petroleum industry for three years, whereas Kang Shi'en worked in the administration of the petroleum industry until his retirement in the 1980s.

In 1952, as the country was recovering from the destruction of war and was able to start new construction, more specialized central organs were established. The top government body, the State Council, was established to replace the former Government Administrative Council to oversee the specialized commissions and ministries. The State Planning Commission began to play a key role in managing China's centrally planned economy. It was expected to focus on long-term strategic and comprehensive macroeconomic issues and to have firm control over the basic factors of the national economy, most importantly, finance, material supplies, and the labor force, among others. The majority of the planning commissioners had backgrounds as regional military and Party leaders rather than as economists or technical specialists. Gao Gang, vice president of the central government and formerly "King of the Northeast," served as the first chairman of the State Planning Commission, whose members included Chen Yun, Peng Dehuai, Lin Biao, Deng Xiaoping, Rao Shushi, Bo Yibo, Peng Zhen, and Li Fuchun, all of whom were core Party leaders. This was in sharp contrast to the composition of the Central Finance and Economy Commission.

The Ministry of Geology, led by Li Siguang, was established in 1952. The Ministry of Building Construction was authorized to organize and oversee construction of major state projects as well as the central administration of urban planning and architecture.[20]

The State (Basic) Construction Commission was founded in 1954, with responsibility for the management of national basic construction. As the function of the State Construction Commission overlapped to a certain extent with that of the State Planning Commission and the Ministry of Building Construction, there was a great deal of minor restructuring among the organs. In general, the State Construction Commission focused on construction planning, whereas the implementation functions rested with the Ministry of Building Construction. Therefore, the Bureau of Urban Planning was under the State Construction Commission, and the Bureau of Urban Construction was under the Ministry of Building Construction. The State Construction Commission was disbanded on two occasions, once for several months in 1958, and a second time for four years, between 1961 and 1965. The Bank of Construction, the state bank specializing in support of basic construction, was established in 1954.

In 1956, the State Economic Commission, under Bo Yibo, was established to ease the burden on the State Planning Commission by auditing and examining implementation of the annual state plans, coordinating among the industrial sectors, and balancing plans and resources among the central ministries. At the same time, the Ministry of Urban Construction was separated from the State Construction Commission. As a result, more emphasis was placed on urban planning and design, urban construction, and urban infrastructure, but the Ministry of Urban Construction was dissolved after the end of the Great Leap Forward.

THE FIRST FIVE-YEAR PLAN

It took exactly five years for the new People's Republic to establish its First Five-Year Plan. The plan focused on major industrial projects to develop the basic industrial sectors. Power plants and the steel, mining, machinery, chemical, and national defense industries were among the top priorities. Transportation and communications received considerable state investments, as did national surveys of mining resources, to support the industrialization plan. The plan placed great demands on Chinese agriculture and peasants. Since the opening of the treaty ports in the late nineteenth century, China had been relying on grain imports to feed its people. But the First Five-Year Plan stipulated that imports would be restricted to machinery. The goal of achieving self-sufficiency in food production placed a heavy burden on the already heavily exploited land. The 500 million Chinese peasants were required to feed themselves and also to support the growing industrial-sector workforce. Conflicts between the construction of heavy industry and the technically backward agriculture sector, subject to acute population pressures, resulted in a very low per-capita food supply. To resolve this problem, the first step was to bring different segments of the economy under the direct control of the State Council so as to enable them to channel resources into the most desired areas at greater speed and with maximum flexibility. Thus, in the early 1950s the centralization of fiscal administration, food rationing, price and wage controls, the nationalization of banking, transportation, industry, and trade, the state monopoly on grain purchasing and marketing, and a variety of other regulations were all designed to achieve this goal.

The First Five-Year Plan mandated heavy use of energy, but the tense international situation required self-sufficiency in oil production. Exploration and drilling played a fundamental role in the production of crude oil. These are highly difficult tasks, involving huge costs and heavy investments. The enormous expenses incurred during the early exploration and drilling were often excessive for individual companies, which explains many of the early oil-exploration failures in China prior to 1949. This type of production, rather than being labor-intensive, requires modern technologies, advanced equipment, and the input of highly skilled labor. However, this rule seemed to have been overturned in the PRC with its "people mountain people sea" strategy that played an important role in the successful exploration of mining resources, assisted by advanced technologies and heavy investments (see fig 1.5 for another example of this strategy in action).[21]

Comprehensive prospecting for natural resources was among the top priorities of the First Five-Year Plan. At the National Geology Planning Work Conference, held in Beijing near the end of 1952, Chen Yun declared, "The geology industry is the most important industry in the national economy."[22] The conference determined that by 1953 "technical" human geological resources could increase tenfold from their level in 1952. Huge investments were poured into mining-resource prospecting and workforce training. Geological prospecting alone received 1.7 billion yuan in investment. Mining-machine factories were built in the early 1950s, and the number of geology students in higher education and technical schools was scheduled to increase 70 percent annually during the First Five-Year Plan period. By 1957, the number of geological technicians had jumped to more than 19,000, as compared to only 644 in 1952.[23] In 1949, it was reported that only eighteen petroleum geologists with eight drilling machines were engaged in oil exploration, including the two machines earlier abandoned by Standard Oil; by 1955 there were over six thousand geological workers, with several hundred drilling machines at their disposal.[24]

The search for petroleum was led by both the Ministry of Geology and the Ministry of the Petroleum Industry. A Survey Committee for Mineral Resources under the Ministry of Geology was led by Minister Li Siguang. Xie Jiarong and Huang Jiqing, the principal petroleum geologists who had worked for the republican government, were both members of the committee. After these geologists outlined the key areas to be surveyed, the Ministry of the Petroleum Industry would send troops to do the detailed prospecting and drilling, work that demanded intensive manual labor as opposed to intellectual inputs. Many of these personnel

FIGURE 1.5 "People mountain people sea": massed peasant laborers at a reservoir construction site, north of Peking, 1958. Photo courtesy of Magnum.

had formerly served in the PLA and then received simple drilling training.

The labor force in the petroleum industry increased dramatically, and the Ministry of the Petroleum Industry became one of the most ambitious ministries in the country, recruiting thousands of young students and peasants into its workforce. On August 1, 1952, the 57th Division of the 19th Route Army of the PLA was transformed into China's first petroleum army.[25] These eight thousand soldiers and officers became the core workforce for drilling, exploring, and constructing in the petroleum industry. The Beijing Oil Institute, with resources mainly from Tsinghua University and Yumen Oil Field, was founded in October 1, 1953. Other training institutes and schools were established in tandem at promising oil sites and the exploration frontier, attracting students with free tuition and generous stipends.

A nationwide mass-prospecting campaign was conducted in 1956. As a result, within an area of half a million square kilometers more than three hundred geological oil structures and 240 oil seepages were discovered. It was declared that the possibility of finding oil was promising in several basins in the west and on the North China plain.[26]

China's economic performance during the First Five-Year Plan period was relatively upbeat. The average annual rate of increase in industrial production reached 18.7 percent between 1953 and 1957.[27] The total production of steel and coal exceeded the planned growth. The mileage of national highways doubled. Freight traffic increased 144 percent and passenger traffic increased 159 percent as compared to five years earlier.[28] However, the state planners still faced some serious unresolved problems. Agricultural production was characterized by an inherent cycle of advance-retreat-advance. The harvest was subject to sharp fluctuations in response to changing climatic conditions, and whenever the harvest declined markedly, industrial production and state construction had to be drastically curtailed. Grain production was growing slowly, barely sufficient to keep pace with industrial production. A poor harvest would inevitably lead to food shortages and result in tighter rationing and/or rising prices. Added to these difficulties were sharp increases in the rate of total population growth and even sharper population growth in the urban sectors. Between 1952 and 1957, the urban population grew by 30 percent, whereas total government collection of grain remained more or less unchanged throughout this period. Pressures from the growing population further aggravated the exhaustion of land resources. Given that the priority of heavy industrialization continued, and that the capital, resources, and technology that the state could afford in order to support the rural sector could not be increased in the short run, it was impossible to extract any more surplus out of agriculture. Agriculture thus became a bottleneck on China's industrialization path.

The petroleum industry was another weak link in the national economy. Capital investments greatly exceeded the amount in the initial budget: actual investments totaled 1.9 billion yuan, which was almost three times that in the original plan. But output was 27.5 percent short of fulfilling the First Five-Year Plan goal, supplying only one-third of domestic consumption.[29] Seven percent of state capital was spent to import petroleum products. There was also an unbalanced regional distribution between energy and industry. The productive oil fields—Yumen, Dushanzi, Yanchang, and Kalamayi—were all more than 1,500 miles away from China's industrial and population centers. Kalamayi was the only oil field discovered after 1949, and Yumen was still contributing more than half of the national crude oil production. Long-distance transportation was a critical problem for this poor start-up country. Shipping millions of tons of crude oil from the west to the east exhausted the only railroads serving these regions. Globally, tensions with the Soviet Union were increasing in the late 1950s, and it appeared very likely that Khrushchev would withdraw technical support and the USSR would suspend its supply of crude oil and petroleum products to China.

A STRATEGIC TURN

The failure to attain the oil-production target of the First Five-Year Plan and the call for a Great Leap Forward in 1958 had a significant impact on petroleum policies. In September 1956, the Second Five-Year Plan (1958–1962) was submitted to CCP's Eighth Party Congress. Disregarding the previous poor performance of the petroleum industry, the plan's output target for crude oil in 1962 was still set at 5 or 6 million tons, 3.4 to 4.1 times that of the output in 1957, thus requiring an average annual growth rate of 27.8 to 32.7 percent.[30] But the plan was soon abandoned and replaced by the far more radical Great Leap Forward goals. The major goal of the Great Leap Forward in the petroleum industry, as in other sectors, was to extract as much oil as possible using the most accelerated methods available.

On February 11, 1958, as recommended by Minister of Defense Peng Dehuai, Yu Qiuli replaced Li Jukui as the new minister of the Ministry of the Petroleum Industry. Yu Qiuli was from Jiangxi province's Jinggang Mountain area, the first Soviet base built by Mao Zedong and Zhu De in southeastern China. Yu Qiuli had joined the Red Army while still a teenager, became a Party member at the age of seventeen, and survived the Long March despite the loss of an arm. He was rewarded with the position of lieutenant general before entering the Ministry of the Petroleum Industry at the age of forty-three. Yu had been responsible for "political work" in the army for two decades. During the war period, he proved to be a capable political leader who could keep his soldiers well mobilized and disciplined. Despite the lack of a formal education, he successfully ran the high-level infantry training school in the Southwest Military Region during the early 1950s. In 1955, he was put in charge of the Financial Department of the Central Military Committee of the PLA, which was later merged into the Central Logistics Department, the equivalent of the Central Planning Commission in the army.

The mandate of the new Ministry of the Petroleum Industry led by Lieutenant General Yu Qiuli was to fulfill the state goals. By 1958 the existing oil fields were already under full operation, with oil workers filling both day and night shifts. The workforce of oil prospecting was further expanded and the intensity of labor inputs was increased dramatically. Extensive mass movements became the mark of the Great Leap Forward, but the Ministry of the Petroleum Industry had transformed the movement into a true battle. Mobilization and operations were called *hui zhan*, literally "joining a battle." In 1958, thirty-six thousand people and 916 petroleum prospecting teams were working in the petroleum industry. The total footage of drilling in 1958–1959 exceeded the total footage during the entire First Five-Year Plan period by 124.6 percent.[31] The number of wells drilled in 1958 was four times greater than that in the previous year.

The extensive prospecting work during the First Five-Year Plan period enabled Chinese geologists to outline the most promising oil structures in the country. Entering the Second Five-Year Plan period, Deng

Xiaoping replaced Chen Yun as the State Council vice premier who was in charge of supervising the energy sector. According to Yu Qiuli's memoirs, it was due to Deng's advice that the search for oil altered its strategic focus from west to east, and this advice was well received in the Ministry of the Petroleum Industry.[32] After 1958, petroleum-prospecting institutions in the northeast, North China, East China, the Ordos of Inner Mongolia, and Guizhou were established, and the regions with better infrastructure and higher demands for energy were given greater priority.

Compared to the great northwest, the eastern regions have much more complicated geological structures, with potential oil deposits likely hidden much deeper under the earth. But science and technology advances during previous decades had enabled Chinese geologists to face the challenges of exploring in the east during the Second Five-Year Plan period. Furthermore, Soviet assistance, in terms of both expertise and equipment, helped to accelerate progress. In 1955, Kang Shi'en led a petroleum delegation to the USSR. The group not only visited oil fields, such as Baku, and oil institutes, but it also brought back the most advanced seismographic machinery, thus greatly contributing to the growth of Chinese oil prospecting during the following years. Soviet geologists worked at many Chinese worksites during the mid- to late 1950s.

The first campaign to search for oil, initiated by Yu Qiuli, began in Nanchong, Sichuan province. In March 1958, three wells in the central Sichuan region managed to produce a high volume of crude oil. The Ministry of the Petroleum Industry soon set up the Sichuan Petroleum Management Bureau and brought in more than 3,400 laborers from the Yumen Oil Field to join the campaign. The Sichuan provincial government mobilized tens of thousands of workers to build mining roads, to dredge watercourses, and even to open a new airline from Chengdu to Nanchong. In April, an on-site working conference on national petroleum production was held in Nanchong.[33] In May, 194,000 tons of equipment was shipped to Sichuan and sixty-eight drilling teams were working in the field. In August, the newly established Sichuan Oil Institute welcomed its first class of 643 students. Within less than three months a total workforce of more than thirty thousand had been summoned to the field. The campaign initiated waves of mass movements to mobilize workers and to facilitate drilling, such as workload competitions (*jing sai*), working skills contests (*bi wu*), and vow and swear ceremonies (*shi shi*).

Unfortunately, during the following months the Sichuan campaign did not produce good results. Further drilling came up with nothing, and even the early promising wells dried up. The campaign was officially ended in 1959. But the campaign turned out to be a practice rehearsal for the next real battle.

Daqing: The Great Celebration

Songliao Basin, located in northeast China, in geological terms is a large nonmarine sedimentary basin covering an area of 260,000 square kilometers. It is in the tectonic framework of the North China–Mongolia tract. Geologists had long thought that China's oil resources were limited to the northwest. In the 1930s and 1940s, both American and Japanese geologists failed to discover any oil in the northeastern region, which was then under Japanese occupation. Therefore, during World War II, the Japanese army had to rely on synthetic fuels and had to move its front to the British East Indies for crude oil.[34]

Figure 1.6 shows how oil prospecting in the Songliao Basin first began later in the First Five-Year Plan. In 1957 the area attracted attention, and further resources were thus poured into the region. In April 1957, the Songliao Petroleum Prospecting Team was established under the Ministry of the Petroleum Industry. Two months later, the team was upgraded to the Bureau of Songliao Petroleum Prospecting. More than a thousand staff members were transferred from Beijing.

After the geological structure of the region became clear after months of prospecting, the location for the first deep test well, a "wildcat" well, was selected to determine whether or not oil actually existed there.[35] In July, the first drilling location in the Songliao Basin, the Songji No. 1 Well, was set in the northeast of the geological structure near Anda. Drilling continued for about three months, reaching a depth of 1,879 meters, but still nothing was discovered. A second drilling attempt began in the southeast, but within several months it too had failed to find oil. Fearing repeated failures, the location for the third test well was not decided until February 1959. But due to a lack of efficient moving vehicles, it took an entire month for the drilling team to move from the site of the Songji

FIGURE 1.6 Oil prospecting on the Songliao Plain, 1959. Source: Daqing geming weiyuanhui, *Daqing.*

No. 1 Well in the northeast to the Songji No. 3 Well in the south, near the small town of Datong, whose name translates as "Great Harmony," as a representative of Confucius's utopian dream. On April 11, 1959, drilling began at the Songji No. 3. After three months of intensive drilling, at a depth of about 1,050 meters, oil finally appeared. The drilling was intended to continue for about one year so as to reach a depth of 3,200 meters in order to provide a full sample of the earth's structure in the area. But Vice Minister Kang Shi'en, after visiting the site, decided to end the drilling and to begin testing for oil right away.[36] On September 26, 1959, four days before the tenth anniversary of the People's Republic, oil spewed forth with ever-increasing force from the Songji No. 3 Well. The oil field was named Daqing after the forthcoming "great celebration" of the country marking the establishment of the People's Republic on October 1. It turned out to be the largest oil deposit ever discovered in China and substantially changed the development path of modern China.

Construction (Jianshe): Building a New China

The relentless search for resources has been a constant theme in Chinese history ever since modernization attempts dating back to the Qing dynasty. The discovery of the Daqing Oil Field occurred at a critical moment and in an ideal location. Just four years after its discovery, Daqing accounted for well over 50 percent of China's crude-oil production, and for almost three decades it was the country's most profitable state-owned enterprise and its largest single source of revenue. Without the discovery of Daqing, progress in the development of China's industrialization and modernization would have suffered greatly.

This successful discovery can be attributed to the country's continuous efforts to build a "new" China. Whether monarchists, republicans, or communists, they all shared a similar sense of crisis and a vision that the future China required rebuilding upon a solid foundation of an industrialized nation-state. Based on this common conviction, cumulative nation-building (*guojia jianshe*) efforts, despite many ups and downs, were passed down from one generation to the next, each of which focused on the needs and goals of the state. On March 19, 1949, during the final stages of the Civil War, the Chinese Society of Engineers, founded by Zhan Tianyou, the first Chinese engineer in the late nineteenth and early twentieth centuries, submitted an open letter to the leaders of the two parties, the communists and the Guomindang. In this letter, Chinese engineers earnestly requested that the two armies pledge not to destroy industrial and mining enterprises and transportation and public facilities during the course of the war, and that both parties share mutual responsibility for protecting China's valuable urban construction and production facilities. The letter contained the heading "If the Civil War destroys Chinese cities, such as Shanghai, the Chinese economy will be set back for at least twenty years and the two parties will end up being national criminals." The letter was evidence of the strong desire on the part of the Chinese "technical intelligentsia" to save the country from self-destruction and to protect industrial plants and railways as important means for the nation's revival. This explains why many of the socially minded engineers of the NRC remained on mainland China and made great social efforts to preserve industrial assets during the shift in regimes.

The People's Republic put an end to China's prolonged nightmare of war. A country that had faced extinction as a unified nation-state was finally pulling itself together, with a vision to become strong and wealthy through industrialization. With the greatly enhanced capacity of the central government to exert control over strategic resources, a strong and effective army to assert territorial control even under the toughest of conditions, and a growing industrial workforce with the necessary scientific and technological training, the new socialist state was able to fulfill China's long quest for energy. Indeed, many of China's most important oil fields were discovered in the 1950s and 1960s. These early oil-prospecting efforts finally provided China with a capacity to develop an independent oil industry by the end of the 1960s.

CHAPTER 2

Production First, Livelihood Second

Hua was a sensible and intelligent young twenty-one-year-old woman when she first arrived at the Daqing Oil Field. She had bright black eyes, chubby rosy cheeks, and long black braids. She was one of the few women who had received a higher education in the 1950s, majoring in urban planning at Tongji University, a renowned technical university in Shanghai, where she met her fiancé, Song (fig. 2.1). When they heard that the northern frontier needed city planners, the young couple volunteered, hoping to "draw a new and beautiful picture on a blank sheet," that is, to build a new socialist oil city for their motherland.

Hua was a city girl from Nanjing, the former capital of the Republic of China. Her father had worked for the republican government, so her family background was classified as "staff" (*zhi yuan*), a category that was looked down upon by the Communist Party. Song was born into a merchant family in Wenzhou, Zhejiang province. They were both southerners, that is, from south of the Yangzi River, which divides China's north and south into two distinct social, cultural, and geographic areas. In the 1950s and 1960s, all university graduates were provided with jobs by state allocation. Refusal to accept a state assignment usually meant there would be no other possibility of a potentially promising career. By volunteering to go to the Daqing Oil Field, Hua and Song had hoped to overcome their unfavorable family backgrounds. They also thought that volunteering to work on the country's industrial frontier would be their best chance to remain together in the same physical location.

Before heading north, Hua returned to Nanjing to bid farewell to her parents. Her mother, already in her early sixties, was sad to see her youngest daughter depart for work so far away. Hua comforted her mother, telling her she would be able to visit every year, as by law unmarried state employees were allowed three weeks of family leave annually. Her mother appeared not to be convinced.

The family was already unhappy because of an incident that had befallen Hua's father that summer. He worked at a one-man postal kiosk near the Ming Palace in Nanjing. At the time, it was a sparsely populated district. Toward the end of a long workday, he found that his postal bag, which had been tied to the back of his bicycle, was missing. The bag happened to carry a 3,000-yuan remittance that he had collected that day. This was a huge amount of money for their family. Without any eyewitnesses, her father could not prove that the loss had not been his fault, so he had to repay the entire sum. The post office would deduct 30 yuan from his 60-yuan salary every month until the sum was completely repaid. In Hua's memories of her childhood, her father always had a troubled look on his face, but this was the first time she ever saw him actually in tears. She promised to send home 30 yuan every month until the debt was cleared. That was the moment when she first felt the responsibility of being an independent woman.

The journey to the north was filled with lingering sorrow about her departure. This was October 1962. Hua had refused to allow her mother to accompany her to the Pukou Railway Station on the northern banks of the Yangzi River; she didn't want to see her mother's tears. But she would have welcomed her mother's company had she known that she would not see her mother again until five years later.

Song met her in Pukou, where they took the Jin-Pu Line to Tianjin. The Jin-Pu Line was part of the most traveled railway in China, linking Tianjin to Pukou, outside of Nanjing. For decades, until the Nanjing Changjiang Bridge was constructed in 1968, all travelers and goods along the Jing-Hu (Beijing to Shanghai) line had to stop at Pukou, take the ferry cross the Yangzi River, and then reboard the train to Shanghai. It was the same for the trip between Tianjin and Beijing. When Hua and Song arrived in Tianjin, a government-run boardinghouse provided free accommodations for all graduates who held official dispatch letters. In the boardinghouse canteen, Hua had her first taste of *wo wo tou*, a

FIGURE 2.1 Hua (sitting on the ground, lower left, with straw hat, clapping hands) and Song (just behind Hua, in white shirt) visiting Songjiang county, Shanghai, as college students, 1959. Photo courtesy of Zha Binhua and Yang Ruisong.

northern-style cornbread. People had told her that northern grain was "difficult to swallow," but Hua liked the taste. It was the couple's first visit to Tianjin, so they decided to spend an extra day there to tour the city. Their feelings were mixed with both excitement and anxiety as they looked forward to a fresh start in the country's northern frontier.

A day later, they boarded the train for Harbin. This part of the trip took twenty hours. The green iron railcar was full of passengers. As they headed toward the far north, the train windows were shut tight as the weather outside became increasingly cold. Then the air in the train became thick with all kinds of odors. With the hypnotic clickety-clack sound of the train, Hua's head began to feel heavy, and, leaning on Song's shoulder, she finally fell asleep sitting on the stiff seat. Song remained alert all the way to Harbin to keep an eye on their two suitcases on the rack above them, which contained all they had.

At twilight, the train finally arrived in Harbin. The Harbin Railway Station was still unfinished, with rough brick walls and bare openings where there should have been doors and windows. They had heard that construction had suddenly been halted when the station's design was criticized for pursuing the "grand, old, and foreign style." The couple ate a warm breakfast purchased from a street peddler in front of the station before they again hopped on the train to begin the next leg of their journey to Anda.

As night fell, the conductor called, "Passengers to Anda, be ready to get off! Arriving at Anda!" Song took out the dispatch card and again puzzled over the address: "Heilongjiang Reclamation Farm No. Fifteen." The discovery of the Daqing Oil Field remained a state secret until 1964. Their families knew only that they were being sent to a state farm in Heilongjiang province, near China's northeastern border with the Soviet Union. Meanwhile, the graduates had been told to report to Anda City. Song showed the conductor their dispatch card to see if they should get off at the next stop.

The young conductor displayed an air of confidence with his response: "Stay put. You should get off at the next stop, Saertu. One yuan and twenty cents for the extra fare," he added.

Hua and Song searched their pockets but found only fifty cents. Their graduation dispatch money had been carefully calculated for the journey, and the three extra meals in Tianjin had put them over their budget.

The conductor shook his head sympathetically and said, "Students? Forget it. I'll call you when we arrive in Saertu."

One hour later, the couple descended from the train in what seemed to be the middle of nowhere. A large group of young men and women disembarked with them.

It was almost midnight. They were welcomed by the darkness and a cold chilly wind. The locomotive departed, leaving clouds of steam in its wake. They couldn't see a thing—no station house and not even a single sign at the stop. Some people quickly disappeared through the loose cuts in the barbed wire that bordered the railway. Hua and Song weren't sure if they should follow. Suddenly a man stepped in front of them. "Are you newly assigned students?" he asked. Song put down their suitcases and took out the dispatch card.

The man scanned the card quickly, then ordered, "Follow me."

In the dark, they could barely see the man's face. But they were not the least bit suspicious. This was a time when people basically trusted each other, years before everything changed in the late 1960s. They picked up their two suitcases and followed the man without questioning him. He seemed used to walking in the wilderness without a flashlight, but Hua and Song proceeded awkwardly, often tripping over the uneven ground. People quickly passed these two clumsy southerners, laughing and talking in excited voices. Hua could see a weak red light flickering far in the distance.

Finally they arrived at the dim red light, marking a cluster of mud houses surrounded by a broken-down courtyard. To the eyes of well-trained designers, the mud houses were strangely shaped, without any right angles and with walls that were barely standing, as if a young country boy had just been playing in the mud. Inside, more than half of the space was occupied by a *kang*, a northern-style mud-and-brick bed with a stove underneath. A young woman who had also graduated from the Department of Architecture at Tianjin University was fast asleep on the *kang*. It was very late, so after Hua exchanged a few brief words with her, she climbed in beside her. Hua was so tired that she quickly fell asleep, despite the strange odor coming from the quilt. Suddenly she was woken up by a sharp scream coming from her roommate. A rat had bitten her nose! The two women sat for a while, unsure what to do. Then they went back to sleep. This time they left the light on.

* * *

Drilling continued along the Songliao Plain. More test wells in the south brought good news on New Year's Day 1960. On January 7, Yu Qiuli traveled to Shanghai to attend an extended Politburo meeting.

"Any good news?" Chairman Mao asked when Yu entered the room.

Yu answered with confidence, "From what we have found so far, in Songliao we have the possibility of discovering a big oil field!"

Mao responded with surprise, "A big oil field?"

Yu replied, "Yes, I just returned from Heilongjiang province. Conservatively speaking, it is quite possible; frankly speaking, we've already found it! We are accelerating the prospecting—there will be a final report within six months."

"That's good enough, even if it takes another half-year," Mao responded.[1]

In 1960, the shortage of oil had slowed industrial production and had threatened national security. More than half of China's crude oil was being imported, mostly from the Soviet Union. But after the Sino-Soviet split, further imports from the USSR were not guaranteed, and the state faced significant financial difficulties due to its huge foreign currency payments. Many vehicles turned to alternative sources of fuel, for instance, charcoal, alcohol, or coal. Fuel for the military almost entirely relied on imports, so large-scale operations that required substantial supplies of fuel became increasingly difficult to maintain. The serious shortage of fuel even influenced pilot training and daily operations in the air force.[2]

In February 1960, the Ministry of the Petroleum Industry plotted a 200-square-kilometer area in the south of the Songliao Basin and discovered that the oil deposits there exceeded 100 million tons, an amount equal to that in the Kelamayi Oil Field in Xinjiang province. Furthermore, it was very likely that the oil was not limited to the south but also stretched over a much larger 2,000-square-kilometer area—the so-called Songliao placanticline. At the current speed, comprehensive planning likely would take another year. But in light of the national energy crisis and insistence by the state leadership, the Ministry of the Petroleum Industry decided to concentrate all of its resources and to launch a vigorous nationwide campaign to complete the comprehensive prospecting and put the oil field into production within the year.

Daqing: The Battlefield

The Songliao Plain was an ideal place for oil extraction. Rich in mining resources, it was also an unusually fertile area that was perfect for grain production. It was a piece of underdeveloped land in China's most industrialized region, the northeast, a place known to foreigners as Manchuria. The plain was well connected to Chinese industrial centers and to the major Soviet-assisted construction projects through dense railway networks. However, by the end of the 1950s it was still sparsely inhabited, an unusual situation in populous China.

The northeast region had been a battlefield during centuries of conflicts between the Manchus, Mongols, Koreans, Japanese, Russians, and Chinese because of its strategic location and rich natural resources. In 1668, development in Manchuria was banned by the Kangxi emperor, who considered the area to be the original homeland of the Manchu people and wanted to preserve it as their cultural and economic heritage. Hence Manchuria remained a vast hunting ground for the Manchu people, and for hundreds of years it remained almost entirely unsettled. A willow palisade was erected to isolate it not only from the rest of the mainland but also from Inner Mongolia. However, driven by pressure from the rapid population growth in North China and frequent natural disasters, including severe droughts and famines, over the years there had been periodic waves of illegal migration to Manchuria. Beginning in the mid-eighteenth century, Manchu bannermen in and around Beijing, who had become increasingly idle and impoverished, were encouraged to return to Manchuria to cultivate the land. These bannermen took with them Han Chinese immigrants to work as tenant farmers.

Beginning in the mid-nineteenth century, after ceding to Russia some 350,000 square miles of territory north of the Amur River and east of the Ussuri River, the Manchu government opened the fertile land of Manchuria to immigration, hoping to counter Russia's growing territorial ambitions in the Far East. But several years later, China faced yet another aggressive regional power, the Japanese Empire, which had acquired the Korean peninsula after its victory during the first Sino-Japanese War. In March 1890, the future tsar personally inaugurated construction of the Trans-Siberian Railway to better connect Russia's newly acquired territories in Asia to its European base. In 1896, the Qing Court agreed to lease the land south of the Amur River to Russia in order to support a more convenient line to Vladivostok, the new port city on the Pacific, and Chita in Siberia, and to develop Sino-Russian relations so that China could defend itself from Japanese aggression in the northeast. As the prestigious Qing dynasty diplomat and statesman Li Hongzhang insisted, the railway was named the Imperial Qing Eastern Province Railway (Da qing dong sheng tie lu), the China Eastern Railway (Zhong dong tie lu) for short. The lease included the land corridor along the railway and the settlement areas surrounding the important railway stations. Construction of the railway in Manchuria gave birth to a series of booming rail towns, including Harbin, the capital of Heilongjiang province, and it invited Russian influence to extend even farther south. In 1898, under the threat of a Russian fleet in the harbor, the Qing Court and Russia negotiated another treaty to lease Port Arthur (along with the surrounding Liaodong peninsula) to Russia as its only warm-water port along the Pacific coast.

The Russo-Japanese War erupted as the rival empires sought to seize control of Manchuria in 1904. The war exhausted Japan's military resources, ignited Russia's own revolution, and shifted the regional power structure in both Manchuria and Asia. In 1905, after nineteen months of fierce fighting, Russia signed the Portsmouth Peace Treaty, transferring to Japan all its rights and interests in South Manchuria, including the leasehold over the Liaodong peninsula (fig. 2.2)—which became known as the Kwantung Leased Territory—and the southern part of the Russian-built Manchurian Railway, including the adjacent railway zone. Control over northern Manchuria changed frequently, split among the Chinese, Japanese, and Russian (later Soviet) governments. Colonial investments in port facilities, communication networks, and heavy industry completely transformed what had previously been an underdeveloped region. Chinese and Japanese railway and steamship companies sponsored competitions to attract migrants to the region by offering discounted or free fares. The average inflow of Chinese to Manchuria in the early twentieth century is estimated at 500,000 to 1 million people per year, representing one of the greatest migrations in Chinese history.[3] At the same time, an increasing number of White Russian families, escaping from the new Bolshevik regime, entered northern Manchuria, and Koreans and Japanese migrated to southern and eastern Manchuria. Figure 2.3 shows a ship of immigrants on their way to Manchuria from Shandong. By 1930, the population of Manchuria had increased to about 30 million, from only 3 to 5 million in the mid-eighteenth century, with more than half of the population settling in southern Manchuria.

The railway zone became the scene of extensive urbanization and industrialization. Much more than a colonial railway company, Mantetsu (the South Manchurian Railway Company) owned and operated numerous properties within the leased—and unleased—territory. It launched various new industries and set up its own research department to carry out extensive economic and scientific research.[4] In 1932, claiming that

FIGURE 2.2 Port Arthur (now Dalian), Liaodong peninsula, 1930s. Photo courtesy of Modern Library of Japan.

FIGURE 2.3 A ship of immigrants on its way to Manchuria from Shandong province, 1927. Photo courtesy of Modern Library of Japan.

Manchuria was separate from China, Japan established Manchukuo, installed former Qing emperor Puyi as a puppet ruler, and presented Manchukuo to the international community as a modern "independent" nation-state. By 1933, the Kwantung Army had seized full control of the northeast, including Jilin, Liaoning, Heilongjiang, and Rehe. To support Japan's expanding pan-Pacific ambitions and warfare, Manchukuo implemented an experimental state-controlled industrialization plan and built an extensive industrial infrastructure in the territory.[5]

Despite the destruction wrought by war and regime changes, Japan's investments in the region helped the CCP build China's first industrial base during the First Five-Year Plan. In 1947 the northeast was already home to more than half of the nation's heavy industry. It produced 87.7 percent of the raw iron, 93 percent of the steel, 78.2 percent of the electric power, and 66 percent of the cement in China (fig. 2.4). In 1949, 42 percent of the total length of China's railways was situated in the northeast.[6] The Anshan Iron and Steel Works, originally built by Mantetsu, was the most important industrial enterprise in the region until the discovery of the Daqing Oil Field. In the First Five-Year Plan period, the

FIGURE 2.4 An open-cut coal mine in Fushun, 1940s. Photo courtesy of Modern Library of Japan.

region continued to receive a lion's share of state investment. During the construction of the 156 major heavy industrial projects assisted by the Soviet Union alone, 44 percent of the investment was directed there and 54 new factories were built. Apart from Shanghai on the east coast, the northeast was the most industrially developed region in China in 1960. As Deng Xiaoping commented on the good news, "This is an ideal place [to discover oil]!"[7]

Total Mobilization

Even with the existing advanced infrastructure, putting the Daqing Oil Field into operation within one year was an immense undertaking, requiring tens of thousands of laborers, millions of yuan, and vast quantities of steel, pipes, cables, cement, and machinery. The undertaking tested the capacity of the young People's Republic just as it was undergoing a catastrophic socioeconomic breakdown. The miscalculation of the Great Leap Forward obliterated years of progress. However, the state machine, which had been tested in the past, proved to be both persistent and stubborn.

FROM BEIJING

Total mobilization for the Daqing campaign took place at both the central and the local levels. On February 6, 1960, Yu Qiuli sent a report to Li Fuchun and Bo Yibo, who were the heads of the State Planning Commission, asking for extra investment funds beyond the annual plan and logistical support for the oil campaign. Li and Bo forwarded the request to Vice Premier Deng Xiaoping, who was in charge of the energy sector. Deng requested that the petroleum leaders submit a report directly to Premier Zhou Enlai and the Central Committee of the CCP. On February 20, seven days after receiving the report, the Central Committee approved the proposal and forwarded the report to the North China Bureau, Heilongjiang province, the State Planning Commission, the State Economic Commission, the State Construction Commission, the Ministry of Geology, and other related departments, as well as to the local governments, mandating full support from all sectors and governments.[8] Ten days later, the State Planning Commission, the State Economic Commission, and the State Construction Commission jointly sent a telegram to the Ministries of Metallurgy, Water and Power, Agricultural Machinery, Foreign Trade, Communications, and First Machine-Building (the national defense industry), and the provinces of Shanghai and Heilongjiang, among others, asking for 19,000 tons of steel, generator sets capable of producing 6,000 kilowatts of power, one hundred motorized trucks, thirty jeeps, sixty tractors, fifty machine tools, two road rollers, 10,000 tons of cement, four thousand to six thousand industrial bearings, and millions of square meters of timber. On March 9, Bo Yibo organized a special meeting of the top leaders from the related ministries and local governments to support the Daqing oil campaign. On March 21, the extra investment from the Central Government outside of the plan (*jihuawai touzi*) totaled 400 million yuan; 57,000 tons of steel were also issued.[9]

The Ministry of the Petroleum Industry also mobilized its military connections to channel more strategic resources to Daqing. In February 1960, the Ministry sent a letter to Marshal Luo Ruiqing, chief of the army's General Staff, asking for the transfer of thirty thousand soldiers and officers to Daqing. A few days later, Yu Qiuli flew to Guangzhou, where Mao and Luo were attending an extended meeting of the Central Military Committee. Yu received permission on the spot. On February 22, a document entitled the "Central Committee Decision on Mobilizing Thirty Thousand Retired Soldiers to the Ministry of the Petroleum Industry" was issued. The transfer also included three thousand officers who were veterans of the Korean War. These thirty thousand retired soldiers became the core labor force for the Daqing campaign, mainly in the construction and transportation sectors. The army in the Shenyang Military District helped during the early construction of roads, water supply infrastructure, and housing and to lay cables. Many scarce resources were collected from the PLA. Yu Qiuli later recalled that he went to Marshal Luo again when Daqing was seriously short of electric welding rods. Luo had replied, "Take anything we have in the warehouse," then immediately asked the air force to ship five tons of welding rods to Daqing.[10] One hundred kilometers of cables from the PLA's communications department were acquired in a similar manner.

To respond to such calls, the Ministry of Railways established in Harbin the Headquarters for Supporting the Daqing Campaign so as to guarantee railway transportation for the thousands of tons of equipment and thousands of passengers who would be headed to Daqing over the next several months. The China Eastern Railway, which had been built by the Russians in the late nineteenth century to ship their goods and soldiers to the Far East and had been renamed the Binzhou Line, served as a vital communications link for the campaign. Anda and Saertu, which were the smallest train stations within the oil field, were updated to second-class status to accommodate the increase in traffic. Extra stations at Ranghulu and Wolitun were added, and the three to four lines in Saertu were quickly expanded to twenty-three lines to receive the supplies and troops. In 1960, the daily number of cars that loaded and unloaded at the four stations exceeded the total number during the entire year of 1959. More than 700,000 people arrived in Daqing by train annually. In 1964, the Ministry of Railways opened a new 138-kilometer-long line from Ranghulu to Tongliao to relieve the traffic on the Binzhou Line and established fifteen more stops along the Rang-Tong Line to better serve the oil front.[11]

The Ministry of Water and Power sent four sets of train-borne power stations to the oil field in the spring of 1960 before a permanent network could be installed. In 1961, a large, 110-kilowatt power station was built in Ranghulu, receiving its power supply from the Qiqihar Fularji Power Plant, one of the 156 major projects built during the First Five-Year Plan period. In 1962, the Longfeng and Xinhua power plants began operations.

Before the water supply system was built, the water-intensive drilling processes had depended on the deep natural ponds and lakes on the Songliao Plain. Tanker trucks carried the water to the production front, and the first several drilling rigs were quickly built at locations that were close to the water resources.

TO THE FIELD

The provincial government of Heilongjiang became the "landlord" for the campaign. It was immediately informed of the successful drilling at the Songji No. 3 Well. Party Secretary Ouyang Qin and Governor Li Fanwu, together with other provincial officials, visited the drilling site near Datong Township, on November 7, 1959. At that time, Datong was still a small town with only some five hundred households living in primitive mud houses. Looking ahead, the provincial leaders realized that Datong would become an important oil city in the future. Because there was already another Datong in Shanxi province, Ouyang Qin suggested the future oil city be named Daqing.

The Heilongjiang provincial government promised to begin infrastructure construction for the coming oil campaign as soon as possible. Party Secretary Ouyang regarded the discovery of the Daqing Oil Field an important opportunity for Heilongjiang's industrialization and agricultural mechanization, especially since the region "already had a developed industry and convenient transportation conditions."[12] One week after the successful drilling at the Songji No. 3 Well, on October 2, 1959, the Party Committee of Heilongjiang province approved a decision to make the province a petroleum industrial base. The decision included plans for building refineries and related factories during the coming year. A working team to support the oil campaign was established, and the provincial governor and the vice governors were made responsible for security, food supplies, public services, power supplies, road construction, and so forth.

On February 21, 1960, Kang Shi'en organized the First Mobilization Conference of the Songliao Campaign, held in Harbin, the capital city of Heilongjiang province, 159 kilometers east of Daqing. Representatives from various ministries and bureaus of the central and local governments participated in the conference. The Ministry of the Petroleum Industry moved all its offices to the field. Vice Minister Kang was assigned to be the head of the leading team for the campaign. Tang Ke, then the director of the exploration division before he became a vice minister, and Wu Xingfeng, vice Party secretary of the Ministry, served as vice heads. Half of the ministerial cadres were working on the front lines of the campaign. The leading team was composed of petroleum leaders from the major oil fields, such as Xinjiang, Dushanzi, Yumen, and Sichuan. The conference announced that the thirty-seven existing petroleum bureaus, factories, institutions, and schools would mobilize their most qualified members and best equipment to join in the campaign. The campaign, a *hui zhan*, was organized along military lines. The Daqing Oil Field was zoned into five "sub-battlefields": Putaohua, Taipingtun, and Xingshugang in the south, Saertu in the central region, and Gaotaizi in the north. Each work unit was assigned to a specific battlefield. For example, the Sichuan Petroleum Bureau was responsible for developing the Saertu zone. The Ministry set a strict timeline for the campaign: all units were to have their "armies" and equipment ready within two weeks; they would join the "battle" by April; and they would prepare the field for oil production by May. All drilling workers, installation teams, and headquarters' officials were required to check in at the site before March 15. When the conference concluded on March 3, the regional leaders were brought home by the PLA Air Force, arriving at their work units even before the news of the conference arrived by telegram, thus enabling them to work at full speed in order to prepare for the "big battle in the northeast."

Thousands of people and pieces of machinery were sent to the Songliao Plain via the Binzhou Railway. Anda and Saertu, the railway stops closest to the oil field, became extremely busy (see figs. 2.5 and 2.6). By March 15, over the course of just two weeks, trains had already dropped off more than twelve thousand workers and soldiers. The small towns of Datong and Anda swelled from merely a few hundred farmers and cowherds to thousands of oil workers, soldiers, geologists, engineers, and Party cadres. With only limited loading capacity along the fifty-kilometer railway inside the oil field, thousands of tons of equipment were often simply pushed off the line and left in the empty fields.[13]

The Heilongjiang Provincial Support Office set up temporary shelters at the Anda and Saertu railway stations. The Bureau of Civil Affairs and the Department of Personnel organized the first-arriving soldiers and officers into twelve infrastructure construction teams. All available shelters in the region, including huts belonging to local peasants, cow stables, and warehouses, were registered and assigned to accommodate the incoming troops. Local residents were paid rent in return for providing accommodations, and they too were mobilized to assist in logistical support for the campaign, such as providing food, clothing, and water.

On March 11, 1960, Li Desheng, chief petroleum geologist in the Ministry of the Petroleum Industry, reported the updated prospecting results to Kang Shi'en: it seemed that there might be even more promising oil deposits north of the Songliao Basin (near Saertu) than in the south

FIGURE 2.5 The petroleum army arriving at Saertu station, 1960. Source: Daqing geming weiyuanhui, *Daqing*.

FIGURE 2.6 Goods unloaded along the railroad line, 1960. Source: Daqing geming weiyuanhui, *Daqing*.

(near Datong). In December 1959 Yu Qiuli had decided to carry out several test drillings near Saertu. In usual cases, test drillings would have spread gradually from the first successful site near Datong town. However, Yu decided to immediately move some of the drilling teams north. With the Binzhou Railway running through the area, Saertu had locational advantages compared to Datong, where the workers had to walk one full day from the nearest railway station. Since the railway already served Saertu, there would be no need to wait for the completion of roads, and the development of the oil field would not be delayed due to construction of the necessary infrastructure. Yu's bold move to begin drilling near Saertu turned out to be a wise decision.

Given that good news, the best drilling teams that had arrived in Datong from Yumen, Xinjiang, and Sichuan were asked to pack up their equipment and leave for Saertu, seventy kilometers to the north. Those on their way to Datong from the Anda train station were turned back to head north. The headquarters of the Daqing campaign also moved to Anda, and then, a month later, to Saertu.

* * *

An Alternative Landscape

In the morning, when Hua (fig. 2.7) awoke, her roommate was long gone. Hua met Song in the courtyard, where simple tables and benches had been set up to serve as a temporary canteen. Song brought breakfast for two—corn gruel and dark-colored sorghum bread (*wo wo tou*). The bread was as hard as a rock. Hua frowned as she took her first bite. She quickly gave up and instead drank the gruel.

The check-in office was only a few minutes away from the boardinghouse. In less than ten minutes, their fate was decided. Song was assigned to work in the campaign headquarters in Saertu, right at the center of the oil field. Hua was assigned to work at the Design Institute. The Institute had just been relocated to Ranghulu, a train stop along the Binzhou Line, some twenty kilometers from Saertu. Though she felt somewhat embarrassed, Hua gathered her strength and asked if the two of them could stay in the same place. The answer was a definite no. As the office explained, the job in the headquarters required extensive traveling and outdoor fieldwork, which was deemed too harsh for women. The Design Institute was considered a better fit for her.

"You can take the commuter train or the shuttle between Saertu and Ranghulu. It's free," the receptionist added.

Outside the office, they ran into their classmate Jin. During the Three Difficult Years, from 1960 to 1962, Daqing had been one of the few places that had welcomed university graduates. Hua and Song knew at least twenty students from Tongji University who had been assigned to the Daqing Oil Field at that time. Jin had arrived a few days earlier and was also assigned to work at the Design Institute. He had already received his first month's salary.

"I'm rich now!" Jin proudly announced, patting his uniform, a warm cotton coat with chain stitches, what the oil workers called a *dao dao fu* (literally "striped uniform").

The newly rich Jin happily offered to buy them baked potatoes at the railway stop. While they were on their way, Jin showed them nearby clusters of houses, which were called Compounds No. 1, 2, and 3. Most of these houses were made of mud and hay. Compound No. 2 was the headquarters where Song was going to work. A newly paved road ran parallel to the Binzhou Line, linking the headquarters to a number of the new buildings along the route.

It was a sunny day, and Hua could see the horizon clearly in the far distance where the blue sky met the earth, something she had never seen before in either Shanghai or Nanjing. Several peasants were selling chickens, grain, and potatoes. Jin spent 1 yuan, equivalent to half a day's salary, to purchase four baked potatoes. The locally produced big potato tasted delicious. In 1962, when most Chinese were still suffering from the famine and food was tightly rationed for urban residents, such a large potato was considered quite a treat. The new university graduates received salaries almost double the standard pay, coupled with supplementary compensation they received for working in a remote border region. However, because housewives were rarely on the payroll and an average family generally had three or four children, many of the Daqing worker's families still found it difficult to make ends meet. The price of daily necessities such as soap and vegetables had doubled since the Great Leap Forward. Very often these necessities were not even available for purchase.

FIGURE 2.7 Hua, wearing her work jacket, printed with the two characters *nong ken,* meaning "reclamation farm" (the disguise for Daqing Oil Field), 1966, photo taken by Xu Ke. Photo courtesy of Zha Binhua and Yang Ruisong.

More than half of the local families received monthly incomes that totaled less than 15 yuan per person, the minimum living wage in 1962. Hence expenditures were strictly limited to food purchases, usually only grain. Whether they had vegetables and meat depended on the harvest from housewives' agricultural labor.

In the afternoon, a truck took Hua, along with some chairs and desks, to the Daqing Design Institute in Ranghulu. It drove at full speed. Squeezed in the back with the furniture, Hua felt uneasy, like a grain of rice flipped up and down in a sieve. The sun was beginning to disappear behind dark rain clouds. There were patches of white salt flats and puddles, what the locals called "water bubbles" (*shui pao zi*), mixed with the grassland stretching endlessly along the prairie. After forty to fifty minutes, the truck finally arrived at Ranghulu. It looked like the same plain stretching along the Binzhou Line and was barely distinguishable from Saertu. A new motor road had been constructed to link it to the south end of the drilling front at Datong. Two research units were located here: the Daqing Design Institute and the Daqing Research Institute of Petroleum Geology. Hua could tell that the houses were brand new, with brick frames filled with mud walls and covered with clean paint. This was surely the best-quality housing she had seen that day—far better than the mud houses, mobile tents, barns, cattle sheds, and suspicious-looking holes in the ground that they had passed en route.

After the furniture was unloaded, Hua climbed off the truck, stretching her frozen limbs. She noticed that the entrance to the house was covered with thick quilts, a common practice in the north to prevent the blasts of wind from blowing inside. In the Design Institute, there were eight divisions: first and foremost was the oil and gas transport division, then the water-injection division for oil extraction, the machinery division, the civil engineering division, the electricity division, the laboratory division, the survey division, and master planning division. Hua was assigned to the fourth division of civil engineering. Most of her colleagues were about her age and were also recent university graduates. The young woman she had met the night before was there too. There were several senior designers in their thirties who had some prior work experience, usually at design institutions in Beijing, Yumen, Sichuan, or Xinjiang.

The division head was from the Ministry of the Petroleum Industry in Beijing. He welcomed Hua: "You are lucky. We just moved here from Saertu. The other work units are so jealous, as we have the best working conditions. Of course, it is nothing compared to the conditions in the cities. But this is far better than when we first arrived."

A girl named Xiao Zhong (literally "Little Zhong") helped Hua pick up her "labor protection" package: a leather hat with flaps to cover her ears, a pair of thick "big head" boots (*da tou xie*), a hay mattress, a cotton uniform (*dao dao fu*), and a long green PLA-style military coat. During the following years, Hua would wear this uniform throughout Daqing's long, cold winters. Bundled up in their uniforms, everyone looked androgynous and anonymous.

Before Hua left for the dorm, the division head called her over. "One more thing that you should know. According to the rules of our 'battle-field' we can take a break only every ten days."

Too bad, Hua thought. I can only meet Song every ten days.

"Tomorrow is the tenth day. We've decided to use the day to move the furniture," the head added.

Hua then realized that a visit to Saertu even once every ten days would not be guaranteed.

*   *   *

Saertu first appeared on maps in 1901, when the Russians connected Vladivostok to Moscow via the Trans-Siberian Railway. At the end of World War II, there were only about 150 households living in the area, many of whom were White Russian farmers.[14] After 1949, the PLA established the "Red Plain" Reclamation Farm to receive retired soldiers and to guard the frontier.

Saertu means "windy land" in Mongolian and "big jar of soy paste" in Manchurian. And Saertu was indeed a windy, swampy, mosquito-infested grassland, with sparse and scattered human settlements. By March, the trucks and jeeps could navigate the concrete-hard frozen land, but housing remained a crucial challenge. The sudden move to Saertu from Datong allowed little time to construct additional housing. Figure 2.8 shows the limited supply of prefab mobile houses and tents, as priority was given to the workers drilling on the front and the prospecting teams. For people working in fixed locations, such as the cadres in the head-quarters, engineers at the Design Institute, construction workers, and those in the logistics department, housing was scattered among the existing villages, in peasant huts, cow stables, and holes dug in the ground with only minimum cover. A large cow stable, called Compound No. 2, was reserved for the ministers in the headquarters.

FIGURE 2.8 The first oil troops settling along the Songliao Plain, 1960. Source: Daqing geming weiyuanhui, *Daqing.*

FIGURE 2.9 The army at the Daqing construction site, year unknown. Source: Daqing geming weiyuanhui, *Daqing.*

Summer soon brought torrential downpours. The water was good for drilling but bad for transportation. The plain thawed into a spongy prairie land and became hostile to motor vehicles, as figure 2.9 illustrates. The priority of construction work was to complete a road network so as to achieve the goal of putting the oil field into operation by the end of the year. But along the Songliao Plain winter could come as early as September. Without proper shelter, a single blizzard could kill thousands of workers. In 1960, because famine was devastating the entire country, many workers' families began showing up at the oil field, relying on the men to support them despite the minimal food and shelter. However, Daqing's leaders summarily dismissed the idea of withdrawing the troops to the nearby cities, such as Harbin or Changchun, to ride out the winter. That would have left only six months for construction and would thus have delayed oil production. For Yu Qiuli, who had led numerous battles under cruel and harsh conditions and who had walked the Long March with a critical injury to his arm, retreat would have been an even bigger humiliation than defeat. Speaking from his Beijing office to Kang Shi'en, Minister Yu made it very clear: "This campaign can only go forward, not backward! Whatever the difficulties, you must persist. There is no question about this."[15]

TEMPORARY HOUSING, COMMUNAL BUILDING

Was there any way to build houses for all the workers and their families in only three months? Where would the headquarters find a sufficient number of laborers? Ouyang Qin, the Party secretary of Heilongjiang province, suggested that the oil workers and their families should construct their own temporary residences out of locally available materials. Such houses, widely used by the locals, were made from mud and hay and were commonly called *gandalei* (literally "dry pounded earth walls"). The dry mud is mixed with hay, poured into a wooden frame, and then pounded repeatedly to make it solid enough to stand up as a wall. The roof is made of layers of hay and finished off with mud. With their thick earthen walls and mud roofs and heated by an interior fireplace, the houses were warm enough to endure the tough northern winters and were comfortably cool in the summer. Except for the wood needed for the windows, doors, and beams, *gandalei* houses were constructed primarily using the locally available earth and hay and they could be built by the workers during their spare time, just as the peasants did, without professional training or tools.

Taking Ouyang's advice, a *gandalei* building headquarters was established, headed by Sun Jingwen, vice minister of the Petroleum Industry. Sun had previously worked in urban construction for six years, where he served as the first head of the Urban Construction Bureau under the Ministry of Building Construction (1953–1955), and then as vice minister for the newly established Ministry of Urban Construction (1955–1958).[16] The headquarters organized the Gandalei Youth Commandos, who built several thousand square meters of experimental mud houses north of Saertu, where the No. 1 Oil Extraction Factory had been established. After learning the technique from the local peasants, they developed building manuals and guidelines and prepared the basic building tools for mass construction. The Youth Commandos summoned all Youth League members and young workers to join the "communist volunteers" to build *gandalei* housing in their spare time. The nearby forestry farm at Daxing'an Mountain, which probably had the richest timber resources in China, provided the needed timber. All of Daqing's workers, engineers, and cadres joined in this building movement. As they were all busy during the day working on oil production, at night the oil field would become one vast construction site. Many workers labored until midnight to construct houses for their families and colleagues. There was no master plan for the construction of the temporary housing. Each work unit chose a convenient location in the vicinity of their respective worksites. Figure 2.10 shows the building of *gandalei* by Youth League members in process.

Beginning on June 1, every work unit organized a specialized building team to accelerate the "voluntary" building process. They shipped timber from the mountain and made the doors, windows, and braids of hay—jobs that were more technically demanding. The local governments and the PLA also participated. The Shenyang Military District helped make 6,050,000 mud bricks and Heilongjiang province provided scarce timber resources.[17]

By mid-October, when the first snows fell on the plain, 220,000 square meters of *gandalei* housing had been completed, providing housing for thirty thousand people, though half of the houses still had unfinished windows and roofs. Finally, in November, after 120 days of accelerated housing construction, the remaining ten thousand workers and staff, who had been living in tents, moved into warm and safe *gandalei* homes. As stated in a report by the Ministry of the Petroleum Industry sent to the State Planning Commission, the cost for building the *gandalei* housing was less than 30 yuan per square meter, without taking into account the voluntary labor performed by the workers, soldiers, dependents, engineers, and cadres. Elsewhere in the country, the standard cost to build housing was 200 yuan per square meter. During the campaign, "nonproductive" investments for housing totaled only 9 million yuan, less than

FIGURE 2.10 Youth League members building a *gandalei*, year unknown.
Source: Daqing geming weiyuanhui, *Daqing.*

1 percent of the more than 1 billion yuan that was invested in Daqing. This was significantly less than the "nonproductive" investments in other state projects, which averaged 9.3 percent in 1957 and 3 to 4 percent in 1958 and 1959.[18]

FIGHTING FAMINE, COLLECTIVIZING THE WOMEN

Extreme hunger accompanied the snow. In September 1960, on the eve of the forthcoming harsh winter, the Heilongjiang provincial government realized that its food reserves were already depleted and it was facing the sudden rising demand of an industrial army. Thus grain rations for cadres and Party members were significantly reduced, to about 13.5 kilograms per month, in order to save the small amount of food that remained for the oil workers. Drilling workers, who received supplementary allowances, received monthly rations ranging from 22.5 to 28 kilograms of food grain, and extraction workers received from between 16 and 22.5 kilograms of grain.[19] Other food groups (*fushi*), including vegetables and meat, completely disappeared from people's diet. Even with such drastic reductions, however, the sustainability of Daqing's food supplies was seriously threatened. Furthermore, many workers had to share their limited grain with wives and children who had followed them to the northeast. In the spring of 1961, there were more than 6,900 families living in Daqing. People hunted desperately for food to supplement their limited rations. Food prices on the local black market skyrocketed. Nearly half of the people in Daqing exchanged their belongings, including their clothes, radios, and bicycles, for food.[20] Before long, the oil field was covered with thick ice and snow, and people could no longer search for food on the prairie. As elsewhere in the country, many of those who were deprived of adequate nutrition developed dropsy. It was reported that by the end of 1960 more than 4,600 people in Daqing had swollen limbs.

When Kang Shi'en was called back to the Daqing Oil Field in January 1961, he realized that productivity on the oil-drilling front had been seriously impacted by the famine. According to a report by the drilling headquarters, more than eight hundred workers had left for home after the New Year's Mobilization Conference; many others had submitted sick-leave applications and were waiting for approval. Using his personal connections and prestige within the PLA, Yu Qiuli was able to guarantee an extra 75,000 kilograms of grain per month for those in Daqing and an additional 1.5 kilograms of soybeans per month for every worker, but this still fell far short of demand.

In every work unit, supplies in the canteens were the main focus of the leaders. All commanders were required to learn how to cook food and how to maximize its utility. The canteens were under strict supervision in order to provide quality food. Exhibitions and conferences about cooking in the canteens were held throughout the year. Many work units developed creative recipes that utilized wild vegetables and grain alternatives.

Kang therefore withdrew 20 percent of the workforce from the production front, and the sick were provided with extra food rations. The remaining workers were mobilized for a campaign to fight hunger. Following the pattern of the oil campaign, people were organized into specialized teams for hunting, fishing, digging, and reclamation. After receiving simple training, they set off for the plains that, after the mass mobilization conference, had been divided into different "battlefields." On January 15, the first hunting team, consisting of one hundred retired soldiers, left for the forests of Daxing'an Mountain. The other, less capable teams, each with more than one hundred people, hunted for rabbits, foxes, birds, fish, rats, wild vegetables, and anything else that was edible on the prairie. The harvest was enjoyed communally; the headquarters collected the food and then allocated it equally to all the units.

In the spring of 1961, some housewives who came from peasant backgrounds picked up their hoes and began reclaiming the nearby land in order to ease the burden on their families and to provide food for their hungry children. After they completed their daily work, their husbands would join them in the fields. Such reclamation of farmland was welcomed by the headquarters. *Zhan bao* (Battlefield News), Daqing's official internal newspaper, began to publish advice about farming and reclamation. Families were encouraged to reclaim all available lots for farming, raising poultry, building fish ponds, and so forth. Five women were honored as model "dependents."[21] The event marked the beginning of a movement to organize all of the housewives in collective farms.

INTEGRATION OF LIVING AND WORKING, INTEGRATION OF INDUSTRY AND AGRICULTURE

The Daqing Oil Field is huge, totaling about 6,000 square kilometers and running 140 kilometers from north to south. The *gandalei* houses were usually built next to the worksites, whether they were oil wells, drilling sites, or offices. Production of crude oil followed a dispersed pattern. Because the oil field was so large and the production sites were so scattered, the workers and their families found it convenient to live in close proximity to their worksites, especially when the roads were still under construction and transportation was difficult. As an oil well entered into production, it became less labor-intensive, so at that point the oil workers could help their wives with the farming. The open, fertile prairie enabled people to farm wherever they wanted. In the years following the Daqing oil campaign, villages and settlements began to spread all over the Songliao Plain.

*   *   *

The women's dormitory was located to the southeast of the Daqing Design Institute compound. Like the offices, it was a one-story brick house. The single room was spartan but clean. Eight hard bunk beds, with personal belongings stored underneath, were situated along the walls. In the middle of the room there was a gas stove and two tables. That's all. Everyone tried to live as simply as possible, with minimal personal belongings, usually just one suitcase, one or two pairs of shoes, and a washbasin. Hua was familiar with such frugality, as the situation closely resembled her student life. Xiao Zhong quickly moved her belongings from the upper bunk to the lower bunk and then helped Hua to set up her things.

"This house is newly built, and it's cold at night. There's only one gas stove. The upper bed is warmer than the lower one. I'm a native here in the northeast. As a southerner, you're surely not yet used to the cold," Xiao Zhong explained.

Hua was grateful for Xiao Zhong's kindness. Not only was it warmer, but the upper bunk was also more private, since the lower bunks were often used as seats for roommates and visitors.

Xiao Zhong showed Hua the well and the lavatory in the yard. This was the third year of the Daqing campaign and the living conditions were improving somewhat but were still relatively primitive. There was no running water. A container truck brought drinking water to the canteen every day. The so-called well in the yard was merely a long pipe that ran into the ground, and its diameter was only wide enough to fit a cup tied to a bamboo stick. This was used for both washing and laundry. There was an outdoor lavatory beside the dormitory, enclosed by hay curtains. Hua knew what it was like inside. At school, as a consequence of the "revolution in education," students had been required to go down to the countryside to engage in manual labor. It was a typical toilet used by rural peasants: an open pit with two wooden planks perched loosely on the sides above the hole. For students, such facilities were temporary; they knew they would return to the city after just a week or two. But for Hua, now living in Daqing, such conditions would be permanent.

"Be sure to bring a flashlight to the toilet at night. You can find it on the table. The planks are thin and the ground is very slippery. It won't be funny if you fall off," Xiao Zhong warned her.

Noticing that Hua was upset, Xiao Zhong added, "We girls usually don't go to the toilet at night. Prepare a chamber pot. I have one."

Xiao Zhong was one of the senior staff members at the Daqing Design Institute. She had arrived in Daqing in 1961, when the Institute was still scattered among a few prefab mobile houses in Saertu. She recalled the first few days when she didn't even have a fixed place to sleep. They worked day and night to draw up the blueprints for the most urgent construction projects. There was never enough time. After a hard day's work, she would search the local hostels, usually at midnight, and squeeze into any spare space she could find on the wide bed (*da tong pu*), regardless of whether it was with men or women. Everyone was so exhausted that they would fall asleep immediately without even noticing their neighbors. There was modest grain rationing and everyone was hungry all the time. Learning from her peers, Xiao Zhong bought a bottle of soy sauce. Whenever she felt too hungry to work in the late evening, she mixed soy sauce with some hot water to make "soy sauce soup," a bowl of which would temporarily ease the hunger pains in her stomach. Unlike many others, she was lucky not to come down with dropsy, but malnutrition was inevitable.

"You are lucky. This is far better than when we first arrived here," she told Hua, repeating what the division head had told her.

During winter in the northeast, the days become dark very early. Hua followed Xiao Zhong to the canteen, whose walls were covered with big-character posters (*da zi bao*). While she stood in line for food, Hua would read the posters. The criticism focused on two former heads of the Design Institute and a young college graduate from Shanghai. Originally the Design Institute had been based in Fushun, in Liaoning province. When the campaign commenced, however, the headquarters required that the Institute move its offices to Daqing, but the former heads of the Institute had refused. They argued that Daqing's temporary situation was insufficient for design work and that it was preferable that they remain in Fushun. This reaction was seriously criticized, and the heads were replaced by PLA officers. In the winter, the college graduate, who had also complained about the harsh living conditions, the food, and the uselessness of design at an oil field, bought a ticket to Shanghai and never returned to Daqing. Hua felt the man had made some good points, but she would never openly admit this. She could not imagine how that young student was going to be able to survive in Shanghai. In the 1960s, urban residents could obtain goods and services only through their place of work. Without a proper work unit and a household registration, the student would not receive any food rations or daily essentials. The criticism must have made his life even more difficult. Since then, Hua hadn't heard any news about him.

After getting her dinner, Xiao Zhong said goodbye to Hua. She had extra work to do that evening. It seemed everyone always had extra work. No one had yet returned from the office. Hua sat in the dorm alone, concentrating on chewing her sorghum rice; it was hard to digest, but it was easy to grow and resistant to heat and drought, so it served as the basic food for poor rural families in the north. She began worrying about Song and whether he would be able to deal with the food in Saertu, as he often had stomach troubles.

Before long, Hua fell asleep without even taking off her coat. When she woke up in the early morning, everyone had returned but they were all sound asleep. Hua put on her full armor and headed out to the lavatory. It had snowed during the night and the land was covered with pure white snow. While walking awkwardly in her new boots, Hua was impressed by the beauty of the plains. The boots had been designed for resisting the harsh winters in Daqing, but they were as heavy as iron. Just as Xiao Zhong had warned, after taking her second step Hua slipped off the plank. Fortunately, the pit was frozen solid. Hua quickly picked herself up. There was nothing on her boots, but she could not help brushing them again and again with the snow. When she finally returned to the dorm, she was surprised to find that everyone had already gotten up and some had already left. Those who remained were dressing at lightning speed and then rushed out, as if to battle.

Over the following years, battles became part of Hua's daily routine. Very seldom could she return to the dorm before midnight, so the amount of time for sleeping was far too precious to maintain her former standards of hygiene. She usually got up at the last minute, rubbed her face roughly with a dry towel—it took too long to get water from the pipe well, and if you prepared the water at night it would have turned into a basin of ice by morning—and rushed off to work. Breakfast had to be skipped if she was not fast enough. The open lavatory continued to haunt her.

At the Institute, most of her colleagues were either single or living separately from their spouses. They were at the "work unit" (*danwei*) day and night, for both working and living. Her colleagues were mostly young, enthusiastic, and friendly. Everyone tried hard to put the interests of the collective before self interests, practicing the same kind of selflessness that Xiao Zhong had when she unhesitatingly gave up the best bed in the dorm for Hua. Men and women always wore the same uniforms, without any marks or ranks. During that period of time, Hua felt that she was embarking on a new way of life, a life of frugality and hardship, a life with innocent dreams.

Hua's first battle at the Institute was against the bed bugs. Almost every room was infested with bugs, and the Institute decided to kill them all at once. The administrative office purchased insecticide powder for every unit. Xiao Zhong was appointed the commander in chief. In the early morning, the battle began when the men brought boiled water provided by the canteen to the yard and helped the women move their bunks outside. Xiao Zhong showed them how to pour the boiled water thoroughly over the planks and bed frames. The hot water kept spilling on the ground, thawing the snow and ice. When the beds had dried, Xiao Zhong instructed everyone to pour the insecticide into the gaps in the frames. The "battlefield" was full of steam, mud, and the excitement of the young men and women. Afraid of bringing the mud and bugs inside, everyone ate their lunch outdoors, sitting on the bed frames, despite the freezing weather. They talked and laughed, turning the bug battle into a collective picnic.

Their lives were becoming routine. Work began at 7:30 a.m. and ended at 5:30 p.m. After supper, it was time for political study, from 7:00 to 9:00. After 9:00, everyone was back at their drawing boards. The leaders never left their offices before midnight, and no one else felt comfortable about leaving before the leaders.

However, there were also moments of relaxation. For Hua, who had a sweet voice, it was the choir after supper. A young man from Chongqing Architectural Engineering School played the accordion, and another man from Shanghai played the violin. Melodies often floated from the fourth division between supper and political study time. They sang popular Chinese songs from the 1950s, mostly about wars and patriotism. "Sing for the Homeland" (Ge chang zu guo), "Song of the Youth League" (Gong qing tuan yuan zhi ge), "On Taihang Mountain" (Tai hang shan shang), "Ten Times Farewell to the Red Army" (Shi song hong jun), and "Song of Guerrilla Fighters" (You ji dui zhi ge) were among their favorites. They sang Russian songs and other foreign folk songs as well. The Russian song "Singing Our Turbulent Youth" (Gechang women dongdang

de qingchun) was a favorite as it was about love, friendship, and youth-
ful yearnings to accomplish great deeds during hard times. The singing
of the choir warmed up the room as well as their young hearts.

The mandatory political study session usually included study of
Chairman Mao's writings "On Contradiction" (Maodun lun) and "On
Practice" (Shijian lun) and stories about model workers and the history
of oil exploration. There were also regular ritual sessions of mutual criticism and self-criticism. Sometimes a comrade from the Headquarters Division of Policy Research, Compound No. 2, would deliver a talk about
international or domestic issues. He was a really good speaker, intelligent,
and with a good sense of humor. Hua could not really understand China's
complicated relationship with the Soviet Union, or the conflicts among
Mao, Tito, Stalin, and Khrushchev, but she knew that the formerly
united communist bloc was undergoing dramatic change.

In addition to political study and the making of blueprints, the designers shared responsibility for maintaining the compound. Usually the
dependents were responsible for cleaning the toilets and the open septic
tanks, and they would use the waste as organic fertilizer. In 1962, the
Institute organized the rural housewives into a collective farm, based on
a spirit of "self-sufficiency." Because there were fewer than twenty rural
housewives at the Institute who were involved in land reclamation and
raising livestock, the Institute leader decided that every division would
share in the responsibilities of contributing to communal living. Every
week, Hua and her colleagues joined the dependents to clean the toilet.
In the cold of winter, the septic tank often looked like an upside-down
karst cave, piled high with frozen human feces. When a pickaxe hit the
frozen surface, fragments would fly out in all directions. After the second shift, the women learned to wrap their faces with scarves to protect
themselves from the contents of the tank. The working situation was
even worse during the summer, when everything melted and became
putrefied.

Because they were bombarded during political study sessions (after
the Anti-Rightist Movement of 1957 and the Revolution in Education of
1959) with stories about Daqing cadres and intellectuals who had learned
from the workers and the peasants and who were not afraid of engaging
in difficult manual labor, none of the members of the Design Institute
would dare to shirk their toilet-cleaning responsibilities. How could they

claim that being better-educated university graduates from the big cities they were superior to the peasant housewives?

* * *

Battlefield Communism: Integration of State and Society

Although the famine cast a huge shadow on China's contemporary history, the Daqing campaign shed a light on that dark period and eventually became a model for Chinese industrialization. In the autumn of 1960, Daqing Oil Field shipped its first tank of oil, shown in Figure 2.11, though this was more a symbolic victory than anything else. Nevertheless, within three years the oil field was fully operational. By 1963, Daqing's crude oil production had reached 4.4 million metric tons, already half of the country's oil supply. China stopped importing crude oil from the Soviet Union beginning in 1961 and had significantly cut the import of Soviet petroleum products since 1963.[22]

FIGURE 2.11 Daqing's first shipment of crude oil, 1960. Source: Daqing geming weiyuanhui, *Daqing*.

The Daqing campaign recorded the transition in the CCP from leadership of the Revolution to leadership of construction. Its rich battle experiences were represented in its leadership and administrative styles during the early years of the People's Republic. After a decade of political and economic reforms, the country was thoroughly organized and mobilized under a single widely acknowledged ideology. The Party-state proved adept at extracting and mobilizing resources, energy, and enthusiasm from the masses for a single project within a very short time. This was achieved with heavy capital investments—not only physical but also human capital. The central government concentrated all decision-making power within the state, and the ministries and enterprises became agents for implementing the national state plan.

The year 1960 marked the end of the Great Leap Forward and the beginning of the famine. The first troops to arrive in Daqing were young, energetic, and disciplined. The top leaders were in their thirties and forties, and the workers and engineers were either new graduates or soldiers who had retired after the Korean War. During this period of crisis, they were called upon to follow China's revolutionary spirit of self-sacrifice in order to build a new industrial base for the motherland. The harsh conditions encouraged the young men and women to live communally; they not only worked and lived together, but they also built their houses together and hunted for food together. The physical and human constraints and scarcities contributed to the solidarity of the community. For many first-generation Daqing people, this period was a memorable utopian moment, representing a primitive style of communist life. Every individual was mobilized and integrated as part of the group, becoming both objects of and agents for revolutionary change. During this period, there were no boundaries between state and society or between public and private.

CHAPTER 3

Breakthrough on a Narrow Front

Hua felt restless when it was already past noon on the ninth work-day. The administrative head had not yet announced whether or not the fourth division would be allowed to take the next day off. The last shuttle bus left from Ranghulu to Saertu at 6:00 p.m. If she couldn't catch it, she would have to walk across the desolate prairie for half an hour to take the train. Wild wolves, roaming on the prairie and desperate for food, had been seen attacking the villages.

Ten minutes before 6:00, the good news was finally announced. Hua grabbed her bag and hurried out of the office as if she were about to do something embarrassing. The bus stop was right behind the compound. A Liberation truck, produced by the Changchun No. 1 Auto Plant as one of the major projects completed during the First Five-Year Plan period, had just arrived. It served numerous purposes in Daqing: shipping goods and passengers, everyone and everything, to and from the fields, running both day and night.

The truck driver stuck his head out the window and shouted, "Where are you going?"

Hua shouted back, "Saertu!"

"Climb on board!" the driver commanded before returning to his seat.

It took Hua quite a little while to climb onto the freight truck. She was a small woman, and the cumbersome *dao dao fu* uniform that she was wearing made it all the more difficult. Someone in the truck reached out a hand and helped to pull her up. The truck was half-covered by a canvas. Inside there were iron benches welded to each side. But the passengers couldn't really sit down; the journey was simply too bumpy. Instead, they had to stand and hold tight so they would not be tossed into one another or against the sides of the truck. The earth in the Songliao Plain was flat and frozen hard as concrete in the winter, but by spring it would thaw into mean and nasty wetland; therefore, any solid construction required a very deep foundation. However, construction of the motorway had been carried out in such a hurry that there wasn't time to lay a good foundation under the pavement. After about a year, the foundation had already given way and the road had been destroyed. Because the truck was half-open, frostbite was another deadly danger. In winter, it was necessary to continue to jump and stomp to maintain one's balance and to protect one's body from frostbite. As the announcement of the break at work would often come at the very last minute, Hua always had to rush to the bus stop. Once she was even in too much of a hurry to put on her big-head boots. She almost lost her feet during that trip. The shuttle was free, but this was the painful price that Hua had to pay to be able to visit Song in Saertu.

An hour later, the Liberation truck came to a sudden stop: "Arriving in Saertu!"

It was already dark when they reached the headquarters at Compound No. 2. But the compound was still lit up and people were at work. Song's dormitory was in Compound No. 3, several yards away. Between the two compounds there was no path, only a snow-covered cornfield. Although the corn had been harvested in September, the corn stalks still remained in the fields. Formerly, the stalks could be used for heating and cooking by the peasants during the winters, but in 1962 the Red Plain Farm had given its land to the oil field, so the workers instead used crude oil and gas for fuel.

Hua carefully followed the footprints beside the cornfields until she reached Compound No. 3. Entering the dorm, she realized that the living situation at the Design Institute was much better than the one here. Inside the room there was nothing but a few beds lined up along a heated firewall. The mud wall was about two feet thick. There was a small window at the end of the wall, resembling a deep hole, and the windowsill was stacked with books and daily necessities. The beams and reed cover on the ceiling had turned black due to the smoke from the burning of the crude oil. The different shades of black revealed the different ages of the buildings. The house looked like an old cloth covered with numerous patches. The local-style mud house had been built quickly but required a lot of maintenance; otherwise it would easily collapse. One-third of the mud houses built in Daqing between 1960 and 1961 had collapsed within two years. One night Song and his roommates woke up feeling rather chilly, only to discover that half their house was gone and they were looking directly at the starry night sky.

The dorm could not hold any guests, so Song led Hua to his office, the Office for Living Base (Shenghuo jidi) back at Compound No. 2. There was already one couple there. The two couples reached a tacit agreement that each would occupy a corner as far as possible from the other so as to keep their precious reunion time as private as possible.

Song had lost some weight during the first month due to the demanding work and because his southern stomach could not become accustomed to the hard grains in the north. In 1962 the canteen provided only sorghum, corn, and barley. In addition to the regular office work, at night the headquarters staff would take turns taking care of the several oil wells near the compound in order "to engage in manual labor." Every evening there was a routine work meeting that lasted until midnight, during which the production units were briefed on the day's progress and problems and the various divisions in the headquarters would immediately respond to the problems. If a division could not follow up on time, the top leaders, for instance Kang Shi'en, would criticize it harshly without any concern about "saving face." "It was as if we were engaged in a true battle," Song remarked.

The young couple had much to talk about, and the time passed all too quickly. It was already almost midnight. Hua and the other woman walked back to Compound No. 1, where there was a laboratory and the women's dormitory. The door to the women's dorm was half open. At that time, very few doors had locks, and even if they did, no one bothered to use them. After several accidents of carbon monoxide poisoning from the insufficient burning of crude oil, the doors were intentionally left open to provide some ventilation. Inside the dorm, there was a large communal brick bed. The lights in the dorm had already been turned off, but Hua and the other woman could still see because of the fire coming from the stove. The bed was quite full and everyone was already fast asleep. With quilts borrowed from their fiancés, the two women quickly found an empty spot where they could lie down.

*   *   *

By the end of the first decade of the People's Republic, the Chinese economy was facing a series of setbacks and complications. The difficult task of building a balanced relationship between industry and agriculture had seemingly come to a dead end. Shortages of both capital and inputs limited the growth of agricultural production, which in turn curtailed industrial construction. The problem was addressed on all fronts—stressing heavy industry while promoting light industry and agriculture through both massive construction of capital projects and the full mobilization of labor power. But due to the famine (1960–1962), the country had exhausted any possibility of making further progress by following the existing path.

In this situation, urban expenditures, which were considered a constituent part of "nonproductive construction," were strictly controlled and often were the first to be cut. The state spent most of its revenue on reinvestments in "productive" units. Accumulation, referring to the revenue returned to production instead of used for consumption, was maintained at a high rate, and urgent social needs were ignored. Urban planners faced waves of criticism for their "excessive spending" of state investments, which left little for the construction of urban housing, transportation, education, or public welfare. Frugality, austerity, and self-sufficiency were promoted in society, and the people were asked to curb their rate of consumption and leisure in order to achieve higher rates of economic growth.

Three years after the discovery of oil at Daqing, the following questions were finally raised: What was envisioned in terms of the future of the Daqing mining district? What construction model was to be followed? This was an unusual period, as the urban economy was stagnating because many factories and industrial plants were being closed. Mandatory and voluntary urban-to-rural migration, famine, and the spread of epidemics led to a sharp drop in the urban population. The petroleum leaders dealt with the economic realities by introducing a spirit of austerity in order to close the urban-rural gap, thus creating a new and different Daqing model.

The Political Economy of Building Construction

In a centrally planned economy, cities are characterized by the building of infrastructure for industrial production, thus distinguishing them from the countryside, whose function is to support agricultural production. The priority in socialist China was to transform the cities from places of consumption in the "old world order" to producers in the "new world order." At the first National Conference on Urban Construction, held in 1954, Minister of Building Construction Liu Xiufeng clearly stated that the purpose of urban construction in the PRC was to serve industrial production: "Urban construction should be coordinated with the state economic plans, and the speed of urban construction should be determined by the speed of industrial construction."[1]

The First Five-Year Plan transformed the national geography of industrialization in modern China. The spatial distribution of state industrial projects gave birth to numerous new towns, or, to be more precise, to new factory towns and newly developed industrial districts in the old cities.[2] As clearly stated, the goal was to build industry, not to build cities, and to industrialize but not to urbanize. In the language of the state plans, the term "urban construction" did not appear. Rather, the term used was "basic construction," referring to the fixed assets to be built for industrial projects. Basic construction was divided into "productive construction" and "nonproductive construction," the latter referring to public housing, urban services, and minimal facilities to guarantee the daily operations of industrial production.

Nevertheless, implementation of the state industrialization plans triggered extensive urban growth. As a result of the postwar baby boom, China's total population increased from 541 million in 1949 to 662 million by 1960. The cities faced even more dramatic growth. The total urban population more than doubled, from 57.65 million in 1949 to 130.73 million in 1960.[3] Notably, during the first decade of the PRC, the baby boom affected the cities much more than it affected the countryside because many young men and women of child-bearing age were drawn to the cities by the industrial sectors. Massive movements took place back and forth between the cities and the countryside. The migration was determined by the economic situation, which posed great challenges to the state planners, economically, socially, and physically. For example, in 1955, 2 million people returned to the countryside because of difficulties in the urban economy. However, in the next year, 6.5 million newcomers flooded into the cities as the national economy achieved a "Little Leap Forward."

In 1952, the Central Finance and Economics Commission grouped Chinese cities into four classes based on their construction priorities. The first class consisted of eight "heavy industrial cities": Beijing, Baotou, Xi'an, Datong, Qiqihar, Daye, Lanzhou, and Chengdu. The second class was made up of fourteen "cities that could be rebuilt by industrial production": Jilin, Anshan, Fushun, Benxi, Shenyang, Harbin, Taiyuan, Wuhan, Shijiazhuang, Handan, Zhengzhou, Luoyang, Zhanjiang, and Urumqi. And the third class consisted of seventeen "medium-level industrial production old cities," including Tianjin, Dalian, Changchun, Jiamusi, Shanghai, Nanjing, and Chongqing. The thirty-nine cities in these first three classes were considered "major construction cities." In the fourth class were the remaining cities, classified as "ordinary cities," whose main goal was to maintain minimal daily operations.[4] Many of the designated major cities accomplished their city planning goals during the First Five-Year Plan period, coordinating relations between the existing cities and the designated industrial projects as well as implementing an infrastructure system.

During the First Five-Year Plan period, Soviet influence was overwhelming. This influence extended to the field of urban planning. Soviet planners helped to draft national planning guidelines and standards. The Ministry of Building Construction established special teams to translate Russian planning textbooks and regulations into Chinese. Every planning institution sent representatives to Beijing to receive training from visiting Soviet planners or sent representatives directly to Moscow. Soviet planners also served as consultants for planning in the major cities.[5] City plans in the early 1950s generally followed the principles of socialist city planning based on the 1935 Moscow plan. These principles included preserving the old city core as the administrative center and channeling industrial use to the peripheral areas—usually outside of the inner-city ring, in a downstream and downwind position, and separated from the residential areas by large areas of greenery or parks.[6]

Following master plans that illustrated future blueprints for the next twenty years, many of the industrial districts were located at the far outskirts of the cities. There was not much infrastructure, in particular public transportation, linked to the old city center. The factories were required to build workers' housing and other supporting facilities from their respective budgets, thus creating numerous de facto independent factory towns. The municipal governments were responsible, within their limited budgets, only for providing simple infrastructure in the new districts.

The Soviets were directly involved in the detailed planning of the factories and the workers' housing. The plans typified the Stalinist ideal of "national style and socialist content," including having a strong central axis and green belts, a symmetrical arrangement of the buildings, parameter blocks, and a monumental entrance. All residential buildings followed a historicist style, with traditional Chinese big roofs, and two- or three-bedroom apartments based on the Soviet standard of nine square meters per person—the so-called "scientific standard to live hygienically." Figures 3.1–3.3 show how all these features appeared in the Changchun No. 1 Auto Plant.

ACHIEVING BALANCED DEVELOPMENT

As the state plans were implemented and institutions were established, the national economy became more complex, and the task of planning became increasingly sophisticated. Over the course of the 1950s there was much greater control over the available resources by the central authorities and a decrease in the role of the private sector in industry and agriculture. Ninety percent of the investment in basic construction during the First Five-Year Plan period came from the central government.[7] Prior to 1952, only eight categories of construction materials fell under state control, including iron, timber, and cement. But by 1953, the large-scale industrial construction resulted in a serious shortage of construction materials. To guarantee the timely completion of the major construction projects, the range of materials under state control was expanded significantly. More than 227 categories of "means of production" were included in the state allocation system. In 1957, the final year of the First Five-Year Plan period, the number of controlled categories had been increased to 532. The state distribution

FIGURE 3.1 Changchun No. 1 Auto Plant: main entrance with front square, 1950s. Photo courtesy of Ministry of Building and Construction Archives.

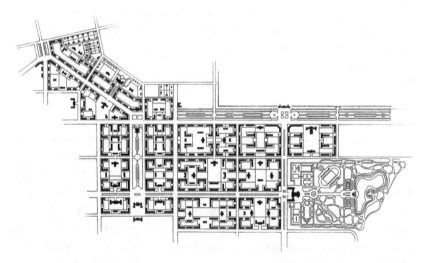

FIGURE 3.2 Changchun No. 1 Auto Plant: master plan for living quarters, 1949. Photo courtesy of Ministry of Building and Construction Archives.

and allocation system basically provided all the materials required for capital construction. Additionally, the purchase of all industrial facilities was planned and ordered by the central government. Local units received their allocations according to the plan and were also required to arrange production according to the plan.

FIGURE 3.3 Changchun No. 1 Auto Plant: workers' housing with traditional Chinese-style roof, 1959. Photo courtesy of Ministry of Building and Construction Archives.

Human capital was managed directly by the central government as well. The State Planning Commission decided on the number of university enrollments. All technical staff in state-owned enterprises and university graduates were under the control of the state distribution system. In 1953 the central government dissolved the industrial administrative departments at the regional levels and redistributed their cadres and technical elite into the ministries and the state-owned enterprises. There were a limited number of experienced modern construction workers, and even they required extensive training. Therefore the construction industry, which was managed by the Ministry of Building Construction, had to be created from scratch at the central level. Many of the state construction workers were soldiers who had retired from the PLA.

The great concentration of both resources and power at the center became increasingly demanding as well as dangerous for the "planning kingdom." The priority of investment was overwhelmingly in the relatively few capital-intensive heavy industries. But for the short term, this "breakthrough on a narrow front" method meant disproportionate growth and a constant need for adjustments to maintain a socioeconomic balance "manually." This "shortages now, surpluses tomorrow" feature is built into many planning economies.[8] It was especially challenging when facing a learning-by-doing process. The state had yet to establish a comprehensive system to collect and interpret data. Furthermore, there was a lack of capacity to respond appropriately to changing circumstances, and there were different interpretations of the responses. The economics of a planned economy are, above all, political. Economic reasoning is complicated by issues of state power versus the power of the branches, local units, and the society, as well as by the battles among the various power holders. Official reports and leaders' speeches often seemed indifferent, filled with empty phrases such as "Place the plan on a . . . completely sound basis"; "Ensure a fairly balanced development of the national economy"; "Proceed gradually as far as conditions permit"; "In accordance with local needs and resources": "When conditions . . . are ripe"; "Build step by step"; "In a planned and well-prepared way"; and so on. But beneath such linguistic ambiguities, disagreements about the direction and pace of socialist construction grew. Debates between proponents of a hard line versus proponents of a relatively moderate line in terms of construction began during the middle of the First Five-Year Plan period. Commitments to different strategies were often linked to different ideological views—being either leftist or rightist—and inevitably were interpreted as revealing personal loyalties to different leaders. As revealed by their language, such differences were not more pronounced than their similarities.

Those state planners whose day-to-day job was to run the country and who were responsible for meeting daily needs and demands were inclined to be more sensitive and cautious about the complexities of the planned economy. The First Five-Year Plan was not approved until April 1955, after a series of critiques and revisions, so until then the national economy was run primarily on the basis of annual plans that were essentially makeshift, perfectly describing the fate of "planning" in many cases. From year to year the planners faced dramatic shifts between shortages and surpluses. The interim adjustment policies often further complicated the situation.

In 1953, the scale of basic construction increased 83.7 percent compared to the previous year, exceeding the projected 75 percent growth rate, which was already a bold number. The number of state employees, that is, those who received food rations and social housing, increased by 15.8 percent.[9] The hustle and bustle in the major construction cities was described by the work team of the Bureau of Urban Construction from the central government as "chaotic scuffles in the sky and on the ground, blind movements of both the dead and the living."[10] In contrast, in 1953 grain production increased only 1.8 percent and cotton production decreased

9.9 percent from the previous year. The country faced an extreme shortage of capital, construction materials, skilled personnel, and, most important, food.

In response to the tense situation, in 1954, in the face of yet another year of grain reductions, the planners proposed a more conservative plan for 1955, directing more investment toward agriculture and significantly lowering industrial growth. The growth rate of industrial production for 1955 was first adjusted downward from 15.5 percent to 12.4 percent, then, in January 1955, it was further adjusted downward to 7.7 percent. Nationwide, only fifty thousand new employees were permitted.[11] To the surprise of the planners, one of the best agricultural harvests occurred in 1955. With the significant cut in the quota for industrial production and nonproductive construction projects, there was a 1.8 billion yuan positive balance in the state budget and a large surplus of pig iron, cement, and timber. Total industrial output increased only 6 percent. The State Council signed a contract with the USSR to export discounted construction materials to mitigate the unforeseen surplus. However, the surplus soon turned into a serious shortage. The contract had to be canceled within a month after it was signed. Premier Zhou Enlai issued a self-criticism for the poor judgment of the State Council.

THE "RASH ADVANCE"

In the mid-1950s, attempts were made to introduce some flexibility to the planning controls, such as allowing more free markets and encouraging the involvement of provincial- and local-level governments. The relaxation from above, which was made public in September 1956 at the Eighth Party Congress, encouraged a series of liberalization policies to relieve the pressure on state planning. Free markets for "minor commodities" were reopened. Peasants were allowed to develop individual sideline occupations, such as handicrafts or raising poultry. The state-controlled prices allowed more flexibility to introduce price and income incentives as supplements to the administrative controls. The provincial and local governments were authorized to have a certain amount of financial power and autonomy and became more involved in the making of the Second Five-Year Plan.[12]

However, in devising the annual plan, the state planners began to feel the consequences of "liberalization" and decentralization. On New Year's Day 1956, *People's Daily* called for "an earlier, extra, and complete fulfillment of the First Five-Year Plan" based on the full devotion of the people. The ministries and provincial governments requested more than 20 billion yuan for construction investment a year, as compared to the original 11 billion yuan. The total budget for basic construction in the First Five-Year Plan was just 53 billion yuan. An additional eight hundred major construction projects were proposed from below. Those requests far exceeded the state's capacity for new construction. At a State Council meeting in January 1956, Premier Zhou stated, "We are facing armies approaching from all fronts," and he urged the "hot-headed leaders" to submit more pragmatic numbers "after taking a cold shower."[13] In February, Zhou, the head of the State Planning Commission Li Fuchun, and Minister of Finance Li Xiannian agreed to downsize total state investment to 14.7 billion yuan in 1956. This number was also supported by President Liu Shaoqi. They all agreed that the time had come to oppose a "rash advance" so that the economy could "steadily advance in a comprehensive and balanced way."[14]

In October 1956, the outbreak of protests and the ensuing violence in Poland and Hungary reverberated throughout the socialist bloc. Chinese leaders warned against the dangers of emphasizing excessive heavy industry while ignoring the people's livelihoods. The Ministry of Public Security collected data indicating that waves of protests and riots were also occurring in many Chinese factories and villages. On November 10, during the Second Plenum of the Eighth CCP Central Committee Congress, Liu Shaoqi quoted Mao, stating, "We want heavy industry, and we want the people." Liu warned Party members about the potential for tense relations with the people if the Party were to continue to ignore their livelihood, and he argued that "industrial construction should proceed on a steady and reliable basis," moving "slowly and with flexible space." What was "a steady and reliable basis"? It meant "the masses would not protest on the streets, and they would be happy and enthusiastic about construction."[15]

During the following Great Leap Forward, the problem was addressed on all fronts—"walking on two legs," which meant stressing both heavy and light industry, urban and rural areas, large- and small-scale industry, and capital and labor. National construction relied on "calls [that] have gripped the imagination of the huge army of hundreds of millions of working people and have been transformed into an immense material force."[16] This illusion of "conquering the sky and battling the land" created a vast industrial conflagration that sucked up all available resources, leaving the people exhausted and starving.

EXERCISING AUSTERITY

The drive to cut costs on nonbasic and nonproductive construction was a constant theme in the planning kingdom. In the second half of 1953, in the face of a serious shortage of construction materials, an Increase Production and Economize (Zengchan jieyue) movement was launched. In June, Premier Zhou brought up the issue of anti-decentralization in the field of urban construction. He argued that many industrial projects did not utilize the existing urban infrastructure but rather favored building new isolated industrial districts, resulting in an unnecessary waste of investment. So the State Planning Commission reviewed implementation of the plan and substantially cut investments in nonproductive construction. At the First People's Congress in 1954, Zhou pointed out that the excessively high architectural standards in basic construction had wasted millions of state yuan.

In November 1954, Vice Minister of Building Construction Zhou Rongxi led a delegation to attend the Soviet All-Union Conference of Builders and Architects in Moscow, at which Nikita Khrushchev attacked architectural extravagance and Stalinist socialist realism. By the beginning of 1955, the lowering of construction standards and avoiding the waste of resources had become constant concerns of Chinese planners, echoing the economic changes in Moscow. The focus was on economizing and replacing the prevalent historicist style of public and residential buildings. In February 1955, the Ministry of Building Construction hosted a national conference on design and construction. The conference criticized the trends of "reactionary capitalist formalism" and the pursuit of building "palaces, castles, and temples." Liang Sicheng, a prominent scholar enthusiastic about classical Chinese architecture and president of the Chinese Society of Architecture, was singled out as an influential "revivalist" who had advocated extravagant big roofs. Furthermore, the plan for the residential district of the Changchun No. 1 Auto Plant was declared to be an infamous waste of state resources.[17]

In June 1955, the CCP Central Committee issued these instructions: "Steadfastly lower the standards for nonproductive construction."[18] In

July, the CCP Central Committee issued the "Decision about Taking Austerity Measures," criticizing wasted investments in unnecessary building ornaments and "luxury" standards for nonproductive construction, such as workers' clubs, theaters, recreation centers, stadiums, and greenery. The "Decision" mandated that the 1954 standard for all basic construction, except for necessary equipment and Soviet-designed factory buildings, be cut by 15 to 20 percent. Vice Premier Li Fuchun, who was also the head of the State Planning Commission, pointed out that a more realistic principle of socialist construction involved integrating modern industry with existing cities, and integrating modern factories with a proper standard of housing, offices, and dormitories.[19] In response to this criticism, the Ministry of Building Construction adjusted its urban construction policies. More industrial projects were to be located near the urban built areas and adaptations in the use of existing facilities were to be encouraged. Many of the big roofs for public buildings were cut from the blueprints or were suddenly abandoned during the process of construction. The nine-square-meter living space standard from the Soviet Union was canceled, and instead 4.5 square meters was set as the maximum amount for living space.

During the "liberal interlude" at the beginning of 1956, the Ministry of Building Construction and the local governments were able to defend themselves, arguing that the dramatic cut in housing and public welfare had created living difficulties. Because Mao had used the metaphor of "bone and flesh" to refer to the relationship between production and livelihood, major construction cities, such as Xi'an and Taiyuan, established an Office of Bone and Flesh to review past construction policies.

However, the central planning authority soon initiated another wave to "increase production and economize." In April 1957, a report written by Li Fuchun and Bo Yibo was circulated by the CCP Central Committee among top cadres. It analyzed the "four excesses" in urban construction: "excessive large scale, excessive large areas, excessive pursuit of novelties, excessive high standards." The authors of the report worried that many projects had been hoarding large areas of land for the sake of long-term development and had produced decentralized and inefficient spatial patterns. The costs of infrastructure construction had increased, and land that could have been used for short-term agricultural production had been isolated. The report suggested six proposals.

(1) The allocation of land should be strictly controlled. (2) Construction standards should be lowered, emphasizing medium and small-scale enterprises and encouraging self-designed and self-made homes. In terms of housing standards, workers' housing was to "follow the same standards as that of local residents in the cities" or "the same standards of local peasants in the mining districts." (3) Cities were to build more collective dormitories instead of family housing; dependents were to be encouraged to return to the countryside and workers were to be allowed periodic vacations (for family reunions). (4) New projects for supporting facilities, such as machinery workshops or labs, were no longer to be built. (5) Existing technical schools were not to be expanded, and those schools that had closed or limited recruitment were to adapt their buildings to serve local middle schools or small factories. (6) Public and service buildings were to significantly lower their construction standards, were to be located close to the factory plants, and were encouraged to be adaptable for various uses.[20]

Housing construction slowed down significantly in the second half of the 1950s. The few houses that were built were mostly single-story economic homes or dormitories. Investments in the construction of public facilities also declined. In 1953, 37.5 percent of the investment that Xi'an received was dedicated to the construction of urban facilities for culture, education, and public health. This figure dropped to 23.5 percent in 1954, 13.13 percent in 1955, and 8.46 percent in 1956. In 1957, it was virtually negligible.[21] The per capita living space for Taiyuan residents decreased from 2.65 square meters in 1949 to 2.27 square meters in 1956, which means that living conditions of the Chinese working class were deteriorating during the socialist regime.[22]

While the April 1960 National Urban Planning Conference in Guilin called for "transforming our cities into new socialist modern cities within ten or fifteen years," no one had expected the forthcoming famine. Within a period of only a few months, China's urbanization program underwent its most dramatic and tragic transformation, a roller-coaster ride from the very top to the very bottom. By the end of 1960, both the cities and the countryside faced huge declines in population.

In June 1961, the "Decision on Decreasing the Urban Population and the Food Supply" was issued by the central government, requiring a downsizing of the urban population by at least 20 million within three years. By the end of 1961, it was reported that 13 million people had already lost their urban status. By June 1963, this number reached 26 million. The definition of a city was modified and the total number of cities declined from 208 to 169.

Urban planning was among the first professions to be dismantled. The building and construction sectors were accused of exercising "departmentalism" and "decentralism." At the end of 1960, Li Fuchun announced at a national conference, "No urban planning is needed for the next three years." Half of the cadres in the Ministry of Building Construction were dismissed, and the remaining planners were required to do "investigation and research" only. In 1961, the State Construction Commission was dissolved, and investment in urban construction was completely canceled from 1960 to 1962.

*   *   *

Planning without Cities

The living situation gradually improved in Daqing in 1963. Tap water became available in the village water house, and after New Year's Day a public bathroom was open once a week. For Hua and her colleagues who had become used to cleaning themselves without water for months, this was a big step toward more civilized living. A child care center with a heating system was also completed. However, in 1963 very few families moved to Daqing together with their children, so the Institute allowed the female staff to move into the empty child care center as their temporary dormitory. Compared to their old dormitory, with its thin brick walls and small stove, the child care center was warm and spacious.

Two pretty women, Xiao Li and Xiao Yang, became Hua's roommates. They had received only a middle school education and worked as drafting assistants to the designers. Their presence in the dormitory provided a sense of femininity. They put up curtains, covered their beds with floral prints, and decorated the room with wildflowers and dolls. They also tailored their work uniforms so that they fit better. Xiao Li even slightly permed her bangs. Naturally they became the center of attention in the male-dominated Institute.

In contrast, Hua was always clad in her loosely cut gray or dark blue clothes—even when she was not working, she never wore brightly colored outfits. To save time and water, during her first year in Daqing she had kept her hair cut very short. Sometimes her fiancé would complain about her plain looks. However, in Daqing, being plain-looking, like wearing clothes with patches, implied a commitment to the Revolution. Hua tended to avoid anything that appeared to be feminine, and she worked just as hard as any of the men. She did not like to hear that the two pretty women had come to Daqing to find husbands with better educations. Nevertheless, Hua could not resist visiting Song in Saertu during the breaks. She was embarrassed to leave the office before 6:00 p.m. on the ninth workday, when everyone else was still at work. Because of her regular leave-taking, she knew she would never be awarded as a model laborer (*lao mo*), no matter how many extra hours she contributed to her work on the other days.

Still, Song was reluctant to stay overnight in Ranghulu. He did not feel that it was right. If he visited Hua, he would arrive in the morning and leave by the afternoon. The happiness of their reunion was inevitably haunted by the gloom of the forthcoming departure. After several arguments, Hua gave up. She was the one who would commute between Saertu and Ranghulu. "Song has a better chance to excel at his work, and anyway I have been doomed since my first impressions at the Institute," she said to console herself.

During the 1963 Chinese New Year, there was a three-day break. It was the longest holiday that people in Daqing had enjoyed in a year. This was the first Spring Festival at the Daqing Oil Field since the three years of famine and hardship. The collective farm operated by the dependents of the Institute staff provided fresh pork and cabbage for the holiday. After dinner there was a party. Every unit prepared special programs for the celebration. The canteen saved a portion of the pork and cabbage for those few staff members who could not join the dinner party. Still, the traditional New Year's family reunions were a real luxury in Daqing. In general, only families that lived in Heilongjiang province could partake in such New Year reunions. Therefore, the majority of workers remained at their work units during the holiday. Very few workers applied for a one-month family visit, even those who had worked at the oil field since 1960, because this would be regarded as "withdrawing from the battlefield." In any case, among those who applied, very few actually received approval because in the past so many who had received approval had never returned. Furthermore, not many families could visit Daqing during the holiday. There was neither adequate housing nor sufficient food for additional family members. The visitors had to stay in the canteens, where the simple beds were separated by thin cloth curtains.

Hua wished she could join Song in Saertu for New Year's Eve, but she was unable to catch the last shuttle at 6:00 p.m. There had been too much work to do that afternoon. Old Song, a structural engineer, saw how upset she was and offered to escort her to Saertu after work. But Hua hesitated, thinking it was too much to ask of a colleague on New Year's Eve, so she expressed her gratitude but refused his offer. "No, Old Song. Don't bother. I can take the train by myself. I am not afraid."

In his strong Sichuanese accent, Old Song insisted, "*Mo de shi, mo de shi.* It's not a problem. I can do it."

After work, carrying one cabbage, 100 grams of pork, and a small bag of wheat flour, Old Song walked with Hua into the darkness. When they got off at the Saertu station, just as Hua had done on the day she arrived, they followed the crowd and exited the station through the opening in the barbed wire. Then Old Song greeted an acquaintance who worked in the headquarters. His acquaintance took the cabbage and pork, then turned to Hua: "You can come with me. I am on my way back to the headquarters." Old Song, relieved of his job accompanying Hua, jumped back on the train to return to Ranghulu. It was at that moment that Hua felt really warm, despite the cold winter of Daqing.

When Hua finally stood in front of Compound No. 3, she heard Song playing the *erhu*, a Chinese two-stringed musical instrument. He was playing a popular song, "Everyone Loves Our Homeland," from the movie *Red Sun*, which recounted a harsh battle in the Civil War. Hua couldn't help but sing along with the melody: "With green orchards on the hills and golden grain in the fields." The music suddenly stopped. Song opened the door, his face full of surprise. Hua looked at him happily.

* * *

Following the Soviet experience in Siberia, a base town for oil workers was to be built before the development of oil fields. In late 1959, immediately after the discovery of the rich oil deposits, the Heilongjiang provincial government raised the status of Anda from a county to a city. Yang Zhumin, the former Party secretary of the Harbin Construction Commission, was appointed mayor of Anda City. In May 1960 Mayor Yang commissioned a new city plan, in which, within fifteen years, Anda would become a big oil city, with an urban population reaching 400,000. A small experimental oil refinery was built in the southeast of the city. However, the Ministry of the Petroleum Industry had other plans.

LOCATING THE DAQING REFINERY

In October 1960, a work team led by Ding Xiu, head of the Urban Construction Bureau, was dispatched from Beijing to Heilongjiang province. The purpose of the work team was to select a site to construct the future Daqing refinery that was expected to process about 1 million tons of crude oil and employ a workforce of about five thousand. As a typical major capital construction project, the Ministry of Building Construction established a construction enterprise, the Sixth Engineering Bureau, to build the refinery. It hired six thousand employees, among whom the core workforce worked for the Lanzhou Xigu Refinery, and the remainder were primarily recruited locally. With the incoming eleven thousand state employees and their families, the location of the plant would very likely determine the location of the future base town.

When the planners from Beijing first visited Anda, they only found a small cluster of dilapidated mud houses without any modern infrastructure, a typical small county town in the northeast. Ang'ang'xi in Qiqihar, suggested by the Heilongjiang provincial government, was another potential location because it had convenient railway transportation to Harbin in the east and to Siping, another big industrial city in the northeast, in the south. Qiqihar, however, was a bit farther from the oil field than was Anda.

In Saertu, the work team met Vice Minister of Petroleum Sun Jingwen, who formerly had been Ding Xiu's predecessor as head of the Urban Construction Bureau. It seems that the Ministry of the Petroleum Industry was not thinking about building an oil base city immediately. As the oil campaign was started before they had fully prospected the oil deposits on the Songliao Plain, the ministers were still not confident that Daqing would be a productive oil field. Just a year earlier, they had encountered the failure of the Sichuan campaign. In the early 1950s the Sino-Soviet Oil Joint-Venture Company had made a huge investment for housing and infrastructure for the Dushanzi Oil Field in Xinjiang province, but thereafter the survey results proved to be unsuccessful and

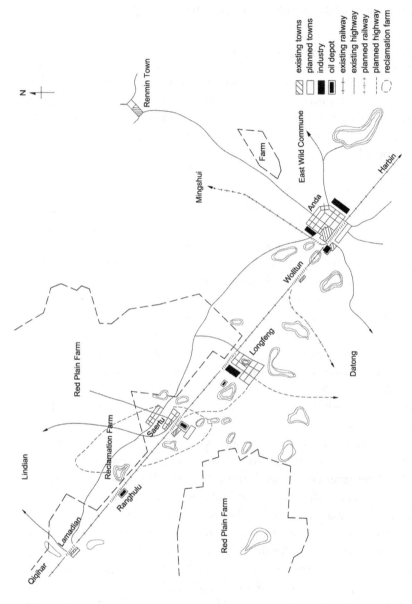

MAP 1 The initial master plan for Daqing Oil Field, with Anda serving as the central city, 1961. Original map by the China Academy of Urban Planning and Design, redrawn by the author.

the construction of the mining residential district had turned out to be a waste of resources.[23] Furthermore, the limited budget that the Ministry of the Petroleum Industry received from the Central Government that year did not permit large-scale urban construction.

Vice Minister Sun was inclined toward developing in a dispersed pattern. He very clearly disliked the idea of building a refinery in Anda. He questioned, "Does Anda have any modern facilities that we can use? Won't it just become another Xigu District of Lanzhou if we put a refinery there?" Xigu District was a concentrated chemical industrial base in Lanzhou, built with the help of the USSR. The planners understood Sun's opposition to the concentration of pollution.[24]

The work team returned to Beijing and submitted its investigation report. In December 1960, the State Planning Commission and the State Construction Commission jointly approved the site of the Daqing Refinery (prior to 1964, it was called the Heilongjiang Refinery) to be constructed in Longfeng (literally "dragon and phoenix"), following the opinion of the Ministry of the Petroleum Industry. Map 1 shows Longfeng, located between Saertu and Anda, 11 kilometers east of Saertu along the railway—a blank patch of land for factory and construction workers. This location would save much time by allowing for commuting by train between the headquarters and the refinery. Workers from the Sixth Engineering Bureau settled at Longfeng and began construction in 1962. The Daqing Refinery was built following the model of the Lanzhou Refinery, but without any assistance from the Soviets. Its first gallon of kerosene and gasoline was produced on November 1, 1963.

VISITORS FROM BEIJING

China's top leaders began to visit Daqing in succession. Deng Xiaoping visited on July 23, 1961 (fig. 3.4). Liu Shaoqi followed on August 7 (fig. 3.5). Although they had different opinions about the mobilization and organization of the campaign, both praised Daqing's attempts to be self-sufficient.[25] Deng declared, "This place is near the railway and the station; motor vehicles can go anywhere on the flat plain; the fertile land is good for farming. This is an ideal place! Qinghai, Yumen, and Xinjiang cannot compare to the situation here, nor can Sichuan."[26] Liu Shaoqi encouraged family dependents to build their own homes supported by

FIGURE 3.4 Deng Xiaoping (left) visiting Daqing, with Kang Shi'en and Zhang Wenbin on the right, 1961. Source: Daqing geming weiyuanhui, *Daqing*.

FIGURE 3.5 Liu Shaoqi (right) visiting Daqing, with Kang Shi'en on the left, 1961. Source: Daqing geming weiyuanhui, *Daqing*.

the public sector, but also said, "Don't let the oil workers engage in agricultural work. It's not worth the 50 yuan per month that we pay." He opined that Daqing provided a good solution for the housing problems and for the "revolutionary" integration of industry and agriculture in the mining district. "Construction of Daqing's mining district and the revolutionization of the dependents have solved those problems that utopian socialists such as Robert Owen and Charles Fourier had not been successful in solving for more than one hundred years. . . . This is the path that world communism should follow." In praise of their achievements, Ouyang Qin from Heilongjiang changed China's traditional agricultural ideals from "men in farming and women in weaving" to Daqing's "men in oil and women in farming."[27]

One year later, on June 21, 1962, Premier Zhou visited Daqing (fig. 3.6). He endorsed the idea of scattered worker-peasant villages and the combination of industrial and agricultural production.

AGAINST CONCENTRATION

In the early 1960s, there were some attempts to centralize production and living services. Daqing People's Hospital was built according to relatively high standards. Located near the Saertu Railway Station and the campaign headquarters, it was a modern three-story building, the first *loufang* (a building with more than one story) in Daqing, boasting advanced medical facilities. Other public services, such as a post office, a bank, and a photo shop, were also built in the proximity of the railway station. Saertu was clearly becoming the administrative and living service center of Daqing Oil Field.

After the "Decision on Decreasing the Urban Population and the Food Supply" was issued by the central government in June 1961, Anda received a downsizing quota of 48,384. In 1961, the urban population in the prefecture of Anda City had increased to 300,000, including 117,200 staff and family members who worked for central enterprises under the Ministry of the Petroleum Industry, the Ministry of Geology, and the Ministry of Building Construction; 47,300 provincial- and local-level enterprise employees and their families; and 35,000 employees of state farms who were categorized as "urban." For an area that was still receiving a workforce dispatched from the ministries, the painful cut in the urban

FIGURE 3.6 Zhou Enlai (middle) making his first visit to Daqing in 1962, with *gandalei* houses in the background. Yu Qiuli and Kang Shi'en are walking with Zhou. Song Zhenming, the tall smiling man with his arms crossed, is standing behind Yu. Source: Daqing geming weiyuanhui, *Daqing*.

population primarily affected those who worked for the provincial and municipal enterprises and their dependents, that is, the women and children. Not only did they lose their salaried work, but, more important, they also lost their grain rations. But many of those who lost their urban status still did not return to the countryside. Instead, they stayed in Anda and remained dependent on their husbands' income. At the same time, the campaign headquarters received many more applications than the size of the downsizing quota to relocate families to the oil field. The number of dependents who did not live with the oil staff totaled 67,000.[28] The oil field was under pressure to permanently accommodate a rapidly increasing population, whether or not they were registered as urban. Otherwise, it would face the danger of losing its workforce.

In 1962, the Heilongjiang Architectural Design Institute was commissioned to design a new headquarters district in Ranghulu, ten kilometers west of Saertu along the Binzhou Railroad. Ranghulu was to be developed as the administrative and research center for Daqing. Architects from Harbin provided a plan with a fifty-meter-wide central boulevard, situated along the north-south axis of the new district, with the headquarters compound and a central park located at the two ends. The headquarters compound—a cluster of T-shaped symmetrical three-story buildings—faced the boulevard and the city park to the south and small hills to the north.

When Yu Qiuli learned about the Ranghulu plan, he rejected it as a "capitalist plan" and criticized the local leaders for being "revisionist."[29] The building was then allocated to the Daqing Design Institute and Petroleum Geology Institute, and the headquarters remained in Compound No. 2 in Saertu.

Daqing leaders were contemplating a revolution in construction. They definitely did not plan to build a "central city" but rather a "new socialist mining district." Initially, a replica of China's agricultural ideal, "the husband in industry and the wife in agriculture" and "one oil well and one family house surrounded by two *mu* of farm land" was considered.[30] But this applied only to oil extraction factories. A certain level of concentration for other production functions was still necessary.

In May 1963, Party leaders in the Ministry of the Petroleum Industry held a meeting to discuss construction of the mining district in the Daqing Oil Field. Yu Qiuli once again stated his opinion that Daqing should "walk on its own," step by step, developing according to the needs of the state. Construction of Daqing's mining district could not follow the foreign models of concentrated oil cities, such as Dushanzi in Xinjiang or Xigu in Lanzhou. Daqing had to build its enterprise frugally and based on reality and emphasize its spirit of self-reliance. Sun Jingwen summarized the current dispersed construction pattern as being "convenient for production, convenient for living arrangements, convenient for the children's education and future employment, and convenient for integrating town and countryside and workers and peasants."[31] Later, at the National Urban Construction Work Conference, borrowing from Sun's summary, Kang Shi'en introduced Daqing's construction experience.

On October 25, 1963, when Zhou Enlai was discussing construction of the Yichun Forestry District and other mining districts, he recommended that the forestry and mining industries follow the Daqing model: "I would like to suggest that all forestry and mining districts not build big cities. There are four phrases, that is, sixteen characters, to summarize the experience of Saertu: 'integration of workers and peasants, integration of urban and rural areas, good for production, and convenient for livelihood' [*gongnong jiehe, chengxiang jiehe, youli shengchan, fangbian shenghuo*]. This will diminish the distance between town and country-side."[32] Thereafter Daqing steadfastly applied the "sixteen-character" principle to the construction of its mining district. Daqing's dispersed, rural-like "mining district settlements," serving both industrial and agricultural uses, represented an attempt to be consistent with the Marxist doctrine of "eliminating the three great gaps" in communist society.

* * *

DAQING'S DESIGN REVOLUTION

In early June, those at the oil field finally welcomed the arrival of spring. The snow and ice had melted into numerous ponds. Wildflowers dotted the grasslands and the women's drawing desks. Wild animals, usually rabbits and ducks, that had survived the hunger and hunting during the previous season, roamed the fields. Weeds and reeds grew five or six feet tall. Thus ended yet another season of hard work. The dependents' farm had reclaimed large areas of farmland, but cultivation still relied on ex-tensive manual labor. All the staff at the Design Institute were required to help with the sowing, fertilizing, and harvesting during the busy seasons. Their inexperience often aroused laughter from among the dependents.

The wind was quite strong in spring. Women wrapped their faces in scarves to protect themselves from sandstorms and sunburns. The mo-notonous physical labor on the land was refreshing for Hua, who had grown up in a city. The farmland along the Songliao Plain was quite large, unlike the small patches of farmland in the south. Hua appreciated laboring for their own food and enjoyed the vastness of the fields. But hoeing the weeds was back-breaking work. Soon Hua's arms and back would ache with pain, and her hands were covered with blisters. But her spirit was comforted by the sunshine, singing, and laughter. Helping one another and working collectively, the young men and women became much closer.

There was a big party for the autumn harvest. The rural housewives would send fresh produce to the canteen, either corn, potatoes, or car-rots. This was a delicious treat after a winter of whole grains. Sometimes the canteen delivered water-boiled fresh corn to the drafting tables at the Institute in the evening. The quiet office would suddenly be full of the fragrant smell of fresh steamed corn, as the young people happily chatted and ate.

The leaders at Daqing had established the rule that the harvest would always be communal. After the harvest at Compound No. 2's fish pond, fish would be served to every work unit in Saertu. One time, several young men on the Road Design Team returned to the harvested land after work and collected an extra basket of carrots for an evening snack. As a result, they were harshly criticized, and their basket of carrots was confiscated and sent to the canteen.

Hua's first design assignment was to work on the cemetery. She was very surprised that a newly developed oil field would need such a place. She was told that the cemetery was to be built to honor those martyrs who had died due to accidents during the installation of the oil wells. Indeed, many lives had been sacrificed after 1960. This was a depressing subject. The senior architect with whom she worked, Mr. Dai, seemed even more depressed. Mr. Dai was thin, in his midthirties, and with obvious signs of malnutrition—a common characteristic among those who had arrived in Daqing two years earlier than Hua. He seldom talked in public, and he intentionally avoided attention, even eye contact. But he never avoided the fact that he was a Catholic, and he prayed before every meal. Hua had mixed feelings about Dai. She admired his courage to pray in public. Hua's mother was also a Catholic. Partly because of her family background, she used to hold back from the intense political movements. She was not yet a member of the Youth League, which was rather rare for someone of her age. But she really didn't like the feeling of isolation while working with Mr. Dai. In her heart, she felt a "loss of face" by having to work under Dai on such a project.

In the spring of 1963, after Premier Zhou's visit, the leaders in Daqing were determined to build *gandalei* to permanently resolve the housing situation. The Fourth Division of Civil Engineering was assigned the job of creating a type of "scientific *gandalei*," that is, mud housing that was to last "at least fifty years." The division appointed work teams composed of its most elite members. Investigation and experimentation were integrated as part of the *gandalei* design work. This time Hua was assigned to the team to plan the oil village, that is, "construction of the living base," under the leadership of Chen Huajin. Chen Huajin was from a wealthy Chinese family in Indonesia. A typical Cantonese, he had dark skin and high cheekbones. His eyes were deep and large. He was a respected figure at the Institute and a well-recognized model labor. Indeed, he reminded Hua of many of the early campaigners who had arrived in Daqing in 1960. He was a thin man, and his back was slightly stooped as a consequence of long periods of malnutrition and stomach ailments. But he never complained about the harsh conditions and he was highly devoted to his work. He was called "Lao Chen," Old Chen, by his colleagues, as a way of showing respect. In his late thirties, he was already considered quite old at the Institute.

During the planning work, Hua became acquainted with the person whom Song most respected—the chief engineer in the oil field, Liu Shuren. At the headquarters Liu was in charge of planning the living base. He had worked for the National Resource Commission of the Nanjing government during the 1930s and 1940s. Immediately before liberation in 1949, he had been made head of the Yumen Oil Mine, which he had helped to save from being sabotaged by the Nationalists. He safely transferred the mine to Kang Shi'en in the PLA. Song worked under Chief Liu in Compound No. 2 and accompanied him on many field trips to the mining district. "You can't tell he was educated in America. He doesn't look like a high-level cadre at all. He works even harder than our young fellows," Song told Hua.

None of these field trips was easy. When the truck got stuck in the mud, Chief Liu was often the first to jump off and help push it forward. Once the truck became so mired in a mud pond that no matter how hard they pushed, the mud would shoot out like bullets as the wheels spun faster and faster and the truck sank deeper and deeper. They tried putting branches and twigs under the tires, but these were quickly crushed. Chief Liu then took off his military coat and placed it under the tires. The driver and the other young men quickly followed. Finally the truck was able to move over the top of the pile of their coats. That scene had made a deep impression on Song. The young men in Compound No. 2 admired Chief Liu with heartfelt sincerity.

Like the other leaders in the headquarters, Liu's work schedule was quite busy. Old Chen and Hua had to frequently brief him about the progress in village planning. Very often these briefings were scheduled in the late evening. They would take the shuttle to Saertu at 6:00 after a quick supper and wait for hours outside of Liu's office, as groups of people went in and out. When they finally entered, Hua saw a tall man wearing an oil worker's uniform, hardly different from an ordinary worker except for his dark eyes that twinkled with alert intelligence.

Hua's plan had followed the principle of building a dispersed settlement, but it positioned a "relatively concentrated" central town for each production headquarters. The plan was criticized by Chief Liu mercilessly: "Why do young designers in the Institute have such outdated minds? Why are you afraid of dispensing with old dead rules? Think of the reality in the oil field. Think of the suffering in the country. You need to ignore the capitalist city planning rules and implement a true revolution in design!"

This was the first time Hua had been so harshly criticized for her work. It was already too late to return to Ranghulu, so she followed Old Chen to the same guesthouse where she had first stayed a year earlier. This time she was alone in the room. Thinking that she might spend the rest of her life planning barrack-like villages, living and working like a peasant, and commuting between Saertu and Ranghulu, she finally broke down into tears. Her naive dream of "drawing a new and beautiful picture on a blank sheet" was gone.

Having sensed her frustration back at the Institute, her team leader, Chen Ruihe, comforted her with his story. Chen was from Jiangsu province, the same province as Hua. He was admired by the young graduates for his talent and his feverish devotion to his work. They called him "Master Chen," Chen da shi. Trained in a classical Ecole des Beaux-art tradition at Suzhou Industrial College in architecture, Chen's hand drawings were like pieces of art, with perfect lines and renderings. He was a "design maniac," who would spend days and nights in front of his drafting table. In 1961 Master Chen was asked to design a housing module for the oil workers and their families, following the Chinese traditional pastoral ideal—"one single family house with two *mu* of farmland" as required by the oil field leaders. This was his first meaningful project, and he worked on it with great enthusiasm. Over time, the experimental house was built according to his design. But when inspecting the model house, the oil leaders became irritated. The house was a typical southern-style rural house, with a red-tiled roof, a white-painted window frame, and a yellow-painted wall. "They said it looked like an old God of Earth temple," Master Chen recalled uncomfortably. The little house, which had been designed to hold two families in four modest rooms, had five doors and eight windows—good ventilation in the south but clearly a waste of energy and material in the north. For a long time thereafter, his nickname at the Institute was "Five Doors and Eight Windows" and he was criticized at several public meetings. Luckily, the criticism did not influence his political standing. Before 1964, Daqing had been a tolerant place for people with different opinions from various backgrounds. But Master Chen said he had learned a lesson from the criticism—that designers should respect the local conditions and should always try to save on construction costs by careful research and investigation about the design.

During the following months, Hua and her colleagues were required to carry out intensive investigations of local mud housing. They visited hundreds of rural families living in rural houses, learned from the experience of the local builders, and talked with the dependents who were to live in the settlements. This was the longest time Hua had spent with peasants in the fields. She was not from a wealthy urban family, but when she visited families with three or four children who were dependent on only one salary, and when she saw those rural housewives who were working so hard for a better life, she sensed the great urban-rural disparities. While standing in front of those suntanned laboring women, Hua began to feel pangs of her previous petit-bourgeois lifestyle. The life that Hua felt was so meaningless and that she was desperate to escape from was their living reality.

* * *

Near the end of 1963, the experimental *gandalei* houses were designed, built, and tested at the Institute. In addition to sun-dried pounded mud-grass blocks, the design team tried to use other locally available construction materials. Small pieces of wood were put together to provide support for the curved roof. Bitumen, a byproduct at the Daqing refinery, was mixed in proportion with the mud and hay for insulation and to provide a water-resistant layer for the roof. One of the difficulties was to design a quickly built foundation for the house that could be adapted to the northern climate. The traditional houses frequently encountered structural failures as a result of the humidity or the thawing of the frozen land in the spring. After several tests, the foundation was finally set at thirty centimeters deep, covered by a five-centimeter layer of bitumen and mud mixture at a ratio of 1:5, along with a building skirt around the outer wall. The ventilation and heating systems were carefully designed to avoid fire hazards and to introduce adequate fresh air. Compared to the typical

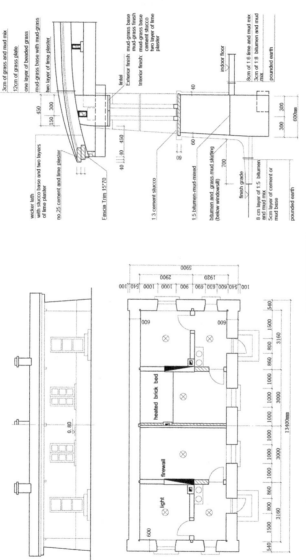

FIGURE 3.7 Scientific *gandalei* house: floor plan, elevation, and sections, Daqing Design Institute, 1964. Original drawing by the Daqing Design Institute, redrawn by the author.

local mud houses, the walls of the "scientific *gandalei*" houses were thinner and the roofs were elevated so as to increase the internal space. The Institute also prepared a construction manual for the dependents and the workers.[33]

In the spring of 1964, the large-scale construction of the "living base" began. Architects and construction workers labored together to build the first worker-peasant village in Saertu. An on-site conference on *gandalei* building was held. All the work units sent representatives to study the new model and to begin their own construction projects. There was no comprehensive planning for the living base. It simply followed the expansion of the oil exploration and production. Figure 3.7 demonstrates how function and economy were the main focus of the house. By the end of that year, the entire Daqing landscape was a product of industrial production.

"More, Faster, Better, and More Economic"

People living in Daqing had developed the ideal socialist city as an industrial production machine in a "more, faster, better, and more economic" way. The planners maintained housing standards that were similar to those of the local peasants, and they built housing according to rural styles, creating an alternative way of lowering building costs. At first glance, Daqing's de-urbanized patterns may appear to be consistent with the Soviet avant-garde proposals of the 1920s, though the latter were based on a utopian vision, whereas in Daqing they were based on reality. Decentralized villages composed of identical houses were indicative of an unprecedented new way of life, an equal society. But the buildings in Daqing were a product of industrial production, and the focus was on function and economy to overcome all difficulties. Ornamentation and decorations were considered simply a waste of state resources. It seems that Daqing had not only discovered rich oil deposits but also low-budget development: industrialization without the burden of urbanization.

CHAPTER 4

Celebrating Daqing

The Correct Path for Industrialization

By the end of 1963, the national economy had slowly recovered from the famine and growth began to resume for the first time in three years. In 1964, China's top leaders were able to turn their attention from immediate survival issues to long-term strategies. On the one hand, they increasingly reflected on past experiences and engaged in debates about future developmental models. On the other hand, the dangers of confrontation with the two global superpowers were increasing. Ideological conflicts between China and the Soviet Union became public. The Party theoretical journal, *Hongqi* (Red Flag), invoked the name of Lenin to criticize the "modern revisionism" of the Soviet Union. The increasing involvement of the United States in the Vietnam War, especially after the Gulf of Tonkin incident in August 1964, and threats of a continuation of China's nuclear weapons program, raised the danger of a Sino-American confrontation.

Daqing initially became well known to high-level cadres at the end of 1963, and in 1964 its name was heard by the general public. But the location of the Daqing Oil Field still remained top secret until the 1970s.

Learning from Daqing

The Fourth Session of the Second National People's Congress was held in Beijing from November 17 to December 3, 1963. On November 19, with Mao Zedong present, Yu Qiuli gave a speech to the congress, in which

he stated that the petroleum industry was the only sector that had fulfilled, and in fact had exceeded, the goals established during the Great
Leap Forward. Not only had Daqing developed at an impressive speed,
but another new oil field, called Shengli (literally "success") the second
largest field in Shandong province, had also begun production. In a
closing speech to the congress, Zhou Enlai announced to the people's
delegates in attendance that the amount of oil required for economic
construction, national defense, and the people's livelihood had been realized. This exciting news was followed by thunderous applause in the
Great Hall of the People, and the announcement was compared to an
explosion of a "spiritual nuclear bomb," thereby cheering up millions of
Chinese and surprising the entire world.[1] On December 25, 1963, the
People's Daily, with great emotion, publicized the following good news:
"Those days when our country relied on foreign oil are now gone
forever!"

On December 24, Peng Zhen, secretary of the Central Committee
of the Chinese Communist Party and Party secretary of Beijing municipality, invited the minister of the petroleum industry to describe the experience of the Daqing oil campaign to a large gathering of cadres in the
Great Hall of the People and at Capital Stadium.[2] More than fifty-six
thousand cadres from the Central Committee, the State Council, and Beijing municipality listened to his report. This was the first time many of
the cadres had ever heard of Daqing. Kang Shi'en first informed the audience that a large oil deposit in Daqing had begun production, and the
state investment, in the amount of 0.7 billion yuan over three years, not
only had already been recovered, but more than an additional 0.45 billion yuan had also been returned. Kang noted, "The more important
achievement of this campaign is that it has trained a capable team of leaders and workers. This team has endured harsh conditions, but the ideological awareness and discipline of its members have increased and their
technical skills have been improved." Kang told some stories about Daqing's model workers, how their heroic spirit and strong will had conquered
hardships, and how the self-built *gandalei* houses and the land reclamation project for agricultural use had contributed to the success of the
campaign.

Peng Zhen made more than sixty comments with great enthusiasm
during the course of Kang's speech. Most of these comments focused on

the "revolutionary management" of the campaign and the heroic spirit of the Daqing people.

> The people in Daqing had indeed suffered harsh times. Someone questioned whether this was a proper way to build industry—was Yu Qiuli crazy to risk so many thousands of lives? But the people in Daqing were not afraid of losing a few lives for the sake of the country, and they tried their best not to risk any. This was also a question of dialectics. They had a team of forty thousand people and were ready to sacrifice two thousand lives. The result was that only two hundred people became ill. This was how Daqing had forged an army for industry. The news that China had become self-sufficient in oil shocked the entire world. This was achieved by enduring hardships. If the entire country were to fight as hard as the people in Daqing had, there would be no limit to accelerating national development.
>
> We need this kind of team, an army for industry. . . . Communists strive to accomplish glorious missions under harsh conditions. Upon what do we rely? The revolutionary spirit, . . . our Party's organization and discipline, the fighting style of the People's Liberation Army originating among the proletariat class, and the self-discipline of the proletariat class. The People's Liberation Army was fighting a battle of "either kill or be killed," and any little problem could become life-threatening—that is why the PLA is well-disciplined and depends on the proletariat class. Our army for industry should follow the same rule. Kang Shi'en was a student at Tsinghua University before he joined the PLA. Can you tell that from him now? He and Yu Qiuli are both young. They are the qualified successors of our country's leadership. We should all learn from them.[3]

Later, this report, modified based on Peng Zhen's comments, was circulated by the CCP Central Committee to lower-level cadres throughout the country. It emphasized the "revolutionization of modern socialist enterprises," "the revolutionary vigor" triggered by the people's "revolutionary spirit" into a "revolutionary work style." Commenting on the report, the Central Committee wrote, "Daqing's experience is unique, but it is applicable not only to the industrial sectors, but also to the transportation, finance, culture, and education sectors, as well as to Party, government, and mass organization organs." Daqing was described as a model of "more, faster, better, and more economical" development. This circular represented the beginning of a national movement to learn from Daqing.

Daqing's success had convinced the central leadership, especially Chairman Mao, that it could serve as a model for China's socialist construction and that its leaders were capable of becoming "revolutionary successors." In January 1964, Yu Qiuli was invited to Mao's office in Zhongnanhai. Also present on that occasion were Zhou Enlai, Chen Yun, Deng Xiaoping, Li Fuchun, and Li Xiannian, the members of the "economic cabinet." Yu was once again asked to report to Chairman Mao on the experience of Daqing. He felt hesitant to repeat the same report that Mao had heard during the session of the National People's Congress, but Mao encouraged him to do so.

Five days after the Party circular on Daqing was issued, on February 10, 1964, the *People's Daily* publicized information about the Dazhai Brigade, Daqing's counterpart in agricultural production. The two production units epitomized Maoist values, such as the power of the masses and their heroic work based on the strength of human will. "In industry, learn from Daqing; in agriculture, learn from Dazhai; and the whole country will learn from the People's Liberation Army!" became the slogan that year.

At many events held during 1964 Mao referred to Yu Qiuli and the Ministry of the Petroleum Industry. In February, at an education work conference, Mao said, "We should learn from the PLA, and learn from the Ministry of the Petroleum Industry. Within three years, the Ministry of the Petroleum Industry has invested 0.7 billion yuan in the Daqing Oil Field and has developed a 6-million-ton oil deposit field and has built a 1-million-ton yield refinery. A little investment, a short period of time, and a great achievement—this is 'more, faster, better, and more economic.'"[4]

In March 1964, Mao once again mentioned Daqing: "The Ministry of the Petroleum Industry has made great achievements. It has not only inspired the peoples' revolutionary spirit, but it has also contributed to our country 6 million tons of oil. In addition to the 6 million tons of oil, it has also contributed a 1-million-ton-yield refinery, producing high-quality oil of international standards. This is indeed persuasive."[5]

On September 12, 1964, when meeting with Li Fuchun to discuss planning work, Mao said, "I think the Daqing Oil Field has its own ethos and logic. While violating the rules of planning, Yu Qiuli gathered all the resources of the petroleum sector to engage in a fierce battle. The people in Daqing had no roads, no food, and no houses, but they succeeded."[6]

On December 26, 1964, Yu Qiuli and "Iron Man" Wang Jinxi, Daqing's most famous model worker, were invited to attend Mao's seventy-first birthday party. The other guests included Chen Yonggui, Party secretary of Dazhai Village; Qian Xuesen, who had played a leading role in developing China's nuclear weapons; and Dong Jiageng and Xing Yanzi, male and female students who had voluntarily gone to the countryside to join in agriculture production. Mao began the event by stating that the purpose was to "eat together" with representatives of the workers, farmers, and soldiers, and not to celebrate his birthday. He again remarked that Daqing should be China's model for industry: "The central government has many ministries. It is very clear that some ministries have made many achievements and have had a good work style, like the Ministry of the Petroleum Industry, whereas others simply ignore the Daqing model and are not willing to learn from it." In the middle of the meal, indicating his resentment toward certain unnamed Party leaders, Mao abruptly declared, "You should never lift up your tails so high [i.e., be too proud]. Some people have not been good, and they have lifted their tails way too high. They should tuck their tails back between their legs!"[7]

MAO BOMBARDS THE "INDEPENDENT PLANNING KINGDOM"

The failure of the Great Leap Forward adversely affected Mao's confidence with respect to national economic issues. On many occasions in 1959, Mao had said that he should allow Chen Yun to lead the work on the economy.[8] The leadership was in the midst of searching for an alternative development trajectory that would not produce catastrophic results just when the successful Daqing model emerged from the debris of the great famine. Assisted by the leaders of Daqing, Mao's attempt to reform the "economic cabinet" served as a prelude for the launch of the Great Proletarian Cultural Revolution.

The formal drafting of the Third Five-Year Plan, scheduled to go into effect in 1966, began in February 1964. At a preliminary meeting focusing on long-term plans in industry and communications, based on a suggestion from Chen Yun, grain production was singled out as the focus for national development. Li Fuchun, Li Xiannian, Tan Zhenlin, and Bo Yibo were the top leaders in charge of formulating the Third Five-Year Plan. It was called a plan for enhancing "eating, clothing, and [items of] daily use" (*chi, chuan, yong*), stressing the need to raise the quality of production and to increase the supply of scarce daily commodities and to downsize expenditures on the military and the national defense industry. Based on their preliminary ideas about the Third Five-Year Plan, agriculture would receive 20 percent of state investment, as compared to 7.1 percent during the First Five-Year Plan and 11.3 percent during the Second Five-Year Plan. It was projected that after five years of construction, national grain production would reach 230 billion kilograms by 1970 and average annual grain consumption would reach a minimum of 212.5 kilograms per capita.[9]

When Mao first heard Li Fuchun's report on his preliminary ideas for the plan, he did not express any disagreement. But his attitude became more critical during the period of extreme tensions with the Soviet Union and the United States. At the height of the cold war, he feared a possible nuclear attack, especially after the October 1962 Cuban missile crisis. Both the Soviet Union and the United Stated had conducted large-scale war games targeting one another. China's border conflicts with Taiwan and the Soviet Union had also increased dramatically, and many Chinese residents were escaping to the USSR from Xinjiang "due to accommodations by the Soviets," as the Chinese government later claimed. A border war between China and India occurred in 1962, and in July 1963 the USSR stationed extra troops in Mongolia.

In May 1964, the State Planning Commission presented a preliminary outline of the Five-Year Plan to a Central Work Conference in Beijing. At the same time, Luo Ruiqing, minister of defense, submitted an evaluation of China's war preparedness.[10] The report raised the issue of an "overconcentration" on industry and on the population. It estimated that fourteen "super-large" Chinese cities (i.e., those with more than 1 million inhabitants) had 60 percent of China's civil mechanical industry, 50 percent of its chemical industry, and 52 percent of its national defense industry. Furthermore, these fourteen super-large cities, plus twenty other large cities with populations ranging from 500,000 to 1 million, were mostly concentrated along the coastal region and could be easily destroyed by an air attack. Mao therefore favored a strategy of developing a "Third

Front," that is, an industrial base in southwest China, which, in addition to focusing on "eating, clothing, and daily use" industries, would be a top priority in the Third Five-Year Plan. Due to the danger that the United States might engage in an aggressive war against China, he pointed out, a concentration of factories in the cities, especially along the coastal regions, might be detrimental to the national development strategy. He argued that the national development strategy should place more emphasis on the hinterlands and should focus on building decentralized plants and institutions. He also suggested that important national institutions, for instance, Peking University, should move some of their activities to the hinterlands.[11]

The state planners saw the Great Leap and the resultant famine as a failure of state planning, and thus they argued that better planning was required. For Chairman Mao, however, the problem was the rigidity of the planning system. Because past planning had been based on the Soviet model—for example, first setting a production quota for steel, then calculating the required amount of coal, supply of power, and transportation capacity, followed by calculating the required labor and the possible increase in the urban population and welfare services—it was difficult to coordinate with the complicated realities. The five-year plans did not take into account unexpected natural disasters, wars, or potential international assistance. Mao thus required a change in the methodology for planning work, insisting, "It needs a revolution." But what type of revolution was envisioned? The state planners did not realize that Mao had already come up with a model that he supported.

The August 2, 1964, Gulf of Tonkin incident was indicative of the increasing involvement of the United States in the Vietnam War. Four days later, Mao wrote in a document distributed to central cadres, "A war is going to break out. I need to reconsider my actions."[12] Furthermore, China's nuclear weapons program had reached a crucial juncture. There existed a possibility that the United States and Taiwan might directly attack China's nuclear weapon facilities in Lanzhou and Baotou.[13] Mao thus began to push even more aggressively for the construction of a Third Front.

Under pressure from Mao, in June the State Planning Commission sent out work teams to determine potential locations for Third Front projects as soon as possible. Otherwise, the state planners and regional governments would not be able to come to agreement within two months on a location for the future steel plants. Many planners questioned the viability of Panzhihua, a mountainous region bordering on Sichuan, Yunnan, and Guizhou provinces, the area favored by Mao, because of its lack of accessibility and of availability of land for construction. Chen Boda, the CCP's leading theoretician, and soon to be a member of the Central Cultural Revolution Group, had become a vice director of the State Planning Commission in 1962 in response to Mao's complaint that the "economic sector is blocking me and Comrade [Liu] Shaoqi." In August 1964, when Li Fuchun asked Chen Boda his opinion about the annual planning-work summary, Chen responded in a letter that the planning commission would have to change its "work style" and accelerate construction of the Third Front and that "many important instructions Chairman Mao has given us since 1958 have not yet been seriously implemented." A copy of the letter was also sent to Mao, who forwarded it to all provincial-level Party committees with the added comment, "Either this year or next year, the planning-work style must undergo significant changes. If it is not changed, then it would be best to completely abolish the current State Planning Commission and establish a different body."

Mao's comments to Li Fuchun were both clear and tough: "If you don't build Panzhihua, I will go there riding on a donkey to attend meetings; if you have no money, use mine! . . . You can choose revolution or no revolution. Either way, I will establish another body either this year or next year if you cannot change this situation."[14]

Li Fuchun and his team worked hard to meet the chairman's requirements. Both he and Bo Yibo personally went to the southwest to convey Mao's choice of Panzhihua as the future base for the steel industry. When Li Fuchun returned to Beijing in November, a plan to restructure the State Planning Commission awaited him.

THE SMALL PLANNING COMMISSION

Mao clearly had Yu Qiuli in mind when he was thinking of reforming the planning sector. After mentioning Daqing and Yu Qiuli to Li Fuchun in September, at the Politburo meeting of December 20, 1964, he called on Yu, who was almost twenty years younger than Li, to "bring new work" to the State Planning Commission. There was some argument that Yu was merely a brave military officer, but Mao responded, "So Yu Qiuli cannot be vice director of the State Planning Commission? Is he only a brave military officer? The Ministry of the Petroleum Industry also makes plans." Premier Zhou Enlai added that this move was to make a "breakthrough in a pond of dead water."[15]

After the morning meeting, Zhou spoke briefly with Yu about his future position. In the afternoon, Mao again asked the members of the Politburo, "Do you think Yu Qiuli is qualified to be the vice director of the State Planning Commission?"

This time there were no voices of dissent. Mao was pleased and said, "I think he can do it. There are some people who only care about small things and they ignore the big things."[16]

Several days later, about the time Yu Qiuli and "Iron Man" Wang Jinxi were invited to Mao's birthday party, Yu's appointment was announced by the CCP Central Committee. He was introduced to the members of the State Planning Commission on the last day of 1964. Based on a suggestion from Mao, a Planning Staff Headquarters, established within the State Council under the direct leadership of Zhou, was to be responsible for "macrostrategic issues." The Planning Staff Headquarters was later nicknamed the "Small Planning Commission" within the State Planning Commission, which focused on routine work. Minister of Building Construction Li Renjun, Zhejiang province Party secretary Li Hujia, Beijing Party secretary Jia Tingsan, and Chen Boda were invited to join the Planning Staff Headquarters. Later, based on a request by Li Fuchun, all Small Planning Commission members also became vice directors of the State Planning Commission, and, until 1980, Yu Qiuli served as the de facto director of the Commission.

Also during the last several days of 1964, local leaders in Daqing received Yu's instructions that all headquarters—meaning all administrative offices—were to remain in their humble *gandalei* houses, and the brick buildings were to be used only for public services. No more multistory buildings (*loufang*) were to be constructed. Planning for the Daqing headquarters in Ranghulu also came to an abrupt halt. Thereafter the economics of the construction in Daqing became the politics of the construction. The struggle between the two lines in the development strategy was represented as mud versus brick, or single-story buildings versus multistory buildings.

BUILDING THE THIRD FRONT

In 1965 Yu Qiuli assumed the leading role for the drafting of the Third Five-Year Plan. The overall goal of the plan was modified to prepare for the possibility that "the imperialists [would] launch an aggressive war against China," and hence a strategic rear base in the southwest was to be built. During the period of the First Five-Year Plan, the Soviet Union and Mongolia were considered reliable Chinese allies. Any invasion by foreign powers would more likely come from the east or the south. Therefore, in the First Five-Year Plan the north served as the defensive hinterland. Based on this logic, and with guidance from Soviet advisers, most major projects were built in northern China.[17] During the period of the Third Five-Year Plan, however, the threat of war was coming not only from the coast but also from the north, plus there was the danger of a nuclear war and intensive air attacks. Therefore China's Third Front program retreated to the mountainous regions in the southwest.

The Third Five-Year Plan significantly increased the share of investment in inland construction by the defense, metallurgy, chemical, and transportation industries, thus inevitably reducing investments in the coastal regions as well as expenditures for agriculture, education, urban housing, and light industry. This departure from the original "eating, clothing, and daily use" plan was, as summarized by Zhou, replaced by the Third Front plan to "prepare for war, prepare for famine, and prepare for the people."[18] Facing these great challenges in his new career, Yu Qiuli retained many of the former senior members of the State Planning Commission, which also remained under the direct supervision of Premier Zhou.

Chairman Mao paid special attention to the formulation of the Third Five-Year Plan. In contrast to his tough attitude toward Li Fuchun, Mao was tolerant with respect to his selected "revolutionary successors." He encouraged Yu Qiuli to significantly lower the target growth rate in order to allow for space to maneuver in the future. During one conversation, Mao asked Yu Qiuli and Gu Mu their ages. When Mao learned that they were both about fifty, he said, "In the future the country will depend on you. We can only be your advisers and consultants."[19]

In terms of investment and production quotas, after the "planning revolution" the Third Five-Year Plan was relatively conservative. The planned growth rate for agriculture was set at 5 to 6 percent, and that for industry at 11 percent.[20] These planning goals were achieved by the end of 1970 despite the significant political turmoil and the deterioration in the central capacity to control the national economy. Agricultural production maintained a steady annual growth rate of 4.5 percent, which was even higher than that during the First Five-Year Plan period. Due to the biggest contribution coming from the rapidly expanding oil industry, the annual growth rate of industrial production reached 9.6 percent. Furthermore, with a massive commitment of resources for the national defense industry, the Third Five-Year Plan had significant achievements. After the explosion of China's first atomic bomb in October 1964, a hydrogen bomb experiment was successful in 1967. The Shengli Oil Field, the second largest oil field after Daqing, entered into production in 1968, and a bridge across the Yangzi River in Nanjing was built in December of the same year. In 1970, China's first satellite was sent into orbit around the earth. Although there was criticism of its inefficiencies and waste of resources, the plan contributed greatly to the development of China's hinterland. Many major railway lines linking the southwest were completed, including the Chengdu-Kunming Railway and the Baoji (Shaanxi)-Chengdu Railway. More than sixty-three major heavy industrial projects were completed and put into full operation, including the No. 2 Auto Works in Shiyan, Hubei. The western provinces, such as Sichuan, Yunnan, and Guiyang, were able to build up their heavy industrial bases due to massive state investments.

The demand for oil increased rapidly during the Third Five-Year Plan period and thereafter. Petroleum was expected to account for a greater share of China's energy supply, and the Daqing model was expected to fuel industrial growth.

* * *

Worker-Peasant Villages on the Oil Field

On December 25, 1963, people in Daqing gathered to listen to a China National Radio broadcast that praised the Daqing Oil Field for its great contributions to the country. The listeners' eyes glistened with tears and their faces lit up as the following statement was read in a strong voice: "Those days when our country relied on foreign oil are gone forever." An overwhelming sense of pride overtook Hua. Their contributions to the country were finally acknowledged. Their hard work and suffering were worthwhile and important, part of the great historical endeavor on which the country was embarked. Thereafter Hua's feelings about "eating bitterness" (*chi ku*) in Daqing began to change. She began to link her behavior to the Daqing work motto, as advocated by the Daqing head-quarters near the end of 1963: "Be honest people, say honest words, and do honest things."

The year 1964 was devoted to planning the *gandalei* villages. For Hua, this began with the field survey and ended with on-the-ground plans. The mining district construction work team visited each headquarters to plan and design the living sites. That meant countless trips to the vast fields on the Liberation truck. Consulting with the clients—the dependents—was a specific part of the design work (fig. 4.1). It was called the Design Revolution: to integrate with the working class, integrate with the masses, and integrate with reality. The dependents usually were more concerned about available public services, such as child care, a canteen, water supplies, and a lavatory. The headquarters wanted to lower construc-tion costs. Learning from her training at school, Hua tried her best to avoid barrack-like master plans, but such efforts were mostly disregarded. Dependents didn't care much about forms and patterns. Workers favored standardized barrack-like plans. Diversity would create extra costs for construction and would be burdens for the laborers.

On sunny summer days, while walking on the prairie (fig. 4.2), Hua could see the simple mud houses with their carefully designed curved roofs from miles away. Wild rabbits provided pleasant company on such field trips. Old Chen and Old Song would walk in the front, exploring the path in the middle of tall grasses and frequent puddles. Hua and other female colleagues followed, guarding against attacks from the giant local mosquitoes. Those invasive quarter-size bloodsuckers could bite through clothing, a much more painful bite than the little ones that Hua was used to. During the first summer, Hua was on a tight budget and could not afford a mosquito net, so she came down with a serious fever from the local mosquito bites.

During the winter, the field work was much less romantic. The freez-ing wind blew snow and ice as sharp as blades into their faces. As the

FIGURE 4.1 Hua (center) and her colleagues investigating *gandalei* houses, 1965. Photo courtesy of Zha Binhua and Yang Ruisong.

FIGURE 4.2 Hua and her colleagues walking on the Daqing prairie, spring, 1965. Photo courtesy of Zha Binhua and Yang Ruisong.

men carried the tools to measure the construction sites, Hua checked the blueprints. If they were lucky, they could find a half-collapsed *gandalei* house to serve as a temporary shelter for a lunch break. Hua learned to eat cold *wowotou* (cornbread) with rice wine to fight off the low temperature.

After an entire year in the fields, Hua wrote an essay for the broadcasting station of the Design Institute. It was from her work in the fields, she wrote, that she began to realize what a designer should do to fulfill the mission of "serving the people" and that the people they should "honestly serve" were not other designers but rather the oil workers and their dependents. The forms and patterns she was taught to value at school were meaningless, sometimes even ridiculous, in the face of the harsh reality. The essay was selected to be broadcast during their political study time. It received a very positive response from the audience. This petite but unyielding woman began to attract the attention of the Institute's leaders.

In 1964 the Design Institute and the Institute of Geology moved into two symmetric three-story office buildings in Ranghulu. A convention center stood in the middle. Hua did not know they had originally been built for the oil field headquarters. Jin called it the "Palace of Heaven," as it truly stood out in the cluster of simple one-story houses, with its extraordinary height, grand pillars, and large steel-framed glass windows. When the Institute moved into its new building, the women staff moved into the Institute's former office. Everyone had more space than before. Because of demand a child care center was also opened for families.

In the midst of the field work, the Design Institute initiated a "technical competition" as part of the nationwide campaign "Learning from the People's Liberation Army." The competition was held in front of the convention center. The Institute organized several games, such as a tracing-blueprint competition, an abacus or slide rule calculation competition, and a surveying and positioning competition. News of these events provided excitement to the busy routine work.

There was also a *pinggong baihao*, which means "evaluation of credits and expression of compliments." The model laborer who underwent the ritual would sit in a chair surrounded by his or her coworkers. Everyone praised him or her with one or two sentences. Good deeds could be sacrificing one's own needs to save state assets and picking up a screw that had been left on the floor. Some talented workers performed the praise in the form of a song and dance duet (*er ren zhuan*) that was popular in the northeast. Often the ritual ended with the model laborers being held up by the crowd and paraded around, while the rest of the audience shouted slogans or sang revolutionary songs. Hua always found this awkward and resisted throwing herself into such events as they seemed to her to be too dramatic.

At the end of 1964, the Four Cleanups movement began. Its purpose was to clean up politics, the economy, ideology, and organization and to expose class enemies and corrupt cadres. It was the first large-scale political movement since the discovery of Daqing. The Daqing headquarters established work teams to engage in the Four Cleanups. Relations among Hua's colleagues suddenly became tense. Everyone was required to make a public self-criticism, beginning with the Party leaders. When Hua heard the division head of civil engineering say that he should not have allowed the singing of "capitalist" songs in the office, Hua lowered her head and felt really sad. She loved singing those songs, and she knew that her colleagues enjoyed them as well. The audience did not reveal any reaction; most people merely remained silent. After the meeting, the work team privately hinted to Hua that she should speak up if she thought the leader's self-criticism was sufficiently honest. Therefore, after the leader made a second round of self-criticism, Hua spoke up: "As a member of the masses, I think our leader has made sincere self-criticism. I think his self-criticism should be accepted." It was then passed. In reality, Hua really did not think the leader had committed any serious mistakes, and she felt uncomfortable about being manipulated. What they were doing seemed to contradict what they were saying in the movement.

When it came to the masses, their self-criticisms were not so readily accepted. Little Huang, one of Hua's close friends on the Road Team and a fellow Tongji University graduate, was charged with violating the state secrets rule. He had mentioned to a friend that he worked at the Daqing Oil Field, not at a reclamation farm. That friend, without realizing that Daqing's location was still a state secret, openly wrote him a letter addressed to "Daqing Oil Field" in Saertu, Heilongjiang province. The fact that Little Huang's father was an overseas Chinese made this careless mistake an intentional disclosure of a state secret. Another colleague was reprimanded because he had lost one of his notebooks; every work notebook was required to be registered and submitted after being used. Master Chen was criticized for his pursuit of exotic designs and extravagant decorations. Hua's sin was the nature of her major—a city planner who was resistant to planning without cities. Her unfavorable family background, the fact that she had an older brother living in Taiwan, and that she was not a Youth League member, all were dutifully noted. The Four Cleanups not only exposed everyone's unfavorable past—it seemed many of Hua's colleagues also had "black" family backgrounds and that the reason that had prompted Hua to go to Daqing was indeed shared by many others—but it also introduced new suspicions in the work unit. From then on, Hua felt the solidarity among the community members had been damaged. The warmth and integrity she had felt in the collective faded away day by day.

Immediately after the movement, Hua was pressured into submitting an application to join the Youth League. Thus, at the age of twenty-four, she finally became a Youth League member.

During Hua and Song's third Chinese New Year in Daqing, the food situation improved a lot. After three years, they were able to buy each other a Shanghai-brand watch as a New Year's gift. Their monthly salary was 50 yuan, plus 6 to 10 yuan in bonuses. Hua sent home 30 yuan per month to help her father pay back his debt. Song sent home 40 yuan per month to ease the burden on his family. So their spending 120 yuan for a watch was considered quite extravagant. But their savings were possible because housing, utilities, transportation, and health care were all provided for free by the oil field. Nor did they have to buy clothing, as every day they wore the same work uniform. The only expense from their own pocket was for food.

One day in the canteen, Xiao Li, the pretty woman who worked as a drafting assistant, was standing behind Hua in line. Suddenly she said out loud, "Who do you think you are, Hua? Aren't you just a graduate of Tongji University?"

The crowd clearly heard her criticism. A flush of embarrassment rose to Hua's cheeks. She picked up her lunch and quickly left. Hua did not know why Xiao Li had said that in public. Before long, people noticed that Xiao Li was no longer working in the office. She showed symptoms of serious psychological problems and was brought home by her parents. Hua did not know if it was because of the criticism she had received or because of the pressure of trying to find a meaningful relationship in Daqing. After several months, Xiao Li was able to return to the Institute for a short period, but her condition grew worse. Her parents came again to take her home, and she was never able to return to Daqing. The miserable fate of this pretty woman and her harsh words burned a deep hole in Hua's memory of Daqing.

In 1965, a detailed design of the living bases had been completed and construction began. The designers had to visit the village construction sites every day. As the central bus station was in Saertu, they first had to go there and then transfer to the various destinations. This could not be accomplished in a one-day round trip, so the Institute was assigned a *gandalei* house in Compound No. 2 as a temporary office and dorm. Hua was happy to move to Saertu, since Compound No. 2 was next to Song's office. There would be no more painful days of having to commute. However, Song and Hua seldom met during the workday. They would set off to different construction sites in the early morning and return in the late afternoon. After political study, it was time for the team meeting. After the meeting, they had to work on the modifications of the blueprints. The workday never ended before midnight.

Nevertheless, on several occasions, either coincidently or intentionally, Song and Hua managed to visit the same site at the same time. Those visits were Hua's happiest moments. One time they both went to "Riding the Wind" (Chengfeng) Village for the transportation sector employees. This was right next to a small pond. During their lunch break they were able to sit by the pond, watching the reflection of the blue sky and the white clouds on the still water and softly singing their favorite songs. Another time they were both assigned to work in Red Satellite Village. After work, as the bus was reported to be late, the young couple walked leisurely through the cornfields and grassland all the way back to Ranghulu.

Near the end of 1965, Chen Huajin, who was in charge of the scientific design of the *gandalei*, and Liu Kunquan, who had contributed to their structural engineering, were named model workers in the Institute. During the year-end celebrations, they were paraded onto the stage and given red silk flowers. It happened to be Xiao Zhong who went up on the stage to tie a big red silk flower on Old Liu. The crowd applauded with extra enthusiasm as everyone knew they were getting married. Quite a few couples in the Institute got married that year. The wedding of Xiao Zhong and Old Liu was quite simple. The Institute allocated to the couple one single room. Basic furniture was provided, including a double bed, one desk, two chairs, and a new quilt. Their colleagues in the Fourth Division of Civil Engineering pitched in to buy them a thermos bottle, a water basin, and enamel mugs as gifts. These were the items needed to establish a new family in Daqing. On their wedding day, there wasn't any ceremony. A group of close friends crowded into their small mud house and served some candy and sunflower seeds. Some men made jokes about the newlyweds and encouraged them to share their love story. Little Zhong and Old Liu smiled shyly and blushed from head to toe.

* * *

Daqing did not have a master city plan. Its planning department focused only on planning for oil production, for example, the division of the oil fields, the spatial distribution of the oil production units, the construction of the facilities, and the infrastructural linkages. The belt-shaped oil field, stretching 140 kilometers in a north-south direction, was divided into several oil extraction fields, following the sequence of their development. The No. 1 Oil Extraction Factory was the area centered around the Saertu Railway Station. The No. 2 Oil Extraction Factory was located several miles to the south of Saertu, and the No. 3 Oil Extraction Factory was to the north. The No. 4 and No. 5 Extraction Factories were farther to the south, near Datong, where the oil was first discovered; the No. 6 Factory was located in the far northwest of Saertu, at the Lamadian Oil Field. Other ancillary departments were located relatively close to Saertu, but still at some distance. For example, the construction headquarters was in Hongweixing (literally, Red Satellite) Village, northwest of Saertu, and the transportation headquarters was in Chengfeng (literally, Riding on the Wind) Village, twenty to thirty kilometers to the south of Ranghulu.

Three types of living settlements were developed based on the principles of integrating industry and agriculture and integrating working and living. First, for those work units that had fixed but dispersed working sites, such as an oil extraction factory, scattered "settlement points" were built close to their production unit. Second, for work units whose locations were fixed and concentrated, such as oil or water pump stations or research institutes, larger-scale "central villages" were built next to the work unit. Remote settlements in the peripheral areas might be built to meet the farming needs of the dependents in these work units. Third, for the mobile basic construction and drilling teams, the living base was built near the oil exploration frontier. There was no viable map for locating these settlements until 1966, so determination of the location was undertaken through on-site investigations. Planners mainly chose higher places (if available) near the work units as the sites for future settlements, as every spring the plains encountered serious flooding problems.

These villages and settlement points began to be linked to roads and electric grids as oil field construction continued on the Songliao Plains. Every settlement had its own waterhouse in the middle, providing piped and hot water, and a public earth toilet on the periphery. The central village might have a few more daily service facilities, such as a grocery shop, a grain station, a barber shop, a bathhouse, or a clinic. Elementary and middle schools began to appear in the villages in the late 1960s and early 1970s, as the first baby boomers in the oil field reached school age. As mud houses could not meet the requirements of large public spaces for school buildings, the schools were primarily made of brick. These individual brick school buildings, in the middle of clusters of low mud houses, were called "camels among a herd of sheep."

The scientific *gandalei* was the standard housing in Daqing for all residents, regardless of occupation, age, or family size. Young couples and singles usually shared two-bedroom units, whereas families with children might occupy an entire unit. There was no more design work on "nonproduction" buildings. Instead, architects saved their time and energy to design "production-related" industrial structures in the oil field.

By the early 1960s, the landscape of the Daqing Oil Field consisted of (1) three small towns—Saertu, Ranghulu, and Longfeng—in the north along the Binzhou Railway, all within five to ten kilometers of each other; (2) an intermingling of oil wells, dwellings, and farmland in the belt-like oil field stretching from the railway to the south; (3) dispersed industrial facilities associated with oil extraction and processing; and (4) a grid pattern of roads linking the *gandalei* settlements and the production points. This landscape was more rural than urban, though it was definitely industrial as well as agricultural. Daqing People's Hospital and Daqing Design Institute were the only two *loufang* in Daqing for more than a decade, serving as landmarks for new arrivals and perhaps convincing them that they were not arriving in the countryside.

RED SATELLITE VILLAGE
(HONGWEIXING CUN)

Red Satellite Village (fig. 4.3) was the first model village built in Daqing. It was the site of the Daqing Oil Field construction headquarters as well as the living base for its workers and families. In the late 1970s, it had 51,846 square meters of housing and provided accommodations for 7,628 residents in 1,428 households.[21]

The site was composed of one central village and four settlement points (Nos. 2, 3, 4, and 8). The central village had 593 households, and each settlement point varied from 100 to 300 households. The settlement points centered around the village at almost equal distances; Nos. 2, 3, and 8 were all within one kilometer, whereas No. 4 was about two kilometers from the village. Map 2 shows how the central village was developed at the intersection of two main work roads, with branches of the road linking the settlement points, while the settlement points also had their own links to the work roads. Map 3 is a master plan of the No. 2 Village. The offices of the three basic construction teams belonging to the Oil Field construction headquarters were located either at the periphery of the village or facing the village across the work road. Public services were at the center of the village, and the schools were in a relatively quiet

FIGURE 4.3 The first scientific *gandalei* village, Hongweixing (Red Satellite) Village, 1964. Photo courtesy of Urban Planning Archives, Tongji University.

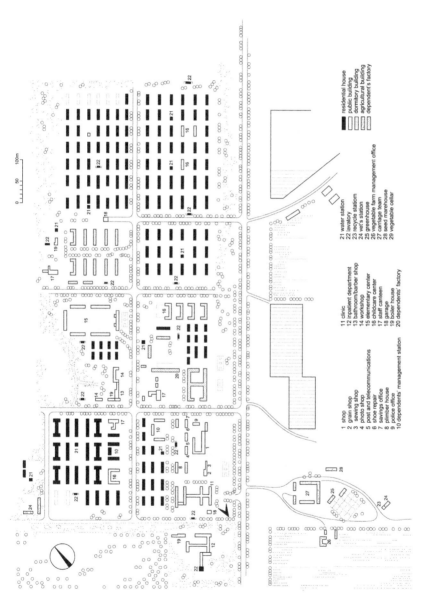

MAP 2 Master plan for Red Satellite Central Village, Daqing Design Institute, 1964. Original map by the Daqing Design Institute, redrawn by the author.

1 shop
2 grain shop
3 sewing shop
4 photo shop
5 post and telecommunications
6 shoe repair
7 savings office
8 plumber house
9 police office
10 dependents' management station

11 clinic
12 inpatient department
13 bathroom/barber shop
14 workshop
15 elementary center
16 childcare center
17 staff canteen
18 garage
19 boiler house
20 dependents' factory

21 water station
22 lavatory
23 recycle station
24 vet's station
25 greenhouse
26 vegetable farm management office
27 carriage team
28 seed manehouse
29 vegetable cellar

■ residential house
■ public building
☐ dormitory building
☐ agricultural building
☐ dependent's factory

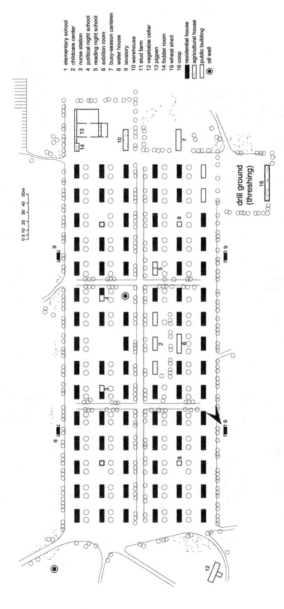

1 elementary school
2 childcare center
3 nurse station
4 political night school
5 reading night school
6 exibition room
7 busy-season canteen
8 water house
9 lavatory
10 warehouse
11 stud farm
12 vegetable cellar
13 pigpen
14 fodder room
15 wheat shed
16 coop

◼ residential house
▭ agricultural house
▭ public building
◉ oil well

drill ground (threshing)

MAP 3 Master plan for Red Satellite No. 2 Village, Daqing Design Institute, 1964. Original map by the Daqing Design Institute, redrawn by the author.

corner (away from the traffic). Structures serving agricultural production were located midway between the village and the farmland.

The layout of the settlements consisted of a simple and universally applicable matrix. Identical mud houses were lined up at equal distances. Black curved oil-painted roofs, brown mud walls, blue wood eaves, doors, and window frames, and green naturally grown poplars surrounding the village constituted the uniform landscape for all the settlements. Inside the settlement points there were no paved roads; instead the roads consisted of pounded ground earth. A grid of electricity poles and cables and gas pipelines provided every household with electricity and natural gas. There was no tap water or piped sewage system. Instead, a public water station provided cold and boiled water to the residents. This was also where the residents did their laundry. Sewage was collected through an open trench that led to the local rivers and ponds, similar to the situation in other rural areas.

PIONEER VILLAGE (CHUANGYE ZHUANG)

Pioneer Village, a model worker-peasant village built mainly by the family dependents, was another early settlement built in Daqing. The emergence of the village was linked to the very beginning of the Daqing oil campaign and the propaganda about the Daqing model dependents. The site was thirty-five kilometers from the Saertu headquarters, close to the early reclamation field of Xue Guifang and her friends, where the Five Shovels' Revolution had occurred. In 1963 and 1964, the village was built as the living base for drilling workers and as the collective agricultural farm for dependents. Eighty percent of the workers in these families worked on the oil drilling frontier and occasionally would return to the village for a short break.

While the men were away on the drilling frontier, the housewives took over all of the responsibilities for building and running the homes. Most of the *gandalei* buildings in Daqing were built with the dependents providing homemade mud bricks and then professional male teams helping to erect the houses. During the construction, some women became skillful carpenters, tilers, welders, or glaziers, jobs that were traditionally done by men.[22] The women met regularly for political and technical study as well as for military training, since they were also members of the women's militia.

Map 4 shows that the Pioneer Village consisted of a cluster of settlements, with one central village and four settlement points: Pioneer No. 1 to No. 4. The distance between the central village and the settlement points was about 1.5 kilometers, with farmland between the village and the settlement points. The central village was located at the geometric center and linked to the four settlement points by paved radius roads. Until 1978, Pioneer Village had 2,255 inhabitants in 667 households.[23] The central village and Pioneer Nos. 1 and 2 each had about 100 to 200 households, whereas the other two settlements were slightly smaller. The central village was a miniature version of Saertu: the courtyard to the headquarters was located to the north of the main east-west road, facing a grid of mud houses to the south. The open space bordering the public buildings was reserved for meetings of the masses or for an open-air theater. Figure 4.4 is a photograph of Pioneer Village.

As a model village, Pioneer Village tried to achieve a high level of self-sufficiency. In the case of agricultural production, the village was a full-scale cooperative commune. It provided grain to all dependents, and livestock farming, fishery ponds, orchards, and vegetable fields offered extra nutrition for both the families and the drilling workers on the front. Every settlement had its own child care facilities, a "barefoot" medical station, boiling water services, and a public toilet.[24] The central village hosted most of the public services, including a dependent management station, a health clinic, elementary, middle, and high schools, a general store, a grain shop, a financial services team (which also served as a post office, a place to make deposits, and a reading facility), a general services team (barber, bathroom, tailor, and repair shop), and a food-processing workshop (producing self-baked goods, soy sauce, vinegar, and wine). The village also offered agricultural production services, such as stations for agricultural research, collective agricultural machines, and a weather observation station and veterinarian services.

The village provided cradle-to-grave services to its inhabitants so as to limit the need to commute to the central town. In the mid-1970s, No. 2 Village consisted of fifty-nine dependents who were engaged in collective production, thirty of whom reported that they had not left the village for seven years; the remaining twenty-nine never left the village after they moved there.[25]

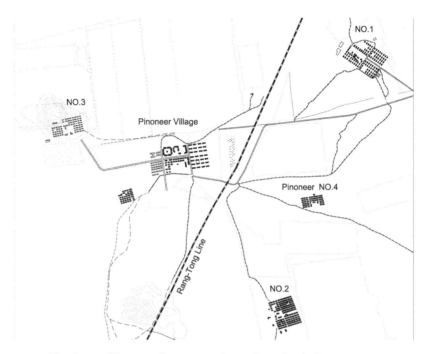

MAP 4 The cluster of Pioneer villages, 1966. Original map by the Daqing Design Institute, redrawn by the author.

FIGURE 4.4 Dependents walking on the unpaved main road in Pioneer Village, with houses on either side, 1977. Source: Daqing geming weiyuanhui, *Daqing*.

STRENGTHENING VILLAGE (TUQIANG CUN)

The No. 2 Oil Extraction Factory was established in November 1964. The oil extraction terrain was a bit south of the Saertu station. As soon as the site of the factory headquarters was finalized in April 1964, about 150 workers were drawn from the basic construction team of the No. 1 Factory to build one hundred units of *gandalei* houses, totaling 7,965 square meters, within a period of six months. By November, the cadres and workers had begun to move in. The *gandalei* houses were used for both housing and offices. In the winter, the Heilongjiang No. 3 Construction Company began building offices, dormitories, a canteen, and a bathhouse made of bricks and wood in the middle of Strengthening Village, occupying 4,966 square meters. In the middle of the construction, the Saertu headquarters issued a call for building mud-painted headquarters in all units, indicating that no "high-standard" buildings—meaning brick-made office buildings—were to be permitted.[26] All unfinished projects were replaced with curved mud roofs, conforming to the *gandalei* houses in the village. In 1965, the No. 2 Oil Factory hired a local peasant construction team to build eight *gandalei* office buildings to serve as the headquarters. Another fifty-two units of *gandalei* houses were built in 1972. The brick buildings completed in 1964 were allocated to the hospital and the middle school.

Strengthening Village served as the administrative and living center of the No. 2 Factory. Figure 4.5 shows its location in the geometric center of the factory, at the crossroads of two main work roads. It had 300 to 500 resident households. The other villages and the nearby settlement points were much smaller; these were owned and managed by subdivisions of the mining districts of the No. 2 Factory. For example, before 1973 Liberation Village, to the north, seat of the Nos. 1 and 9 Mining Districts, consisted of only ten *gandalei* buildings; New Village, built in 1965 and the most remote settlement, where the oil tank and garage were located, consisted of twenty-two *gandalei* buildings. In addition to an oil production unit, there was a work-study school, the July 21 University (a workers' university), and an educated youth team (an organization for unemployed youth engaged in agriculture). Throughout the field a public hoggery, greenhouses, and so forth were dispersed.

Before 1980, Strengthening Village had a middle school, hospital, workers' club (built in 1976), central canteen, food store, food-processing

FIGURE 4.5 Strengthening Village, early 1970s. Photo courtesy of Zhang Qihua.

FIGURE 4.6 Thawed land in front of mud houses, Strengthening Village, early 1970s. Photo courtesy of Zhang Qihua.

FIGURE 4.7 *Gandalei* house in Strengthening Village after a decade of living. Photo courtesy of Zhang Qihua.

FIGURE 4.8 Free outdoor barber service outside of a shop constructed of brick in the *gandalei* village. Photo courtesy of Zhang Qihua.

workshop, management station for dependents, bathhouse, barbershop, child care facilities, and more. Housing and utilities were free, and public services, such as child care and the canteens, charged minimum fees. However, the *gandalei* houses required yearly maintenance and the residents assumed full responsibility for such maintenance, for which they could take off one week per year. Figures 4.6–4.8 provide glimpses of life in the village.

Cities and Buildings Based on the Daqing Model

By the beginning of 1966, the first year of the Third Five-Year Plan, Daqing had become a buzzword in state media. On January 2, after the New Year's editorial "Fighting for the Fulfillment of the Third Five-Year Plan," the *People's Daily* published an editorial entitled "Daqing: The Correct Path for China's Industrialization." Daqing was praised as representative of the true spirit of the general principles of socialist construction and the correct road for China's industrialization. Unlike in the past, the editorial claimed, Daqing's success overwhelmingly relied on the guidance of Mao Zedong Thought, showing that "Mao Zedong Thought not only can guide revolution, but also can guide construction." On the same day, another article about Daqing appeared under the title "Daqing: A Paradigm for Studying and Applying Mao Zedong Thought with Liveliness." As repeatedly reinforced in this article, the spiritual power originating from belief in Mao Zedong Thought had transcended all difficulties in the natural conditions.

By 1966, the production of crude oil in Daqing had jumped to 10 million metric tons, and the number of workers had increased to fifty-eight thousand, more than 40 percent of whom were living with their families.[27] Daqing was depicted as a model community in which individuals could conquer nature.

On April 2, 1966, the *People's Daily* published yet another article about Daqing, entitled "Daqing Has Built an Integrated Industry and Agriculture and an Integrated Town and Country New Type of Mining District." This was the first time that Daqing was mentioned as a new type of industrial community, a village-like city, following the sixteen-character principle of "integration of workers and peasants, integration of the urban and the rural, good for production, and convenient for livelihood," as summarized by Premier Zhou. The article reported, "Daqing is a brand new social organization, inspired by Mao Zedong Thought, created from practice by our people. It is a new thing emerging from socialist construction. It has infinite vigor, a promising future, and it should be a model for the new industrial and mining construction of our country."

In the article, Daqing was called a "new socialist industrial-mining district," not a city, village, or enterprise. It was a modern petroleum production base, a collective farm, and an association of industry and agriculture for both workers and peasants. Daqing's work-study system enabled "everyone to become involved in manual labor, everyone to study, everyone to live within the organization, and everyone to engage in revolutionary work." The past debates on patterns of housing construction, whether concentrated or dispersed, were declared to be an economic as well as a political choice. According to Daqing's leaders, the idea of building a dispersed settlement had been inspired by Mao's instructions to the Wuhan Steel Plant, which stated that large enterprises should play a role in "industry, agriculture, exchanges, education, and the military," and from Zhou's sixteen-character principle, as well as from instructions from the other top central leaders. They argued that they had learned from past oil city construction about the inconveniences produced by the separation between living and working, the problems of unemployment among female dependents, and the waste of money and time on "high standards" and "outmoded guidelines."

The advantage of Daqing's dispersed settlement pattern, as summarized by the *People's Daily*, was that it fostered a complementary relationship between industrial and agricultural production. The integration of production had positive outcomes for both agriculture and industry, as the agricultural production guaranteed the necessary food supply for the industrial workers, and the industry helped with the mechanization of agriculture. The dispersed construction did not require "high-standard" infrastructure because there were no problems commuting between the living areas and the work sites, and the living settlements could take advantage of the nearby "production facilities" without charge, such as the supplies of water, electricity, and natural gas, as well as the availability of roads. Furthermore, the waste produced at the living quarters could be used to fertilize the surrounding farmland. The cost of living to Daqing residents was low, as they did not have to pay for utilities or transportation. The self-sustained community with public services, such as canteens, child care facilities, and a clinic, mainly provided by the dependents, could save the workers time and energy to devote to production and work. The article clearly expressed the idea that Daqing had transcended the earlier differentiation between industry and agriculture and between the urban and the rural, and had the advantages of both. Daqing had established a new Chinese form of ideal socialist society.

The last section of the editorial praised the way Daqing combined enterprises and local government—"centralized leadership, integrated management, and a combined system of administration and enterprises." In the Daqing model, the enterprises organized everyone—workers, peasants, housewives, and students—into a single organization. The welfare provided by the enterprises was also provided for the society. The enterprises fulfilled the function of local government administration, including public services, public security, mediation of civil disputes, and so forth. Such grass-roots units were responsible for the management of production and for the provision of nonproduction services, security, and civil affairs. This combination decreased the number of administrative personnel in the government, reduced the layers of government organs, and promoted efficiency and quality of services. The dual functions of enterprises and a single leadership effectively directed services and management toward socialist production.

THE *GANDALEI* SPIRIT IN ARCHITECTURE

Chinese architects during the first decade of the People's Republic faced criticism that they were alienated from economic reality by pursuing costly, unrealistic modern standards. China was pursuing "more, faster, better, and more economical," thus building the country on the socialist principle of frugality. Aesthetic values were costly, so luxuries were to be sacrificed for socialist production. Many design blueprints were abandoned during the first few years of the People's Republic as they did not match local conditions. For example, the Ministry of the Chemical Industry estimated that 60 percent of completed design work was totally "wasted" during the First Five-Year Plan.[28]

Although Soviet standards were abandoned after the Great Leap Forward and the famine, Chinese architects struggled to determine "our own way" under the socialist regime, that is, to be independent from both the capitalist world and the revisionist Soviet world. During the first decade of the PRC, architectural production swung between the pursuit of a "national style" and the economics of construction. Following Khrushchev's abandonment of Stalin's socialist realism beginning in 1955, the historicist school was strongly criticized, and by the end of the First Five-Year Plan period, national adjustments moved in the direction of thrifty construction. However, the Great Leap Forward offered opportunities for a comeback of the "big roofs," as represented in some of the "Ten Great Projects" completed in Beijing to celebrate the tenth anniversary of the People's Republic. Some modernist architects were classified as "rightists," and on June 4, 1959, during a conference in Shanghai about architectural standards, Minister of Building Construction Liu Xiufeng addressed the issue of "creating a new style for China's socialist architecture." His speech relieved some of the tensions between formalism and functionalism; "economy, function, and appearance when circumstances allow," as later summarized during a conference held by Liang Sicheng, the president of the Architectural Society of China, became the prevailing watchwords in the field of architecture.

In April 1960, although the great famine was moving into full swing, the Second National Urban Planning Conference, held in Guilin, called for "transforming our cities into new modern socialist cities within ten or fifteen years." This call created much resentment among the top leadership, and Liu Xiufeng's Shanghai speech was attacked as an "anti-Party, antisocialist architectural doctrine." As a result, the Ministry of Building Construction was deprived of its administrative functions with respect to urban planning. In 1965, during the Four Cleanups movement, Liu was criticized for exercising "departmentalism" by unnecessarily raising the standards for architectural design and nonproductive urban construction. He lost his position as minister of building construction in May 1965 and never again held a high position.[29]

The old style of design was criticized for its "three separations": separation from the working class, separation from the masses, and separation from reality. Urban planning was criticized because it "only considered the long term and not the reality; for overly pursuing a larger scale, bigger population, beautiful layouts, big squares, big architecture, broad streets, and a low density." The design institutes thus faced another wave of downsizing. The National Urban Planning and Design Institute survived three years longer than the State Construction Commission, until it too was finally disbanded in 1964. Economy and function returned as the most important criteria for architecture. The Ministry of the Petroleum Industry served as the model in this "design revolution." In the *People's Daily* of December 7, 1964, two architects, Feng Lei and Wang Shouchang, from the Ministry of the Petroleum Industry, argued that there was no need to design grand squares or public gardens at the entrance of factory compounds, as the Soviet architects had designed for the Changchun No. 1 Auto Plant, because they only added unnecessary expenditures for non-production-related construction.[30]

*   *   *

Since the official call to "learn from Daqing," waves of tourists began to visit Daqing. Hua was often pushed to the front to explain her transition during the past three years from an orthodox city planner as an example of the "revolutionization of intellectuals" in Daqing. Her story was also chosen to be published in the national media. When the Fourth Annual Conference of the Architectural Society of China was held in Yan'an in March 1966, the Daqing Institute was invited to contribute two keynote speakers. Hua was selected as one of the speakers. This decision surprised both the division as well as Hua herself. As an inexperienced young professional, she did not know what to say in front of a group of such prestigious experts.

The head of the division reassured her: "Don't worry. The Ministry of the Petroleum Industry will thrill those technical experts. At the conference, we are not to talk about techniques; we are to talk about politics, to revolutionize the field of architecture and engineering. You should talk about the changes in your thoughts, not about planning theory."

Hua prepared her speech with mixed feelings. After several rounds of editing, the talk was approved by the Institute. Until Hua got on the train, she still could not believe that she had been chosen to represent Daqing to speak at a national conference on architecture and city planning in Yan'an. Yan'an had been the Mecca for young Chinese men and women during the war, and it remained so in the 1960s. It was also the location of China's first modern oil mine, the Yanchang Oil Field.

First gathering in Xi'an, the capital of Shaanxi province, the delegation consisted of representatives from design institutes and construction sectors from throughout the country. Hua noticed that the delegation members were predominantly middle-aged men. She could easily tell they were all senior cadres or principal designers at their respective institutes and they all wore well-tailored black or gray wool coats and leather shoes. There were very few women, and they primarily served as assistants or secretaries for the delegation. Hua and the other Daqing representative, Director Hu, wore simple cotton-padded jackets covering their old blue uniform and peasant-style black cloth shoes. That was the standard outfit in Daqing, but as part of the delegation, their appearance made them stand out.

It was about three hundred kilometers from Xi'an to Yan'an, through primarily mountainous areas. The roads were primitive, and it took two days for the delegation's bus to reach Yan'an. When Hua saw the pagoda, a landmark in Yan'an and the symbol of the Chinese Communist Revolution, she was too excited to remain still. It was early spring. There was barely any green color on the pagoda mountain. It looked like a huge pile of yellowish-gray earth. The bus crossed the Yan River bridge and entered the county town. The waterbed was wide, but muddy water scarcely covered half of the bed. The land was barren. Under the bright sunshine, the group of modern motor coaches appeared very strange on the narrow unpaved streets surrounded by dilapidated mud houses. Some men and children squatted at the street corners, eating their lunches while gazing at the incoming strangers. The local men wore white wool towels on their heads to protect them from sandstorms, the sun, or blizzards. Under the white towels, their worn weathered faces were dark-colored and carved with deep wrinkles due to the hardships of age. The children wore worn-out cotton jackets with nothing underneath. They looked like they had not taken a bath for a very long time. Even after having lived in Daqing for four years, Hua was struck that there was no trace of the sixteen years of industrial construction among these people or on this land. It was extremely unsettling to see the extreme poverty.

This was two months before the beginning of the Great Proletarian Cultural Revolution, but the theme of the conference was already highly political. A great deal of time was devoted to the study of Mao Zedong Thought and to criticism of Chinese architecture. The doctrine of "function, economy, and appearance when circumstances allow" was replaced by Daqing's *gandalei* spirit. Director Hu and Hua introduced the process of developing a "scientific *gandalei* design" in Daqing. Hua's speech was followed by a talk by a model construction worker, a worker engineer, and a construction renovation worker. It was unprecedented that construction workers would appear on stage at a national conference of the Architectural Society and join the academic discussions on the creative use of local materials. The application of cheap, local construction materials, the adaptation of existing structures, and the maintenance of the same standards for rural and urban buildings were the main topics of the conference.

When Hua finished her speech, she received scattered applause from the audience. The reactions to her speech were complicated. During that year, most senior designers had been seriously criticized or had faced pending disciplinary action. Former president Liang Sicheng had been replaced. Minister of Building Construction Liu Xiufeng had been removed from his position during the Four Cleanups movement the previous year. In February 1965 Sun Jingwen, vice minister of the petroleum industry, was appointed vice minister and Party secretary of the Ministry of Building Construction.

At the end of the conference, the newly elected president of the Architectural Society of China urged all design communities throughout the country to follow Daqing's lead in the *gandalei* style of construction, whereby traditional materials and techniques are combined with modern materials and techniques to save the state money and to faithfully meet China's construction needs. Daqing's dispersed pattern of worker-peasant villages, the benefits of combining working and living spaces, and the introduction of farmland near living settlements were the models of future construction.

Unlike the depressed senior designers and cadres at the conference, Hua was drawn into the revolutionary heat, and she developed a sense of self-confidence. Her willingness to devote herself to a greater purpose was strengthened. She was overwhelmed by the feeling that the heavy responsibility of building a New China now fell upon the shoulders of her generation. What were the members of her generation to do to overcome the hardships and eradicate poverty? Hua became a loyal believer in the Daqing spirit in 1965.

"We should live in *gandalei* housing all our lives in order to build the motherland," she stated proudly during one of the conference discussion sessions.

"We should live by the spirit of *gandalei* housing all our lives," Director Hu carefully corrected her, but she was too excited to hear.

On her last night in Yan'an, Hua submitted an application to join the Chinese Communist Party. In her letter, she pledged that she would dedicate her life to building the oil field, to building her motherland.

This passion lasted on the train from Xi'an to Beijing. When Hua walked into the dining car, she noticed there were many unfinished dishes left on the tables. The local peasants' statue-like faces and their blind stares in Yan'an remained very vivid in her mind. She was annoyed by the ignorance of those people on the train. She made a provocative speech to criticize the waste of food. "Wasting food is a sin in our poor country!" she shouted with emotion.

The speech provoked a reaction from some of the people in the dining car. A young man stood up and said, "This woman comrade is right. We must not waste food. I did not leave this food, but I am going to finish it." As he started eating, several other people joined in.

* * *

RURALIZING THE CITIES

In early 1965, the State Basic Construction Commission resumed its functions. Gu Mu, Yu Qiuli's close partner on the Small Planning Commission, served as the head of the State Construction Commission. Sun Jingwen, vice minister of the petroleum industry, served as vice head. The main function of the State Construction Commission was to organize and reinforce construction of the Third Front. There was some debate about the necessity of maintaining the Urban Planning Bureau under the State Construction Commission. In the end, thirty urban planning positions were retained instead of the hundred positions that existed prior to the great famine. Nationwide there were about five thousand city planners in the early 1960s. By the mid-1970s, there were only about seven hundred people directly engaged in urban-planning work.[31] Accompanied by the petroleum leaders who entered the central leadership,

FIGURE 4.9 Designers working under a tent at the Third Front. Photo courtesy of Tongji Urban Planning Archives.

members of the State Planning Commission and the State Construction Commission served as important agents to promote application of the Daqing model.

Implementation of the Third Five-Year Plan followed the path exemplified by the Daqing model, which was based on the ideology of "production first, livelihood second" and the spirit of "self-reliance" and austerity. During the first year of the Third Five-Year Plan, Daqing had already become a model of development that extended beyond industry, and its heroic working class was highly praised. *Gandalei* housing, representing the spirit of the pursuit of frugality (*jianku fendou*), was applied to workers' housing even in remote areas of China where mud was scarce. The self-reliant, decentralized, "new socialist industrial-mining districts," which integrated industry with agriculture and integrated production enterprises with administrative management and social services, became

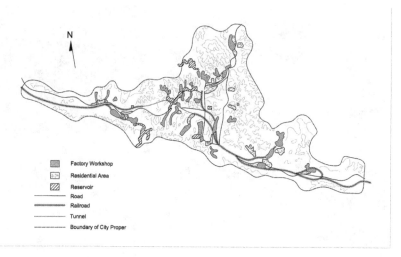

MAP 5 Master plan for Shiyan: "Dispersed and concealed in the mountains." Original map by the China Academy of Urban Planning and Design, redrawn by the author.

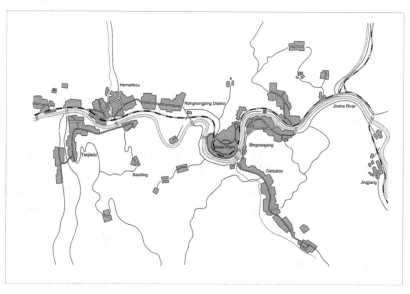

MAP 6 Panzhihua Industrial District Plan, 1965. Original map by the China Academy of Urban Planning and Design, redrawn by the author.

a model for all types of Chinese work units. Even in Beijing one could find mud houses and urban agriculture in the very center of the city—"wherever land was available."[32] The State Planning Commission issued calls for reform with regard to "basic construction planning management," state investment in urban construction was canceled, and the responsibility for basic construction was left primarily to the work units, such as factories and institutions. Large-scale planned state housing construction was replaced by self-built economic housing with the assistance of the work units.

Urban planning, better described as "master planning of industrial development," was active only at the Third Front. Figure 4.9 shows these designers at work. Many planners who had lost their jobs in Beijing found positions in the southwest. Third Front cities, such as Shiyan and Panzhihua, were planned and built based on the Daqing model (see maps 5 and 6). The instructions of the State Planning Commission on Third Front construction called for "dispersal and concealment in the mountains" (*kaoshan, fensan, yin bi*) so as to be fully prepared for imminent war. Housing mainly consisted of *gandalei* houses, conforming to local rural standards and appearances. The goal was to diminish the gap between town and country, represented by methods such as lowering urban housing standards to the level of rural housing standards and placing factories in dispersed rural settings. However, like Daqing, the locations of these national defense projects were state secrets and remained unknown to the public. The rural landscape also served to camouflage industry from possible air-raid attacks.

Industrialization without Urbanization

China carried out its extensive industrialization programs, led by the socialist state, under very premature conditions, with the leading Party members emerging from rural backgrounds, great damage from the previous decades of war, an agricultural society with little industrial infrastructure, and an uneasy international situation. Past attempts, such as the Self-Strengthening Movement during the Qing dynasty or the "Golden Ten Years" during the republican regime, had failed because of financial, social, and political problems. China's communist leaders were fully aware of this, so they maneuvered carefully within what they perceived to be very narrow available space. This was a low-budget path without any margin for aesthetics or amenities. The goals of rapid industrialization and economic growth, intertwined sophisticatedly with communist ideology and scarce resources, shaped the path of China's development.

The downsizing of urban construction, the criticism of the architects and urban planners by the top leaders, and the rise of the Daqing model all originated from an ideology that saw urbanization as an undesirable byproduct that accompanied the state's industrialization goals. With Chairman Mao trusting the petroleum leaders to bring reform to the "planning kingdom," the Daqing model was seen as the solution. Urbanization was controlled in order to limit the costs of industrialization and to satisfy ideological demands. Factories thus assumed responsibility for meeting the basic needs, both material and spiritual, of the workers.

CHAPTER 5

Living in an Urban-Rural Heterotopia

There is not a personal bone in my body!
—Iron Man Wang Jinxi

Extensive state-led industrialization transformed the national geography and created a strong state apparatus; it also gave birth to a new society, an invention of Chinese industrial and urban life. Factories were the training grounds for producing an army of disciplined industrial workers whose collective activities would achieve their highest potential; everyone was expected to be a "worker-peasant-merchant-student-soldier" (*gong nong shang xue bing*) combined into one body. After the geologists discovered the oil deposits, maximizing oil production would require a total commitment. Thousands of workers converged onto the oil field. Machinery was scarce and often arrived at sites that lacked basic infrastructure, skilled workers, and supplies. The veteran oil workers, retired soldiers from the People's Liberation Army, and young graduates served as the core labor force for drilling and construction. This new working-class, primarily from peasant backgrounds, underwent some radical changes with respect to their attitudes toward industrial culture as well as toward their new living environment. Education to achieve higher productivity, greater discipline, more sacrifices, and deeper commitments—the values of the new socialist working class—was to be implemented at the production site. Relying on the principles of "urban-rural integration" for working and living, "a great popular reform," based on the ideology and morality of Marxism-Leninism and Mao Zedong Thought, was under way.

The various groups reacted to these calls in different ways. There were model workers, model dependents, and transformed intellectuals who represented the values that the state sought to reinforce. There was also passive resistance, a reluctance to sacrifice, and runaways. Such differences occurred within a closed, homogeneous space. Collective life could not completely eradicate personal interests, and social solidarity was disrupted in the face of these unsettling forces.

The Factory as a Production Machine

Working conditions were extremely harsh in Daqing. Thousands of workers and staff arrived without adequate clothing, housing, or food, and once there they encountered a desolate prairie and backbreaking manual labor. Workers from the south—many drawn from the Sichuan campaign—were completely unprepared for the cold weather on the Songliao Plains.[1] The factories of Harbin produced winter jackets for them, but the freezing rain, mixed with sweat from their labor, made many of the workers sick. Although the plains were conducive to the free movement of motor vehicles, the frequent rain in the spring and the thawing land soon produced ponds and wetlands, a "big jar of soy paste" as it was often called. Workers had to move the heavy machines to the targeted sites by tractors, horses, or sometimes even by their own "hands and shoulders." Until the water pipes or water tanks were ready, they had to carry the water for the drilling in pots and hand basins. As the production sites were scattered throughout the 6,000-square-kilometer oil field, it was common for three or four persons to work alone at a site. It was once reported that a building team of five, trapped by a snowstorm, lost contact with the headquarters for seven days and were left without any food or water supplies.[2] Even the retired officers who had returned from the Korean War found campaign life unbearable.[3] At the Songliao Oil School, a training base for future oil workers, teachers would make nightly checks to make sure that none of the students had escaped, and they would have to search for the runaway students in the lonely grasslands.[4] However, the hardships did not disrupt oil production; rather, they produced a modern working class "who possessed a level of ideological awareness" that was the goal Mao hoped all Chinese could achieve. Because many of the oil workers had been transferred from the army and engaged in agricultural work in their spare time, they were representative of the three constituencies that were critically important to socialist society—workers, peasants, and soldiers—combined in China's ideal new socialist man or woman.

IRON MEN

Daqing's leaders attributed the campaign's success to the quality of its workforce. The oil workers, especially the pioneer drilling workers, were given the most credit for these achievements. They were assured that they were the owners of the factory and the ruling class of the regime. From the very beginning of the campaign, Daqing leaders honored model workers, who, due to their solid presence, zealous commitment, and moral enthusiasm, set the tempo and tenor of work discipline for the newcomers. The model workers were rewarded generously with moral incentives as well as career opportunities, special allocations, such as extra food and uniforms, and other material benefits.

The first and most famous model worker in Daqing was "Iron Man" Wang Jinxi. A well-known veteran oil worker from Yumen Oil Field, Wang led his drilling team to produce new drilling records on numerous occasions. Arriving on March 25, 1960, he was among the first in Saertu. Born to a poor peasant family in Yumen, Shaanxi province, Wang, thirty-seven, was both thin and frail. But his devotion to the drilling industry and his enthusiasm for competitive work made him the first model worker handpicked by Yu Qiuli. According to his official story, on the day of his arrival, as Wang and his crew got off the train in Saertu, he asked only three questions: "Has our drilling machine arrived yet? Where is the drilling site? What is the drilling record here?" None of these questions had anything to do with his personal interests—they all focused on work and production. Ten days later, while searching along the congested Binzhou line, he and his crew finally found the train car carrying their drilling machine. However, at that time there were not yet any available cranes, trucks, or tractors. Determined not to wait any longer, Wang decided to move the sixty tons of equipment by hand to the work site, which was several kilometers to the northwest of the Saertu Railway Station. It took the team one full day to offload the equipment and three more days to move it to its final destination. On April 11, Wang's team finally finished the installation of the drilling equipment. The headquarters assigned host families in the nearby village to the drilling workers, but Wang never checked in with his host. When his host visited the work site and saw Wang sleeping near a power generator, she was so touched that she said, "Your team leader is an iron man!," thus conferring on him his new nickname.[5]

On April 11, the day that Wang's team was finally ready to begin drilling, Wang was called to participate in the last event of the First Daqing Oil Field Technology Colloquium at the Anda Railway Workers' Club. More than five hundred cadres, experts, engineers, and workers crowded into the Club. Yu Qiuli delivered the closing speech, replete with military language: "We must all have the attitude of fiercely attacking the targets, working as fast as thunder and wind, conquering hardships, and fighting in harsh conditions. . . . Every team, every unit, and every person must have a spirit to charge forward without fear of losing their lives, just like in fighting in a revolutionary war, and with such courage we will conquer all difficulties and never be defeated by any adversities!"[6]

Then Yu Qiuli asked, "Where is Wang Jinxi?" Wang stood up and was led to the center of the stage.

After briefly introducing Wang and his story, General Yu raised his single arm, and exclaimed, "Learn from the Iron Man! Salute the Iron Man!"

The participants at the colloquium all seconded this call. Wang was lifted up by the leaders and carried around the room so that he could be saluted by the people. Iron Man Wang soon became well known to all the workers in the oil field.

The drilling became a symbol of progress. They worked in continuous shifts, day and night. All drilling teams sent observers to the drilling site to learn from Iron Man. Drilling needs a large supply of water to keep the machines from overheating. As the water pipeline was still under construction and the water tank would not arrive for another three days, more than one hundred laborers were organized to fetch the water, basin by basin, from the nearby pond. The drilling was completed on April 19. Nine days later, oil shot forth from the Saertu No. 55 well. This was recorded as the moment when the Daqing Oil Field began production.

On the next day, Kang Shi'en organized a Ten-Thousand-Person Swearing-In Conference for the campaign in Saertu. At the beginning of the conference, Iron Man Wang, whose leg had been injured early that morning while working on the oil derrick, was paraded around the conference site wearing a red silk flower and riding on a horse led by the leader of the drilling headquarters. This was a People's Liberation Army tradition to honor heroes during the war, and thereafter it became a traditional warm-up activity for Daqing's mass conferences. Iron Man Wang, speaking to the thousands of oil workers and cadres, called out his famous slogans: "I am willing to sacrifice twenty years of my life to develop a big oil field for our motherland!" and "Charge when the conditions are ripe, and charge even when the conditions do not permit it!"[7]

After the Ten-Thousand Person Swearing-In Conference, a movement to learn from Iron Man Wang was promoted. Other Iron-Man–style model workers emerged during the campaign. The theme of triumphing over all difficulties through human power and a strong belief in Marxism-Leninism and Mao Zedong Thought, devoting oneself to production regardless of the danger of being hurt or even of losing one's life, was repeated again and again in the stories about the model workers. One Iron Man became "Five Red Flags"—five model workers—during the July conferences, and soon there were one hundred "Red Flag" work units.

Many of the Daqing model workers were incorporated into the leadership. Iron Man Wang was initially appointed vice head of the Daqing Drilling Headquarters. Then, in 1968, he was appointed vice director of the Daqing Revolutionary Committee, which had replaced the government organs. One year later, at the Ninth Party Congress, together with Chen Yonggui, the peasant leader in the model village of Dazhai, Wang joined the Party's Central Committee. Iron Man Wang died of cancer in 1970 at the age of forty-seven, thirteen years younger than the average Chinese lifespan at the time. To this day he remains one of the most well-known models representing the Chinese working class in the People's Republic.

IRON GIRLS

Daqing society was dominated by young males. The first few women to arrive were mainly graduates or engineers who had remained in design research institutes or administrative institutions. During the national wave of recruiting women workers into the labor force, so as to create a more balanced structure in the future society more local women were re-cruited from oil schools to join the Daqing campaign or simply to be-come contract workers.[8] When the young dependents of the oil workers arrived, many were accepted as "temporary workers" due to the rapidly growing need for more laborers. In 1964, the female staff constituted 10 percent of the total employees in Daqing, a record in many heavy in-dustries.[9] The women were first assigned to office positions or jobs in the services industry, such as in the canteens, shops, or child care facilities. Later, more women were sent to the production front to work as oil extraction workers or construction workers. There were also female sol-diers, female logging workers, female truck drivers, female electricians, and female plumbers.

As the oil industry is not overly demanding in terms of physical labor and has a relatively high level of automation, more women in Daqing be-gan to work in oil extraction. In some oil extraction work units, the female workers held more than half of the positions. These female oil extraction workers became representatives of Daqing's emerging new socialist women and a national role model for women. "Iron Girl," origi-nally a model from the Dazhai Young Women's Pioneer Team for agri-cultural production, became an honorary title for those daring young women who worked on the oil front and who were willing to challenge the limits of human endurance and to compete with the men. Teams of Iron Girls, mainly engaged in oil extraction, were established in many units. By the early 1970s, there were 129 teams of Iron Girls and more than sixteen thousand female oil extraction workers at the front in Daqing.

The propaganda about the Iron Girls was similar to that about the Iron Men, emphasizing their devotion to work and their enthusiasm to compete. They wore the same outfits as the men and dispensed with a feminine appearance, such as having long hair. Some of the Iron Girls were later promoted to be leaders in Daqing or even to the ministerial level.

THE DEPENDENTS

Several months after the beginning of the Daqing campaign, despite discouragement by the campaign headquarters, dependents—rural housewives and their children—began to arrive at the oil field. Many were seeking reunions with husbands who for years had served in the army; others arrived simply to escape the starvation in the countryside. But the conditions in Daqing were no better than the conditions at home. Housing was inadequate; there was no extra food; and they faced harsh, cold winters and inhospitable plains. But because of the rapidly growing need for laborers, many of the young dependents were recruited as "temporary workers." They worked on infrastructure construction, building *gandalei* houses, serving in the canteens, working in the shops, or as members of organized teams that searched for wild vegetables. The elderly women offered basic child care for the working mothers.

As previously noted, employment opportunities for women in an oil field usually did not exceed about 10 percent of its total labor force. In Daqing's case, farming not only solved the problem of the food crisis, but it also helped to organize the rural housewives into agricultural collectives, transforming the women from consumers into producers. During the later years of the Daqing campaign, an increasing number of dependents was persuaded to join the collective agricultural teams. Collectivization was much stricter during the Cultural Revolution, when those women who preferred to stay home were referred to as social "parasites." Activities such as individual farming and raising poultry were attacked as "capitalist sprouts" and were collectivized. Model dependents, such as Xue Guifang, who was the dependent of an oil-drilling worker and a pioneer in land reclamation and farming, were selected to encourage housewives to engage in farming and collective labor.[10]

Stories about the Daqing dependents received prominent national attention through the efforts of Sun Weishi, chief director of the Central Experimental Theater.[11] After receiving an education in Moscow, Sun enjoyed enormous prestige by directing Soviet drama on the Beijing stage. But by the 1960s, what was previously Sun's advantage in terms of her knowledge of Soviet drama became a liability. When Zhou Enlai returned from his second visit to Daqing, he suggested that Sun find some inspiration in Daqing to boost her professional career. Therefore, in 1964 Sun and her husband, Jin Shan, a famous actor, moved to Daqing "to live and work with the Daqing dependents." In 1965, the Party's theoretical journal *Red Flag* published an article by Sun that enthusiastically praised the Daqing dependents:

The workers formerly transferred from the industrial battlefront to help the dependents build villages have been sent back with big red flowers and music (as the dependents could now build the villages by themselves). Agricultural production was completed entirely by the dependents. . . . The service staff in the canteens, nurseries, tailor shops, barber shops, public bathhouses, post offices, banks, bookstores, commodity shops, and grain stations in the workers' new village . . . are basically all dependents. . . . The dependents are paid according to their labor contributions recorded by their number of work points, regardless of whether they are working in industry, agriculture, or in the service departments. . . . The items produced by the dependents are publicly owned and redistributed by the public. . . . Babies go to child care and children go to elementary school or to work-study middle schools. Everyone lives in an organization, and everyone lives within the system.[12]

After two years of living in Daqing, Sun Weishi returned to the Beijing theater with the play *The Rising Sun*, a drama performed by the Daqing dependents that depicted their productive lives in the new society. In Beijing, the drama was performed over 180 times within three months to audiences of tens of thousands. Zhou Enlai and his wife, Deng Yingchao, who was the head of the All-China Women's Federation, attended the performance on many occasions. After Ye Jianying, vice chairman of the Central Military Commission, saw the play, he instructed the dependents in the army to learn from the Daqing women.[13] Figures 5.1–5.6 show the many roles that these women undertook in Daqing.

In fact, the dependents represented the grass roots of Daqing society. Their food rations were the lowest, compared to those of the oil workers and the cadres. Initially their rations depended on how much they harvested on their own; thereafter they were set at 13.5 kilograms per person per month, and 3 to 5 kilograms per month for their children (whose household status followed that of their mother). In addition to food rations, as in other rural settings the dependents would receive 50 or 60 yuan at the end of each year based on the number of work points they had earned. The income gap between permanent state employees and collective temporary workers was huge. Moreover, the dependents usually also had to carry the burden of all household and domestic responsibilities.

FIGURE 5.1 Daqing women as child care providers. Photo courtesy of Zhang Qihua.

FIGURE 5.2 Daqing women as schoolteachers. Photo courtesy of Zhang Qihua.

FIGURE 5.3 Daqing women as dependent farmers. Source: Daqing geming weiyuanhui, *Daqing*.

FIGURE 5.4 Daqing women as tractor drivers. Source: Daqing geming weiyuanhui, *Daqing*.

FIGURE 5.5 Daqing women as construction workers. Source: Daqing geming weiyuanhui, *Daqing*.

FIGURE 5.6 Daqing women as soldiers. Source: Daqing geming weiyuanhui, *Daqing*.

YOUNG INTELLECTUALS

Daqing had an extraordinarily highly educated labor force.[14] In this industrial troop, 13 percent were veteran oil workers, 28 percent were former soldiers in the military, and 59 percent were "young intellectuals"— graduates from universities or technical schools.[15] Therefore, Daqing was not only a society under the dictatorship of the proletariat class but also a place where "young intellectuals clustered." In 1962, there were thousands of "technical cadres."[16]

In the early 1960s, national ideology and policies toward intellectuals were still swinging between left and right.[17] Intellectuals were charged with having unreliable associations with capitalists and the working classes and for being ignorant about grassroots conditions when compared to the workers and peasants who "in the last analysis . . . [are] the cleanest people and, even though their hands were soiled and feet smeared with cow-dung, they were really cleaner than the bourgeoisie and the petit-bourgeois intellectuals."[18] In March 1962, at the National Conference of Science and Technology, Zhou announced that most of China's intellectuals were now serving the workers, not the bourgeois classes. However, just six months later, in September 1962, Mao gave a speech entitled "The Problems of Class, Current Trends, Contradictions, and the Integrity of the Party" at the Tenth Plenum of the Eighth National Congress of the Chinese Communist Party, in which he reasserted the existence of class struggle between the proletarian and bourgeois classes and the struggle between socialist and capitalist roads. Clearly, if intellectuals were to be integrated into the Party and into the state apparatus, they had to be transformed. Mao proposed that intellectuals be transformed by engaging in manual labor and work-study programs, not by differentiating them in terms of their treatment toward cadres and workers. Figure 5.7 shows this ideal in action.

During the first several years of the Daqing campaign, all intellectuals, mainly the cadres, were expected to build *gandalei* housing and to engage in agricultural production. They built their own houses and joined in agricultural production to provide their own food. On July 26, 1962, in response to Zhou's speech, the Daqing Campaign Work Committee reaffirmed its policy that all technical cadres were required to join in manual production work in three to five positions and to reach a certain level

FIGURE 5.7 Daqing Oil Field Development Colloquium, where both workers and engineers were invited to join the discussion, year unknown. Source: Daqing geming weiyuanhui, *Daqing.*

of proficiency.[19] Therefore, the first jobs that the young graduates, who had just arrived at Daqing, took were usually on the oil production front, where they worked for two or three years. This became routine practice for all newcomers.

The response to such manual labor training was mixed. Many intellectuals publicly agreed that this helped them better understand the hardships on the production front and the real needs of those at the grass roots. But privately many of them felt this was a form of punishment, and they expressed their opposition to the policy.

However, materially the intellectuals received higher wages than the workers in Daqing, though both were still paid at very low levels. For fresh college graduates, the average starting wage was about 38 to 46 yuan per month. This was about 10 to 20 yuan more than the typical wage for starting field workers.[20] Cadres and engineers also received certain privileges in their housing allocations. Only model workers received the same benefits as the cadres. Moreover, although many model workers were promoted to leadership positions in Daqing, over time the technocrats remained more influential in their management positions.

The Factory as a Work-Study School

In 1964 the *People's Daily* and other state media disseminated abundant propaganda about Daqing. Most of these articles emphasized Daqing's heroic and self-disciplined workforce, its effective political education and serious study of Mao Zedong Thought, the workers' scientific and technical innovations through hard work and democratic participation, their pride in being a member of the Chinese working class, and so forth. One of the most influential reports was "Daqing People, Daqing Spirit," which appeared in the *People's Daily* on April 20, 1964. The article was in six parts: (1) Daqing as an extension and development of the Yan'an spirit; (2) Daqing as a model for the future of the entire country; (3) Daqing as a center of innovation for oil exploration and extraction technology; (4) the positive work style of Daqing workers, starting with the most minor responsibilities; (5) Daqing workers as a stainless all-purpose screw; and (6) Daqing as a close community where everyone cared for others more than they cared about themselves. For the first time Daqing was compared to Yan'an, the center of the CCP base area from 1936 to 1949, where the CCP reestablished itself after the Long March and achieved victory over the Nationalists in the Civil War to assume control over the entire country. The enthusiasm and self-discipline of the people in Daqing, both in terms of their work and their participation in the emergence of a caring and mutually supportive community, contrasted sharply with the cold and ruthless situation in the northern plains. This was a story of revolutionary people conquering nature through sheer human will, a steadfast will inspired by communist ideology and patriotism. In this regard, the Daqing spirit was best summarized in a poem by Iron Man Wang: "If an oil worker roars once, the Earth will shake three times!"[21]

In Zhou Enlai's "Government Work Report" to the Third National People's Congress in December 1964, he attributed the success of Daqing to the innovation of the Chinese geologists, China's increasingly independent design and research abilities, a strong belief in Mao Zedong Thought, the integration of centralized leadership and mass mobilization, and the integration of a revolutionary spirit and a scientific attitude. The article referred to both the "laborization" (*laodonghua*) of intellectuals and the "knowledgization" (*zhishihua*) of the workers, as well as the principles of the design revolution and thrifty construction.[22] In a later official account of the Daqing story in 1966, Mao Zedong Thought was claimed to be the source of action-motivating, norm-setting, practice-guiding, and reality-defining precepts. This highlighted the importance of moral voluntarism and personal faith in the human potential to conquer the difficulties of technology and nature in order to transform society.

Daqing emerged as a national model just as the Mao's personality cult was beginning to grow. In October 1959, after Lin Biao replaced Peng Dehuai as minister of defense, he wrote an article entitled "March Ahead under the Red Flag of the Party's General Line and Mao Zedong's Military Thought," published in the party journal *Red Flag*. This marked the beginning of the political education movement in the People's Liberation Army. Yu Qiuli responded firmly to Lin's call during the Daqing campaign. As Mao's "little red books" were not published until 1964, the Ministry of the Petroleum Industry chose *On Practice* and *On Contradiction,* two of Mao's major philosophical works, as textbooks to be used during the Daqing campaign. On April 10, 1960, the first decision issued by the Daqing campaign headquarters was "A Decision about Studying *On Practice* and *On Contradiction* Written by Comrade Mao Zedong." The decision stated:

> The Party Committee of the Ministry has decided to organize all Communist Party members, Youth League members, and cadres to immediately study Comrade Mao Zedong's *On Practice* and *On Contradiction* and also to call on all non-Party staff to study these two documents, and to use the standpoints, opinions, and methodology of the two documents to organize all the work during this big campaign.
>
> The study should follow the principles of integrating theory with practice, applying the method of study along with discussion, and discussion together with practice. . . . Party committees at all levels must formulate their study plans and report to the higher level. Master the weapons, be daring in practice, understand the rules of oil field development—these are the goals of our study. We call on all staff in this big campaign to promote the study of Mao Zedong's works to a new high level, and to be prepared for an ideological revolution, for the unfolding of a technological revolution, and for a production revolution.[23]

On April 26, at the headquarters' extended meeting, Yu Qiuli further noted the importance of studying Mao Zedong Thought during the campaign: "Mao Zedong Thought is the guideline for all our work: *On Practice* and *On Contradiction* are the soul of the campaign. We must read these works carefully, again and again. After having read the works by Chairman Mao, we will have clear minds and energetic bodies, and we will be full of new ideas to face any problems; without Mao Zedong Thought, we cannot do anything."[24]

As the local bookshops in Anda and Harbin did not have many copies of Mao's *On Practice* and *On Contradiction,* the Ministry of the Petroleum Industry shipped thousands of copies from Beijing by air so as to guarantee that every person on the Daqing battlefield would receive one copy. Each work unit set up its own study programs and study teams.

In 1964, Yu Qiuli reported that the success of the Daqing campaign and the mobilization of the workforce to its fullest extent were due to the constant study of Mao's two booklets and that the Daqing people's revolutionary spirit, hard work, and self-sacrifice had arisen from faith in Marxism and Mao Zedong Thought.

Mao asked, "Which two articles?"

Yu answered, "On Practice and On Contradiction."

Mao laughed, "My two booklets are that useful?"[25]

In 1966, the Nanjing Military Region began to encourage soldiers in Anhui province to follow the Yan'an spirit and engage in agricultural work. On May 7, Mao wrote a letter to Lin Biao in response to the "Report on Further Developing Agricultural Production and Side Occupations in the Armed Forces." In this letter, Mao described his vision of an ideal society:

The PLA should be a great school. . . . In this great school people can receive political, military, and cultural training. They can participate in agriculture and sideline production. . . . The military and civilians are forever mingled together. . . .

Factory workers . . . should concentrate on industrial production, but they should also work in the military, and in political and cultural fields. They need to take part in the socialist education movement and need to criticize the bourgeoisie. . . . The first duty of peasants . . . is agricultural production (including forestry, husbandry, sideline, and fishery productions).

They must also engage in military, political, and cultural activities. They can set up collectively owned small-size factories. And they must criticize the bourgeoisie. The situation with the students is no different. . . . If conditions allow, people working in the commercial sectors, in the service industries, and in party and government organizations should do the same thing.[26]

The letter was called the "May 7th Directive." On May 15, it was forwarded to all Party members, with the following comment by the Central Committee: "The letter Comrade Mao Zedong wrote to Comrade Lin Biao is a historically important document. This is a new development in Marxism and Leninism." On August 1, the *People's Daily* published an editorial entitled "The Whole Country Should Become a Big School of Mao Zedong Thought," calling for a national movement to study the May 7th Directive. The directive became the textual foundation for the thousands of May 7th cadre schools that were established in the late 1960s. Cadres from industrial, bureaucratic, and service units were assigned for specific periods of time to reside in these cadre schools, where they undertook a combination of agricultural work and ideological training.

The Factory as a Battlefield

In 1966, the production of crude oil in Daqing reached 10.6 million metric tons, which was 75 percent of the total national production. Daqing's status as a national model had reached a peak as a revolutionary storm began to sweep across the country.

On July 26, the *People's Daily* published photos of Chairman Mao swimming in the Yangtze River, implying that the chairman was sufficiently strong and ready to resume his command of the party. The Eleventh Plenum of the CCP's Eighth National Party Congress, convening on August 1, passed the "Decision of the CCP Central Committee on the Great Proletarian Cultural Revolution," thus formally launching the Cultural Revolution among the public. On August 5, Mao wrote his first "big-character poster," "Bombard the Headquarters," in praise of the student rebels at Beijing University, clearly indicating that "some leading comrades from the central down to the local levels" were not acting in conformity with Party policy. Mao had the script distributed to the Party plenum.

To celebrate the plenum's decision on the launch of the Cultural Revolution, Daqing held a grand event, at which Iron Man Wang Jinxi gave his signature speech in support of the central decision. Several days later, Wang led a delegation of oil-drilling workers and their dependents to Beijing. They were honored by the top leaders, gave speeches at many public events, and were invited to be guests at the seventeenth-anniversary celebration of the founding of the People's Republic. The image of the Daqing oil workers standing on top of the Gate of Heavenly Peace (Tiananmen) with the state leaders impressed the entire country. During the event, a seriously injured oil worker gave a speech. At the Museum of Revolutionary History in Tiananmen Square, an exhibition entitled "In Industry, Learn from Daqing" was held, receiving thousands of visitors.

THE RED GUARDS

While the model oil workers were enjoying their highest honor during the celebrations, the Red Guards, with Mao's endorsement, paid a visit to the Museum of Revolutionary History, not to learn from Daqing but to critically examine the exhibition. The exhibition featured a photo of Liu Shaoqi visiting Daqing. The Red Guards questioned whether Daqing in fact "had been peacefully transformed into an experimental land for capitalism" by a group of revisionists. They argued whether Daqing's ideal communal life—"both industrial and agricultural" and "integrating the urban and the rural"—was an idea copied from capitalist utopian thinkers. This self-sustaining pattern—"husbands as industrial workers and wives as agricultural farmers," who lived together near oil wells and farming land—was interpreted as a repetition of the old dream of "one house and two units of land" and calling for individualism rather than collectivism.[27] "Economism," one of the charges against Liu Shaoqi and the leaders of Daqing, referred to using not only moral but also material incentives and rewards by bribing the oil workers to produce more.

Beginning in 1966 Yu Qiuli and Gu Mu worked closely under Premier Zhou's leadership in the State Council, carrying out basic functions to keep the revolutionary fervor from damaging economic production. The man handpicked by Mao to "break through the pond of dead water," Yu had developed close relationships with the senior economic leaders in that "dead pond." The fact that he was young and had a "pure red" background, as well as the fact that he had been handpicked by Mao, protected him from serious attacks in later years. Worried about being unable to fulfill the plan, Yu worked hard to keep production on track regardless of the heated revolutionary atmosphere. Workers were encouraged to become involved in the Cultural Revolution only during their spare time. On a number of occasions, his role of guaranteeing industrial production clashed with the Central Cultural Revolution Group, led by Chen Boda and Jiang Qing (Madame Mao). Although the chairman agreed with Yu's suggestion that eight hours of production work should be guaranteed daily, he issued a call to "grasp revolution and to promote production" (*zhua geming cu shengchan*), and the animosity between the "economic cabinet" and the Central Cultural Revolution Group continued.

Zhang Chunqiao, the leading theoretician in the Central Cultural Revolution Group, commented that Daqing was "red in the beginning but black in the end," thus admitting that in 1960 Daqing's experience was communist in nature but that it had changed in later years. The claim that Daqing was a "sham model" and its communist pattern "faked" spread from Beijing to the production front. After National Day in 1966, the official press gradually became silent on the topic of Daqing, and the dependents' theatrical performance *The Rising Sun* was closed down. Similarly, the Central Cultural Revolution Group did not support Iron Man Wang's behavior. Zhang Chunqiao once said, "Iron Man has become part of the vested interests in Daqing. . . . He is now on the opposite side—a member of the privileged class rather than a member of the working class," and he "no longer has any revolutionary vigor."[28]

In January 1967, more than ten thousand Daqing students and workers departed for Beijing to appeal for justice from the central government. Joining the rebels in the State Planning Commission and the Red Guards from Beijing universities, they initiated a meeting to criticize and denounce Yu Qiuli, but Yu was rescued from the meeting by Zhou Enlai. Premier Zhou received the representatives from Daqing, reassured them that the "Daqing Red Flag was erected by Chairman Mao," and persuaded the workers to return to work.[29]

At the same time, Yu Qiuli and Gu Mu became involved in a conflict in the capital between senior generals and the Central Cultural Revolution Group, a conflict later called the "February Countercurrent."[30] In February 1967, Li Fuchun invited the central leaders in industry and transportation, including some members of the Politburo, Vice Premier Tan Zhenlin, Marshal Chen Yi, Li Xiannian, and Yu Qiuli, among others, to his home to discuss "grasping revolution and promoting production." The purpose was to put production and transportation back on track despite the heated climate. The meeting soon turned into a session to criticize the Central Cultural Revolution Group for destroying the social order, threatening the Party's leadership, and purging the senior cadres. The session resulted in a furious face-to-face brawl with the Central Cultural Revolution Group. A longtime subordinate to these senior generals and a member of the economic cabinet, Yu Qiuli seconded the generals, although he did not say anything nearly as outrageous as what was said by Marshal Chen and Vice Premier Tan Zhenlin. Mao and the Central Cultural Revolution Group considered these clashes to be by far the most serious incident against the Cultural Revolution. Chen Boda claimed that they amounted to an attempt to "subvert the dictatorship of the proletariat." Chairman Mao ordered that Tan Zhenlin, Chen Yi, and Xu Xiangqian "request leaves of absence to carry out self-criticisms." Yu Qiuli, as a junior member, was allowed to remain in his position, but he became one of the more popular targets for the Red Guards and rebels in Beijing. He was forced to attend many denunciation sessions, and at one point the students confined him to the Beijing Oil Institute. Zhou had to call the Central Cultural Revolution Group to rescue Yu and let him return to work.[31]

Nor were the other petroleum leaders free from criticism. Kang Shi'en, at that time the minister of the petroleum industry, was told to denounce Yu, and because he refused he was forced out of his position. Song Zhenming was sent to a May 7th cadre school, and sixteen or seventeen high-level cadres in the Daqing headquarters were attacked as "capitalist roaders" or "renegades."[32] By the end of 1966, more than six thousand cadres faced criticism.

REBELS

At the Daqing Oil Field, the young men and women responded enthusiastically to Chairman Mao's call for an upside-down "cultural revolution."

Red Guards from Beijing, mainly from Beijing Normal University, China University of Geosciences, and Beijing University of Aeronautics, established ties with the local Daqing students.[33] Students at the Beijing Oil Institute had been working in Daqing to build their own *gandalei* campus in Wangjia Weizi, a peninsula several kilometers east of Saertu. They were to establish their own half-work, half-study experimental program. But they soon abandoned the plan and joined the battle to fight against revisionism and capitalism. Before long, the workers and the staff joined the students. Big-character posters began to appear on the campuses, in the factories, and finally in Compound No. 2, bombarding the headquarters. Some workers complained about the hard work and the strict regulations, by which they were "controlled, wedged, and suppressed," not much different from the capitalists' exploitation of workers or even from slavery.[34] Corresponding to the Central Cultural Revolution Group's criticism of Iron Man Wang, some young workers joined the battle to attack the senior model workers who "had been part of the privileged class."

The Cultural Revolution repealed the concrete rules that had been established in Daqing, thus revealing and sharpening the existing conflicts within society. Clashes between the leaders in power and the "suppressed" workers, the educated youth and the cadres, and the "royalists" and the "rebels" continued unabated through to the end of 1966.

In June, the Daqing Work Committee issued calls to the "battlefield" to enthusiastically join the Cultural Revolution, inviting the masses to criticize the Party: "Anyone can raise issues, anything can be raised, and anything can be discussed." The Work Committee provided poster frames and free paper, brushes, and ink in the Compound No. 2 canteen. Initially most people remained silent. They had learned a lesson from the past. The vice Party secretary of the Mining District Construction Office, Wang Qingshan, a retired military officer who had an unquestionably "good" class background, decided to take the lead in writing a big-character poster. Several veterans signed his poster, considering this to be a way to participate in the nationwide movement. Because Wang was not very well-educated, the poster consisted of only a very few sentences. No one really knew where this would lead. But posters gradually began to fill the frames, like single trees lining up into woods.

The well-educated young men and women were initially prudent, but eventually they "threw themselves into the movement" due to encouragement from state media and high-level officials. Within eighteen days, thousands of posters had appeared. The people of Daqing were surprised to learn that so many different opinions existed in the oil field. The posters revealed the disagreements among the people regarding the organization of the campaign, their resentment toward certain authorities, and their demands for better treatment. One influential poster, written by Liu Dong from the Planning Department, was entitled "Twenty-one Articles on Criticizing the Political Experience of the Ministry of the Petroleum Industry." The poster questioned the capability of the petroleum leaders and the efficacy of the Daqing campaign. Liu argued that the hasty mobilization and organization of the campaign had caused a tremendous waste of time, manpower, and materials. Some individuals were singled out publicly by name. One poster accused Chief Liu Shuren of being a hidden counterrevolutionary because he had worked for the National Resource Commission before 1949. The poster, written by Chief Liu's right-hand man, stated that Liu had "a black line linking him directly to the sky," implying that he had secret access to the highest authority: his in-law Vice Minister Kang Shi'en. Some posters complained that the forced extra hours and laboring to midnight without any improvements in productivity were merely a political show that deprived the workers of rest. The posters that attracted the most attention would be moved to the center and front of the exhibit, provoking either a sympathetic reaction or harsh criticism, but also resulting in even more posters. The petroleum leaders faced an unexpected high tide of public criticism.

* * *

The summer of 1966 began like a fire as the movement to "Smash the Four Olds" spread to Daqing. As a young man who loved literature, Song, with great pain, burned his books and journals. This was a means of self-protection before these petit-bourgeois items were discovered by the Red Guards. He saved only one diary, the one written by Hua when they first fell in love with each other at the university. He hid it in a secret space inside his suitcase, a rather romantic but bold act that would have been considered deranged during those furious days.

Under normal circumstances, Hua would usually refrain from participating in such political events. But only three months earlier she had returned from Yan'an and she was still reveling in the halo of having represented the Daqing spirit at a national conference. Both she and her fiancé had already submitted their applications to join the Communist Party. So together with two other colleagues, they wrote a long article expressing their reflections on the past Four Cleanups movement. They argued that the movement had effectively protected those in power. It had become a manipulated show. The integrity of the masses was seriously damaged during such criticism campaigns.

On July 9, when Hua entered the canteen, she sensed something was different. People were gathered in front of a large, newly written poster entitled "What Do They Oppose?" There was complete silence in the canteen, and no one seemed to be interested in eating. The poster had been written by the Policy Research Office, the think-tank of the Daqing Work Committee. It praised the Daqing leadership and described the past month as a "dance by ghosts and devils." More than forty cadres who had criticized the leadership were cited by name. The sarcastic language and oppressive tone of the poster produced a strong reaction among the onlookers.

The next day, new posters added more names of people who had excessively "freely aired their views." Vice Secretary Wang Qingshan of the Mining District Construction Office, who had rashly written the first big-character poster, was called the head of many "ox demons and snake freaks" (*niugui sheshen*). Liu Dong's poster was declared to be "the cornerstone of distinguishing the revolutionary from the counterrevolutionary." Others were labeled "rightists," "anti-Party elements," or those who had "committed mistakes," including Hua and Song. Chief Liu Shuren, who could not deny that he had worked for the Nationalists in the past, was called a "reactionary academic authority."

The "free airing of views" was followed by intense "struggle sessions" (*pi dou hui*). It was summer, so the sessions were often held outdoors. Limestone divided the outdoor arenas into three distinct areas: one for the "revolutionary masses," one for the counterrevolutionaries, and one for those who had "committed mistakes." In almost no time, Hua's reputation in the office changed from a radiant red revolutionary to a black "troublemaker." During the first few days, she refused to admit she had done anything wrong. However, the pressure was unbearable. Nightmares and sleeplessness followed. A deep gap developed between the "revolutionary masses" and the counterrevolutionaries. Hua held out for several more days until she could endure the pressure no longer. Then she publicly announced that she had committed mistakes that were both anti-Party and antisocialist. Following her self-criticism, not a word was said. But Hua was crushed by her own statement. The session ended with sounds of Hua's loud crying. People silently proceeded to leave, and no one offered her any consolation.

Facing these challenges, Song was less emotional. He gave Hua the support she needed. He got her a twenty-four-inch bicycle and in their spare time taught her how to ride it. Some of their close friends, including Old Song, left for the newly discovered Dagang Oil Field in Tianjin city. Hua was sad to see her friends depart. As she rode the new bike in the dark plains during her sleepless nights, her feelings of frustration were somewhat eased. But her desire to leave Daqing grew.

*   *   *

After arguing about the importance of "grasping revolution and promoting production," the Daqing Work Committee was soon placed in a defensive position. In the Beijing Workers' Stadium on October 6, Zhou Enlai and the Central Cultural Revolution Group spoke to the assembled 100,000 "revolutionary teachers and students" from all over China: "This is to announce the rehabilitation of all those revolutionary comrades who have suffered such things as repression, attacks, struggle, and even suppression by the hands of leaders at various levels or by work teams."[35] News spread from Beijing to Daqing through the networks of the Red Guards. Big-character posters again began to appear in Compound No. 2 "disclosing the black curtain of the Daqing Work Committee."

In mid-November 1966, the Work Committee organized a rehabilitation meeting and the leaders issued a public apology to those who had been classified as counterrevolutionaries or who had been accused of "committing mistakes." The "black documents" that had been saved in their personal dossiers, including the big-character posters, were burned in front of them. Song Zhenming, the director of the committee, shook hands with all those who were rehabilitated. Those who were newly rehabilitated were issued armbands of the "Scarlet Guard Team" (Chi wei dui) to indicate that they were again considered members of revolutionary organizations.

In December, rumors began to circulate among the cadres in the compound that the November rehabilitation had been just for show. The committee retained all of the self-criticism documents in order to "square accounts after the autumn harvest" (*qiuhou suanzhang*). Those who believed that they were finally rehabilitated were shocked and felt humiliated. On December 9, the central document, the "Ten Points on Industry," affirming industrial workers' right to join the Cultural Revolution and to establish their own "revolutionary organizations," was issued. The veterans were the first to set up "rebel organizations" (*zaofan tuan*), with Wang Qingshan as their leader. Their genuine working-class backgrounds provided them with protection. Thereafter many other rebel organizations were established, all of which claimed they were the true rebels and revolutionaries who were "guarding Chairman Mao." The 828 organization, named after the date (August 28, 1966) on which Chairman Mao had received the Red Guards in Tiananmen Square, was composed of students and young workers. Senior oil workers, who were accused by the young rebels of being "royalists" because of their loyalty to the existing leadership, established the Red United group.

At the beginning of 1967, the state media called on all united "revolutionary rebels" to "seize power" from the existing bureaucracy. Among the rebel organizations there were alliances, rivalries, and conflicts of interest. People often changed their organizational affiliations depending on the prevailing political winds. Everything was happening too quickly to be comprehensible.

THE REVOLUTIONARY COMMITTEE

Maintaining revolutionary momentum instead of meeting economic requirements remained a central conflict in Beijing. However, Daqing Oil Field was too important to be tested for its revolutionary vigor. During the first two years of the Cultural Revolution, oil production had been seriously interrupted, thus contributing to a grave oil shortage in 1967. In March 1967, under the command of Premier Zhou, the People's Liberation Army from the Shenyang Military Region was called to Daqing to maintain order and resume production, making Daqing one of the earliest places during the Cultural Revolution to be placed under military control.

The PLA tended to protect the senior cadres in order to utilize their production experience. The Daqing Revolutionary Committee was established on May 30, 1968. Iron Man Wang Jinxi was appointed as vice director of the committee.[36] The conservative workers, the so-called "royalists," joined together under the leadership of the PLA to maintain order and to increase production. By August, some big-character posters in Beijing revealed that the conflicts between the royalists and the rebels were becoming violent. Some three thousand workers from Qiqihar were called in to join the battle against the rebels.[37] Finally, in the autumn of 1967, the PLA succeeded in restoring order in Daqing to protect the oil production. As early as mid-1969, many Daqing cadres who had been purged during the early days of the Cultural Revolution were reinstated in leadership positions. With the return of the experienced workers and cadres, normal oil production was resumed. But the social conflicts and political struggles continued. No bonuses were issued to workers from 1969 to 1971.[38] In February 1969 Kang Shi'en returned to work in the Ministry of the Petroleum Industry. Premier Zhou and Yu Qiuli encouraged him to focus on increasing oil production as quickly as possible, both to save China from the acute energy shortage and to rescue the national economy that was on the verge of collapse.[39] The oil field remained one of the leading growth engines in the Chinese economy during the Cultural Revolution.

Beginning in 1969, Daqing was once again a prominent topic in the Chinese press, frequently noted in connection with the Fourth Five-Year Plan (1971–1975). Praise for Daqing focused on its contribution to China's technological capabilities, and public attention was once again directed to Daqing as a model community. These articles repeated many of the same descriptions of Daqing that had been used in 1966, sometimes even using precisely the same phrases. The only change was that Daqing as a frontier region was played down and the community was presented as well established rather than a forbidding and sparsely inhabited area.

*   *   *

June 10, 1967
To the Revolutionary Committee:
    We are to marry on July of this year. We wanted to wait until after the conclusion of the revolutionary movement so our wedding date was postponed on several occasions. Now it seems that the end of the movement will not be imminent. The path from seizing power to struggle, criticism, and reform (*dou pi gai*) will not be easy, and there will definitely be changes

back and forth during the course of the movement because this is a struggle between two classes and two lines. Such ups and downs will occur more than once. The counterrevolutionary current will not come to an end in the short term. Therefore, we plan to marry this year on the birthday of our Party. For these reasons, we are applying for the following:

First, we both have been away from home for five years. Our parents are already elderly. We will need fifty days to visit our two families as one family lives in Nanjing, Jiangsu province, and the other family lives in Wenzhou, Zhejiang province. Also, the latter is not yet accessible by rail.

Second, if conditions do not allow for fifty days of leave, as permitted by the senior authorities, we instead will apply for a two-week wedding holiday in Tianjin. Hua's sister and her family live in Tianjin. The two sisters also have not seen each other for five years.

Please consider our application.

Applicants: Song and Hua

June 20, 1967

Comrade Song and Hua have worked in Daqing since 1962. They have not visited their families for five years. The Revolutionary Committee hereby approves their fifty days of leave (including the time spent for the journey) for their wedding and home visits.

The Revolutionary Committee of the Daqing Mining District Construction Office

Feeling disoriented during the Cultural Revolution, Hua and Song decided it was finally time for them to pay attention to their private life, that is, to start a family. After their application was approved, they began to prepare for their trip. At a time when all Chinese urban residents received their daily necessities through a rationing system, their first step was to change their rationing coupons, especially those for grain and cloth, from local to national coupons. After five years, they had saved coupons worth 97 kilograms of grain and 13 meters of cloth. They thought this would be sufficient to cover their fifty days of leave. They sent most of the coupons to Nanjing and Wenzhou by post because it was too dangerous to carry them en route. They acquired several copies of an official reference letter from the office for their room and board, for a marriage certificate, and for possible identity checks.

FIGURE 5.8 Hua and Song's wedding photo in Tiananmen Square, Beijing, July 1, 1967, photo taken by Yang Zhenhua. Photo courtesy of Zha Binhua and Yang Ruisong.

On June 24, 1967, they finally began their journey. The road from Compound No. 2 to the Saertu Railway Station was full of slogans painted by the various rebel organizations. Some of the characters were as large as Liberation trucks, written on the bituminous pavement with lime water. In the dim light, one by one the couple stepped on these characters advocating rebellion as they made their way to the railway station.

Hua and Song first spent a few days in Tianjin and Beijing. On July 1, the Communist Party's birthday, they took a wedding photo in front of the national flag pole and Heavenly Peace Gate (Tiananmen), as planned (fig 5.8). But then their planned journey was interrupted.

They did not know that at the time of their projected departure, a central order was issued to the rebels "not to take to the streets to demonstrate, not to fight, not to arrest people, not to obstruct rail, road, or river traffic, not to erect roadblocks, not to steal weapons, and not to shoot." This order accurately described the anarchism in China at the time. Indeed, by the summer of 1967 China had descended into a state of civil war. The Great Cultural Revolution had turned into a great military revolution. Violent clashes between rival groups were taking place all over the country. Regional transportation was interrupted. As a result, the couple was delayed for two months in Wenzhou, where the city center was literally burned to the ground by the revolutionary rebels. For

Hua and Song, it turned out to be a mind-blowing journey. On the one hand, it was their honeymoon, and they were far away from the center of the conflict. They could enjoy each other's companionship, and they were pampered by their families, relatives, and friends. On the other hand, all along the way they witnessed the fighting, demonstrations, explosions, burned-down buildings, and corpses. The faces of those determined young people who were sacrificing their lives to seize power were unforgettable. Hua could not help but ask why this had been worth the sacrifice of lives. It was the trip that turned the direction of Hua's life and her view toward politics.

After regional transportation was finally resumed, on September 25 the couple was able to report back to Daqing from their extended leave. Because of the unexpected delay, all their national coupons had been spent. They became just as penniless as when they had first arrived. Hua wrote in her diary that day, "Face the reality!"

CHAPTER 6

Challenging the Daqing Model

When the large-scale housing construction in the Daqing oil district was completed in the winter of 1967, Song and Hua began a new stage in their lives. In November 1967 the married couple was assigned a scientific *gandalei* house near Compound No. 2 (fig. 6.1). The standard unit had two rooms, one large and one small, with an entrance room that also served as a kitchen. Housing was still in short supply due to the rapidly growing population, but Hua and Song had priority in housing allocation as they both worked as permanent employees in the headquarters (*shuang zhi gong*) and both had college degrees. However, Song felt uncomfortable occupying an entire unit while so many others lived in much inferior accommodations. One of his colleagues had just had a baby girl. His wife, as a dependent, had a much lower value than a full-time staff person, so the family still lived in a small cellar. Song brought Hua to visit the family. The cellar was called a *di yin zi* by the locals. Half of the room was underground so as to retain heat during the cold weather and save on construction materials. The unit lacked natural sunlight and good ventilation and so was humid and dark. The baby's little face and nostrils were stained black due to the smoke from the burning of crude oil. Hua felt sorry for the family and also felt uncomfortable about their own much better living situation.

Song and Hua wanted to give their larger room to the family, but the second room was too small to hold all of their furniture. However, Song, a talented architect and a good carpenter, was able to convert the two single bed frames into a double folding bed. He built a drop table and floor-to-ceiling bookshelves from leftover timber at the construction site. In the following months, he even built an addition to the house to serve as an extra kitchen. After Hua put up simple linen curtains she had bought at the Saertu department store, the room felt cozy and comfortable. "Finally we had our own space, a place to store both our happiness and our sorrow," Hua thought kindheartedly.

When their colleague visited their home and saw their well-furnished room, he was convinced that Hua and Song's offer to give them the larger room was sincere. So the family of three moved in.

FIGURE 6.1 Hua and Song's first home, a scientific *gandalei* house in Saertu, 1968. Photo courtesy of Zha Binhua and Yang Ruisong.

The following year was tense due to class struggle. A number of political movements occurred in succession: "cleansing the class ranks," "consolidating the Party," and the endless "political study." But for Hua and Song it was also a year of warm companionship. Song was asked to work in the propaganda office as a graphic designer, editing the newspaper, and painting political murals. He liked his new job and was happy to be removed from the political turmoil at the headquarters. Hua was selected to give solo singing performances on tour in the oil fields. She was warmly welcomed at the oil production fronts, the railway stations, and the villages for dependents. Their small room was often filled with the sounds of laughter from their friends. Song became close friends with a journalist, who two years earlier had been one of the famous big-character poster writers. They both were obsessed with the classical Chinese novel *Dream of the Red Chamber* (*Honglou meng*) and would spend many days and nights discussing it. Hua learned to cook, though her neighbors often gently teased her about her awkward final products. Most of the time, the couple ate in the canteen.

Hua's pregnancy changed everything. She soon began to feel nauseated and lost her appetite. The only foods available to eat in Daqing were sorghum, cabbage, and potatoes. Song bought Hua a jar of preserved fruit in Harbin. The jar of fruit was very expensive for their salaries, so Hua would eat only one or two pieces when she felt really ill. After six months of pregnancy, she was pale and weak. She had even fainted several times during work. Song suggested that she consider giving birth back in Wenzhou, where medical conditions and the food were much better. Song's family promised to take care of her. Because Hua's parents in Nanjing were under political investigation, they were unable to help her.

Thus one month before her due date, Hua traveled on her own to Wenzhou. Her mother-in-law was as kind as she could be, and she welcomed Hua warmly. The living conditions in Zhejiang province were much better than those in the northeast. Freshwater fish, chicken, and seafood were expensive, but at least they were available. Nevertheless, during her two months in Wenzhou Hua could not have felt lonelier. She missed Song, who remained in the far north. In addition, Song's family did not speak Mandarin and Hua could not understand the local Wenzhou dialect. A baby girl was born in late October. Her mother-in-law treated Hua the same as before she gave birth, but Hua could tell from her face that she was a bit disappointed. Deep in her heart, Hua too had wished for a boy. Her past experience made her think that life would be much easier for a boy.

Song wrote a letter home and suggested that Hua leave the baby in Wenzhou, as Daqing was too harsh for a newborn. The pain from the delivery, the frustrations of being an inexperienced new mother, the feelings of isolation due to her inability to understand the local dialect, and her fears about her forthcoming departure from the baby resulted in Hua's serious postpartum depression. According to Chinese tradition, a woman who just gave birth is forbidden to walk around. Hua felt like she was in prison in the small attic of Song's family house, and she was handicapped by the new identity of being a mother.

Song's sister helped Hua find a wet nurse in Leqing county, near the Song home. The family lived in a decent southern-style courtyard, and the wet nurse had recently given birth to a baby boy. Hua was thus reassured about leaving her baby, Xiaohua, meaning "Young China," with the wet nurse. Several days later, she bought a return ticket to Daqing. But first she went to Leqing to bid farewell to Xiaohua. When she arrived, Xiaohua happened to be crying in her bed while the wet nurse was busy nursing her own son. The scene caused Hua much pain. Later, when she calmed down, Hua could understand the behavior of the wet nurse. But she was still upset when she heard Xiaohua crying. "Why should the needs of a boy always come before those of a girl?" she asked herself. "Why could a rural woman cater to her baby's needs first but I could not?" Impulsively, she took her baby and announced that she would take her back to Daqing. All of Song's family members, including her mother-in-law with her tiny bound feet, escorted Hua to the ship she was to take back to Shanghai. Later, when Hua recalled her mother-in-law's look of sorrow, she regretted her imprudent decision, which resulted in many years of burden for both families.

Before heading farther north, Hua and her baby stayed with her family in Nanjing for a month. Hua almost lost her courage to bring the baby back to Daqing. It was an extremely harsh winter, and the atmosphere at home was thick and cold. Hua's older sister had moved back home with her son; thus she was separated from her husband. She also came under political investigation, so often she could not return home for many days. Her son appeared to be too mature for his age. Most of the time he sat quietly on his bed, waiting for his mother to return. Hua's father had just been released from investigation, but he still was required to report to the residents' committee every day to make a self-criticism.

Remaining at home all day, Hua found no relaxed conversations and no smiling faces. She felt even more depressed than when she was in Wenzhou. She knew she could never leave Xiaohua in Nanjing.

The trip back to Daqing was a nightmare. The railway system had not fully recovered from the anarchy of the Cultural Revolution. Even though the worst of the violence had ceased, disorder persisted. The trains were crowded with all sorts of people. Even the lavatories were filled with travelers. Passengers crawled in and out of the windows. Additionally, there was growing distrust of strangers. Although people seemed to be sympathetic to a young mother traveling with a newborn, Hua did not dare to let Xiaohua out of her sight. During the entire journey, Hua did not eat or drink much to avoid the need to go to the lavatory, and soon she was no longer able to produce breast milk for her baby. Gathering all of her strength, following a brief stop in Tianjin, after another seventeen hours on the train from Tianjin to Harbin, Hua finally saw her husband standing on the platform, with a deeply worried face.

* * *

In the late 1960s and the 1970s, oil prospecting occurred throughout the country and the Chinese petroleum industry entered its heyday. More oil fields were discovered in northern and central China. Crude oil production maintained an amazing annual growth rate of 20 percent from 1968 to 1978, from 15.99 million metric tons to 1 billion metric tons, sharply contrasting with mediocre agricultural performance and industrial production.[1] Within a decade, China was transformed from an oil importer to an oil exporter. The dramatic growth in the supply of oil changed the national economic landscape and served as a "lubricant" for China's relations with former enemy states; it also allowed the "petroleum group" in the leadership to gain more control over national politics. Expectations were growing about drafting ambitious new development programs.

The Red Flag on the Industrial Front

Work stoppages from 1967 to 1969 led to a serious energy crisis in China. Even Liaoning province, a region rich in coal resources, sent an emergency telegram to Premier Zhou Enlai requesting state support.

In contrast, the decline in petroleum production was less serious, and after 1969 it quickly resumed. In fact, it represented China's brightest star during the Cultural Revolution, "the red flag on the industrial front." It is no exaggeration to say that during the ten years of the Cultural Revolution, oil production saved the national economy from collapse. In 1970, as an emergency measure, 10.75 million metric tons (MMT) of crude oil, one-third of the nation's annual national production, instead of the 2.34 MMT in 1966, was burned at power plants instead of being sent to be refined. This was a great waste of resources. However, the use of crude oil did not change much after the energy crisis eased. In 1975, crude oil production reached 77 MMT, and more than 30 MMT were sent directly to thermal power plants. After so much blood, toil, tears, and sweat, Kang Shi'en was heartbroken to see the oil being wasted in such a way. "Burning oil is a great waste of money!" he declared. "This amount of crude oil could have achieved a much greater value!"[2]

In the early 1970s, China's stagnating industrial development did not correspond to its rapidly growing oil production. The country still faced a severe shortage of refining facilities. The need for better equipment and technology to refine petroleum was so great that the petroleum leaders became pioneers in turning to the outside world. After China severed relations with the Soviet Union, there was a slow opening to the West, especially to Japan. French president Charles de Gaulle recognized the People's Republic in 1964. Unofficial Sino-Japanese trade resumed even earlier.[3] As early as the mid-1960s, the Ministry of the Petroleum Industry began to import oil refineries, synthetic fiber textile plants, chemical fertilizer plants, and petrochemical plants from Japan and Europe, all of which consumed petroleum-derived feedstock.[4] However, these were piecemeal deals made in the face of great political risks due to the unfavorable domestic and international climates. In the 1960s, China's ability to import technology was crippled by the lack of agricultural surplus; since the outbreak of famine, China had had to use its foreign exchange to import food. The Fourth Five-Year Plan (1971–1975), endorsed by Mao, still emphasized decentralization and called for development projects that were "small scale, indigenous, and labor intensive" rather than projects that were "large scale, foreign, and capital intensive." Thereafter, due to the threat of war, about 40 percent of the state budget was allocated for military purposes.

THE RISE OF THE HYDROCARBON MEN

From 1969 to 1972, under Mao's banner of "continuing the revolution," another wave of decentralization was attempted to oppose bureaucratism and support populism. On numerous occasions Mao had warned the Party about the danger of an overconcentration of power and resources. Hence localities were given control over small-scale industrial enterprises and the large-scale economy was decentralized. In May 1969, Mao specifically ordered that management of Anshan Steel Plant, one of the largest state industrial enterprises, be decentralized to the Anshan municipal government. In May 1970, the State Council drafted a reform plan to decentralize the state-owned enterprises, which included both Daqing Oil Field and Changchun No. 1 Auto Plant. Management of more than 86 percent of the centrally owned enterprises was to be transferred to the provincial administrations.[5] This policy corresponded with national defense goals that sought to establish regional industrial systems that could survive and operate independently in case of the threat of war. These measures resulted in a decline in central control during the early 1970s.

In 1970, as more autonomy was granted at the regional level, the State Council underwent a major reform. More than eighty ministries and commissions were either eliminated or downsized, resulting in twenty-seven remaining ministries and commissions, and the total number of employees was reduced by 72 percent. During this restructuring, most of the petroleum leaders were rehabilitated and many rose to prominent positions in the central leadership. The State Economic Commission, the Office of Industry and Transportation, the Bureau of Material Supplies, the Ministry of Geology, the Ministry of Labor, the State Statistical Bureau, and the Central Relocation Office were all merged into the State Planning Commission, where Yu Qiuli remained as director. The Ministry of Building Construction and the Ministry of Construction Materials were merged into the State Basic Construction Commission, under the directorship of Gu Mu, who had been Yu's colleague in the 1960s. In 1973 Gu joined Yu as a vice director of the State Planning Commission. The Ministry of the Petroleum Industry, the Ministry of the Chemical Industry, and the Ministry of the Coal Industry were merged into the Ministry of Fuels and Chemical Industry, under Kang Shi'en as minister. Tang Ke, who had played a major role in supervising the development of Daqing Oil Field through the early 1960s and had been a vice minister of the Ministry of the Petroleum Industry, became Kang's vice minister.

The 1971 demise of Lin Biao, Mao's "close comrade-in-arms" and hand-picked successor, in a plane crash, possibly caused by running out of fuel after a failed coup attempt, signaled an end to the focus on the national defense budget and China's tense international relations. The visits of Richard Nixon and Kakuei Tanaka to Beijing in 1972 marked the beginning of China's turn to the outside world. The deferred payment of loans to China by the Japanese Export-Import Bank was a direct result of the diplomatic normalization between the two countries in September 1972. This ushered in a new era of economic relations between China and the outside world.[6]

Accompanying the changing political and international climate were intense debates about ideology and strategy in the socialist state. Although Daqing Oil Field was constantly promoted as a model of self-reliance, the rising petroleum leaders understood the importance of advanced technology for sustainable growth and the limitations of an indigenous and labor-intensive model. They thus boldly introduced dramatic changes when drafting state plans.

THE 4-3 PLAN AND LIQUID ASSETS

In January 1972, the State Planning Commission, under the leadership of Yu Qiuli, submitted a report titled "Importing Technical Equipment for Chemical Fibers and Fertilizers" to the State Council.[7] The plan, which involved US$0.4 billion of foreign purchases, was quickly approved by Mao on February 5, 1972. Feeling encouraged, Yu Qiuli worked with the vice premiers to submit several import plans, focusing on purchasing entire industrial production lines and equipment for the chemical, petrochemical, steel, fertilizer, synthetic fiber, and power generation industries, amounting to foreign purchases totaling US$4.3 billion. This "4-3 Plan" was considered the second wave of large-scale foreign imports after the First Five-Year Plan.[8] Twenty-six major industrial projects were built, including the Shanghai Jinshan Refinery, Beijing Refinery, Daqing Refinery, and new rolling mill production lines for the Wuhan Steel Plant. In addition, ocean freighters and planes were purchased. Chen Yun and Deng Xiaoping, who again assumed their positions in 1972 and 1973, respectively, were strong supporters of the 4-3 Plan. In 1974 Deng, as the first representative of the People's Republic to participate at a meeting of the General Assembly of the United Nations, declared, "Self-reliance in no way means 'self-seclusion' and a rejection of foreign aid."[9]

In 1973, with the outbreak of the fourth Arab-Israeli War, oil became the most powerful weapon held by the oil-rich countries. Within one year, the price of oil on world markets increased from US$2.59 to US$11.56 per barrel, sparking an international energy crisis. Japan was the worst hit among the industrialized countries as its petroleum consumption depended completely on imports. Riding the wave of its increasing domestic crude oil production, the dramatic rise in world petroleum prices, and improved Sino-Japanese, Sino-U.S., and Sino-Western European relations, Chinese petroleum found receptive foreign destinations instead of being wasted in boilers.

Replacing agricultural products and other mineral resources, oil became China's most important source of foreign revenue. In 1973 China exported 1 MMT of crude oil to Japan. In 1975, total exports of oil were estimated at 11.6 MMT, and Japan was China's largest customer.[10] Additionally, China no longer withheld information from the rest of the world about its oil reserves. Instead, Beijing began to speak in lofty tones about its new discoveries and its rapidly growing oil production. In fact, after the mid-1970s, the location of Daqing Oil Field was no longer a state secret. In 1975, Beijing invited a twenty-member delegation from the American Society of Newspaper Editors to visit Daqing, indicating the government's confidence in the accomplishments of its oil industry and its willingness to trade on world markets. William Giles, a reporter for the *Wall Street Journal* who was a member of the delegation, described his impressions of Daqing:

> The sun sneaks up over the vast, dusty plain here in northeast China at 3:45 am, but daylight only deepens the strangeness of this place. A wasteland inhabited by gazelles and wolves in the 1950s, Taching [i.e., Daqing] today is a major center of China's fast-expanding oil industry . . . [a] forbidden territory for outsiders. . . . Yet an American reporter stands here now, looking over a wheat field and a patch of yellow squash, vainly searching for recognizable signs of oil country. . . .
>
> China's crude-oil production has more than doubled since 1971, to an estimated 1.1 million barrels a day currently. This is small compared with

U.S. output of 8.4 million barrels daily, but the trend is sharply upward, and it's likely to continue. Vice Premier Teng Hsiao-ping [i.e., Deng Xiaoping], third-ranking official in China's hierarchy, stated last month that the petroleum industry would get front-ranking priority in China's economic plans, along with agriculture and steel production. . . . It's quiet and unhurried for a place with 400,000 inhabitants. The wandering hogs, goats, and ducks make more of a stir than the people, who live mostly in simple adobe or brick quarters. An occasional oil spill on the landscape and isolated gas flares only temporarily remind you that this is oil country. The smells are of the fields, not of industry.[11]

TESTING NEW WATERS

With rising exports, the petroleum leaders became more aggressive in importing new technology and equipment. Although the growth of oil production was dramatic, there were still questions about its sustainability. Production had been pushed to the limit with respect to the traditional high-labor inputs, and urban investment still faced serious constraints.

At the end of 1969 and the beginning of 1970, the British and the Norwegians discovered huge oil reservoirs in the North Sea. Global oil exploration extended to the continental shelves, and there was a frenetic rush to discover oil in the sea after the 1973 oil crisis. Not only was this oil more expensive to produce; it was also more demanding with respect to technology. Optimistic foreign assessments of the potential bonanza in the Gulf of Bohai and the South China Sea stimulated China's expectations and actions.[12]

In addition to whole plants for producing downstream petroleum products, China entered the world market for oil-drilling rigs, oceanographic vessels, computers, and equipment to process seismic exploration data, updated pipelines, and so forth. Japan alone accounted for 63 percent of China's plant and technology contracts during the Fourth Five-Year Plan period.[13]

But the foreign purchases were expensive. In the 1970s China lacked both sufficient bargaining power and adequate knowledge to make large-scale international purchases from the Western countries. The price of sea-drilling equipment rose rapidly in the rush to discover oil in the Gulf

FIGURE 6.2 Daqing Fertilizer Plant, built with bricks and concrete in an economic industrial style, 1974. Source: Daqing geming weiyuanhui, *Daqing*.

of Bohai and the South China Sea. In 1972 China bought a used oil rig, the *Fuji* (renamed *Bohai No. 2*) from Japan for US$9 million. A year later, Beijing unsuccessfully sought to strike a deal for a new submersible barge at a cost of US$22.6 million. The Chinese turned to a Norwegian company, and the final price for an equivalent vessel was set at US$38 million.[14]

After 1973, China's purchases of foreign plants and equipment grew rapidly, very soon outpacing its exports. Criticism of the large-scale imports increased due to balance-of-payments difficulties. In 1974 China's trade deficit reached a historical high. The ideology of the Cultural Revolution had scarred relations with and dependency upon the capitalist world. This sense of fear and frustration can be traced back to China's defeat during the Opium War. Trading Chinese resources for foreign capital goods was regarded as inviting imperialist exploitation. The Central Cultural Revolution Group, especially Jiang Qing and Zhang Chunqiao, criticized the 4-3 Plan for "transferring the energy crisis in the capitalist world to China." In its stead, they advocated an import-substitution strategy. Conflicts between these two strategies intensified after the SS *Fengqing* Incident in 1974, as the radical group celebrated the successful launch of a domestic-made product and criticized the purchase of expensive secondhand foreign ships.[15] Because the chief architect of the 4-3 Plan, Zhou Enlai, was hospitalized with cancer, Deng Xiaoping was blamed for the "foreign slave" (*yang nu*) mentality. He was compared to Li Hongzhang and Zeng Guofan during the Self-Strengthening Movement a hundred years earlier for being a "bourgeois comprador." In the petroleum industry, Kang Shi'en was criticized by Wang Hongwen, Mao's second hand-picked successor after Lin Biao, for importing foreign drilling machines from Romania.[16] Construction of Daqing's fertilizer and ethylene plants were strictly scrutinized and temporarily put on hold. Figure 6.2 is a photograph of Daqing's fertilizer plant.

Growing Industrial Agglomeration

At the outset of the Cultural Revolution, the anarchist state slowed down production machinery and loosened command controls. Gradually, private space and private time began to grow. Workers were allowed to have regular days off and were granted more holidays. The majority of the young men and women who arrived in Daqing in the 1960s had now entered their thirties. With its relatively homogeneous population, the oil field saw its first great baby boom in the early 1970s and with it an increased demand for housing. Figure 6.3 shows the state of the *gandalei* village at this time.

The population boom and growing livelihood demands were evident not only in Daqing but also throughout the nation. Beginning in 1962, after restoration of the national economy, there was a surge in the birth rate over the next decade, setting a historic record. Rural birth rates were increasingly outstripping those in urban China. On average, a rural woman gave birth to five or six children, as compared to an urban woman giving birth to only two or three.[17] During this period, there was also a huge exchange of urban and rural people and a great mix of agricultural and industrial laborers. Urban youth were sent to the countryside and

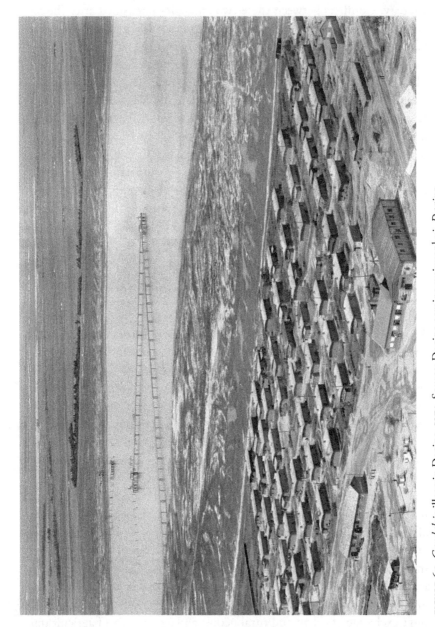

FIGURE 6.3 *Gandalei* village in Daqing, 1974. Source: Daqing geming weiyuanhui, *Daqing.*

cadres were sent to work on farms, and a substantial number of peasants were recruited by the labor-starved urban work units as temporary laborers, usually without issuing them nonagricultural household registration permits. Reclamation and farming were encouraged in the cities, and small industrial enterprises boomed in the rural villages.

The agricultural harvests in 1969 and 1970 were bountiful. In 1970, according to plan, national grain production reached 240 billion kilograms. But with the population growing by almost 200 million during the previous thirteen years, per capita grain consumption was even lower than the record low in 1957. On average, each Chinese person could obtain only 0.79 kilograms of grain per day from domestic production. Average consumption of other foodstuffs was so modest that it could be counted only on an annual basis, for example, 7.5 kilograms of pork, 2.1 kilograms of edible oil, and 1.6 kilograms of sugar per person per year.[18] This was far from adequate, essentially only slightly above starvation levels. As a result, China continued to import grain from the outside world.

Despite the tightened state controls and the mass deportations from cities, rural-to-urban migration remained positive. The annual urban population growth rate between 1962 and 1972 actually remained at about 2 percent per year, which is a fairly remarkable number considering the size of the outflow. At a national planning conference at the beginning of 1972, Premier Zhou announced that nationwide the population of state-employed workers and staff exceeded 50 million, wage expenditures exceeded 30 billion yuan, and the sale of grain exceeded 40 billion kilograms. In a planned economy, these "three-exceeds" were not regarded as positive indices of development; rather, they represented a burden on state resources that should have been reserved for industrial production.

* * *

The family of three did not return to their home in Saertu. The national movement of "going down to the countryside" had begun three months earlier. As a result, millions of urban youth were sent to the countryside, and cadres were sent to May 7th cadre schools. The May 7th cadre school in Daqing was located in the far northeastern corner of the oil field, on a former dairy farm called the *gongnong tuanjie* farm (literally "the integration of workers and peasants"). In 1965 the Beijing Oil Institute was relocated there. Students from Beijing spent months building a campus for the institute, consisting of *gandalei* buildings. Before long, after Mao had bombarded the "capitalist headquarters," the students returned to Beijing to participate in the Cultural Revolution.[19] The campus of the institute was abandoned until it was finally reopened as a work-study school for May 7th cadres. Hua and Song were on the list of those who were to participate in a special training program at this school. This is why Song initially suggested Hua leave their baby in Wenzhou. After Song heard from his family that Hua was bringing the baby back to Daqing, he tried his best to make them feel at home.

There were plenty of *gandalei* houses on the site, so they were able to live in more spacious quarters. After moving home-made furniture and belongings, Song rearranged them. But the supply of natural gas was insufficient. Fearing that the room would be too cold for the infant, Song installed an extra stove made of an empty gasoline can and some asbestos pipes. He painstakingly cut a hole in the roof to allow for better ventilation. Crude oil was stored in an open pit. In the winter, the oil would freeze like pieces of bean curd. Residents used shovels to chip away at a cube or two, which they then took home to use as an extra supply of fuel. Song neatly stored some oil cubes outside their kitchen. When Hua entered their humble mud hut, she was touched by his efforts. "However harsh it might be, at least we are able to stay together," she said to herself (fig. 6.4).

In early 1969, there was little sign of a thaw. Winter gripped the entire country. Tuanjie Farm was like a lonely peninsula facing a sea of snow. Beyond the farm, the white uninhabited plains stretched as far as one could see. There was a shuttle that ran from Tuanjie Farm to Saertu twice a day. Without the shuttle, on good days it would take at least two hours to walk to Saertu.

The first two months of living on the farm passed quickly. Preoccupied with the baby, Hua was unable to sleep through the night. Luckily, her work during the day was not difficult. There were several labor teams, most of which were for agricultural production. The farm also had a daycare center, a canteen, and a clinic served by two "barefoot doctors." The cadres took shifts working at the different jobs. Hua was assigned to work on a carpentry team, making simple desks and chairs for the school. The neighbors knew Hua was not good at needlework, so they helped her make baby clothes for Xiaohua. Xiaohua was sent to the daycare center, and Hua went there twice a day to nurse her. Life was simple and primitive,

FIGURE 6.4 Song and Hua in their second *gandalei* house, Tuanjie Farm, 1969. Photo courtesy of Zha Binhua and Yang Ruisong.

but it was endurable. Before long, Hua became fully engaged in preparing for the first Chinese New Year for their family of three.

Three days before New Year's Eve, Hua suddenly vomited after dinner. She felt terrible pains in her lower abdomen. The clinic doctor gave her some painkillers, but they did not help. The next morning, Hua and Song left Xiaohua in the care of a neighbor and boarded the shuttle to Saertu. Diagnosed with acute appendicitis, she was to be hospitalized. She then made a decision that later she would come to regret.

Worried that there was no one to take good care of her baby at home, she insisted that the hospital only provide her with very conservative treatment. So the hospital doctor simply prescribed some penicillin. She did not have time to have the injection in the hospital as they had to hurry to catch the last bus home. However, back at the farm, the barefoot doctor said that he was not sure whether it was safe to give her a penicillin injection because of the results of a suspicious allergy test. This barefoot doctor had not had extensive medical training, and it was already very late in the evening. So the couple had no choice but to wait until the following day. They spent a sleepless night and in the early dawn Song hurried to the road in search for any vehicle passing by. When he finally found a pickup truck to take Hua to the Saertu hospital, she had already lost consciousness. Even worse, there was no doctor at the Saertu hospital that day. The hospital's best surgeon, who had been denounced as a "capitalist reactionary authority," had been sent to clean the streets. The head nurse had to begin Hua's surgery before they could find a qualified doctor. Hua survived the operation, but there were a number of complications and she was afflicted with various infections during the following months. On several occasions, she struggled between life and death.

While Hua remained hospitalized, Song had to commute daily between Saertu and Tuanjie Farm. Hua could see that Song was losing weight, and his face was deeply lined with fatigue. Hua felt too guilty to even ask how he was managing to take care of a three-month-old baby and a sick wife. It was only several years later that she learned Song had gone one day to their former home near Compound No. 2, which was only a few steps from the hospital. He wanted to ask their former roommates to allow him and Xiaohua to temporarily stay in their small room so he would not have to make the long journey to Saertu every day and so they would be closer to Hua, who was still breastfeeding. But the wife of his former comrade, who then had a much larger family and who might have been afraid that Song wanted to reclaim their old home, barred the door and refused to allow him to talk with her husband. Song said that at that time his heart felt as cold as the Daqing winter. His beliefs in a "collective spirit" and "self-sacrifice" were shattered.

Luckily, there were some helping hands on the collective farm. Although as weak as a small kitten, Xiaohua survived with cow's milk, sympathy from the other nursing mothers, and some baby formula that had been sent from Nanjing by her grandparents.

In the summer of 1969, after a second operation, Hua was finally discharged from the hospital. Despite her strong desire to made amends, she soon realized her responsibilities as a wife, mother, laborer, and homemaker were much more complicated and difficult to fulfill when living on an isolated farm. She constantly felt pain in her lower back and abdomen. The agricultural work had become a source of real torture. In addition to their inadequate living conditions, her domestic chores were exhausting and time-consuming as everything had to be done by hand. She struggled to split their limited supplies of rice and wheat between her baby and her husband, both of whom suffered from malnourishment. Shopping was also an exhausting undertaking due to the long lines. Thin and weak, Xiaohua often became ill. But Hua did not trust the barefoot doctors on the farm. Every time Xiaohua had a fever or a cough, Hua insisted on taking her to the Saertu hospital. Within a matter of several months, Hua was already stretched to her limit.

At the time, after the Zhenbao (Damanskii) Island incident in March 1969, conflict with the Soviet Union along the border was intensifying.[20] Daqing Oil Field was close to China's northern border with Siberia and would be an easy target were a war to break out. Many people began to send their family members to the countryside. Song's family suggested that they send Xiaohua to Wenzhou. At first Hua stubbornly refused. She refused to let these past months of hardship be in vain. Above all, she wanted to keep her family together.

Before long, the political study meetings ended and Heilongjiang province was placed on high alert. The cadres at the Daqing May 7th cadre school were organized to build air-raid shelters and to stockpile grain and food. Students in the large cities were evacuated. Hua became extremely worried about the safety of her daughter. Her family in Nanjing wrote and urged her to send Xiaohua to stay with her grandparents. Hua finally succumbed to reality. On the train heading south, she could not help but regret her past decisions. It was she who had dragged Song to Daqing in the first place, causing much suffering for both her husband and her daughter. There were no freezing winters in the south, and the food and the health services were both much better there. Why had she been so naive, forfeiting all these comforts and causing her family so many hardships?

*   *   *

RESTORATION OF URBAN EXPENDITURES

In November 1971 the State Basic Construction Commission organized a symposium on urban construction as a prelude to resuming its work. In December 1972, the Urban Construction Bureau was reinstated under the State Basic Construction Commission. This was accompanied by the resumption of urban investment. Urban planners who had been sent to the May 7th cadre schools began to return to their posts.

Statistical data were released to review the current state of Chinese cities. The lack of investment had left urban areas in a dilapidated state. In 1973 many cities faced great shortages of water. For instance, large cities, such as Beijing, Tianjin, and Xi'an, lacked one-third of their daily water needs. Because of the lack of a sufficient number of pumping stations, many urban residents living in multistory buildings had to carry water by hand from the ground level to their apartment every night. In Qingdao, factories were regularly shut down to save on water for the summer. To avoid disputes, the city government issued water stamps. The quota for each resident was 15 liters per day.[21] There were no urban traffic problems as vehicles were rare, but the buses were always overcrowded. There were 15,831 buses registered in 176 Chinese cities, with an average of 90 buses per city, though many cities actually had no buses at all. Typically, there were long queues in front of the bus stations, food shops, water stations, and other places providing daily necessities.

The shortage of housing was serious. In 1974, the newly established Housing Division under the Urban Construction Bureau drafted a housing policy to improve the existing housing stock, but the policy did not place priority on initiating new construction. Urban construction was primarily carried out on a patchwork basis, like "inserting needles wherever there is a seam" (*jian feng cha zhen*). Due to these incremental efforts, the average living space per capita reached 3.6 square meters in 190 Chinese cities by 1976.

The booming Chinese petroleum industry contributed to the slow but steady improvement in urban infrastructure. Liquefied petroleum gas began to be widely used in the cities. The number of customers who benefited increased fortyfold between 1972 and 1975. Bitumen, a byproduct at the oil refinery, contributed to the pavement of over 140,000 kilometers of highways in 1978.[22]

EXTENSION OF THE OIL FIELD

Construction in Daqing became less utopian and more practical during the late 1960s and the early 1970s. Housing increased with self-built additions and expansions of existing settlements. With the improved economic situation and fewer political mandates, the villages grew larger, with new houses primarily made of bricks instead of mud and hay. Many of the remote single households, the so-called husband-wife oil wells, were abandoned when more shuttles became available. Schools were filled with children, and hospitals, shops, and buses were ever more crowded. Total completed housing in the 1970s reached 1.79 million square meters.[23]

The belt-shaped oil field, stretching 140 kilometers in a north-south direction, was operating at full capacity in the 1970s. Oil reservoirs in the far north and south, even the Lamadian field, which originally was reserved for wartime crises, were quickly opened for development. Construction of a 1,157-kilometer pipeline to transport oil from Daqing to the port of Qinhuangdao on the Bohai Gulf was completed in 1974. Some 90 percent of the crude oil exported to Japan was produced in Daqing.

Human settlements in Daqing closely followed the path of industrial oil production. The industrial plan crisscrossed the landscape with lines and grids, defining the living settlements. This was an open structure, which could be extended when the production fields were broadened. Heavier clusters of administration, management, research, and transportation headquarters and refinery plants were located along the narrow transportation corridors, with identical settlement points and villages linked by rectangular road grids spreading out from the middle. The first level settlement consisted of three workers' towns, Saertu, Ranghulu, and Longfeng, each with populations of forty thousand to sixty thousand, located along the Binzhou Railway. Self-contained living accommodations, as well as educational, cultural, and sanitation services, such as shops, banks, post offices, restaurants, hotels, photo studios, high schools, and hospitals, were available. The administrative headquarters for the production units were located in the central villages, which provided modest-scale living facilities for 2,500, to 4,000 people. These were usually located in the geometric center of the units' "command domain." The production brigades, which were linked together by mining roads, were located at settlement points—the grass-roots living bases and basic services for the oil field—for populations of 1,000 to 1,500 people. The settlement points were usually surrounded by farmland or production wells that were within a thirty-minute walk from the residents' living places.

Two railroads, the Binzhou Line from east to west and the Rangtong Line from Ranghulu to the south, were the key transportation corridors in Daqing. Three major vertical roads, running parallel to the Rangtong Line, linked the production sites in Saertu in the very north to Datong town in the south. One major horizontal regional road, at a small angle parallel to the Binzhou Line, provided linkages between the workers' towns—Saertu, Ranghulu, Longfeng, and Wolitun (which was developed later)—and other cities, such as Harbin and Qiqihar. The other main east-west roads, stretching from thirty to sixty kilometers, together with the north-south roads comprised the grid linking the working and living areas. The naming of the east-west roads followed their position and sequence in the grid, such as Middle 7th Road, lying in front of the Saertu headquarters, and South 2nd Road, referring to the road passing Strengthening Village (No. 2 Factory). North-south roads were given more meaningful names, such as Iron Man Avenue, which was the most important north-south artery (see map 7).

* * *

The closing of the cadre school was as unexpected as its establishment. In mid-1970, just when Hua thought they would live such a life forever, the cadres began to be "liberated." They were all reassigned jobs. Hua and Song returned to the Daqing Design Institute in Ranghulu. Thus their third home in Daqing was a simple brick house inside the Institute compound. They brought back from the farm some of their home-made furniture: a small cabinet for the kitchen, a heavy irregular chopping board, and an old chest that served as their dining table. The former residents in their new home had left them a small cellar that served as a natural refrigerator. The cellar was soon filled with canned food and baby formula sent from their families in the south.

Eight years had passed since Hua had first arrived at Ranghulu with her single suitcase. The young men and women she had met at the Institute had become husbands and wives, mothers and fathers. They were all equally bewildered by their rapidly changing circumstances. The families struggled in the face of the serious food shortages, the lack of urban amenities, anxieties about the political situation, and various other family disruptions. Some families felt completely lost. Others were tougher and were able to withstand the hardships. Little Huang, now Old Huang, and his wife were a source of support upon whom Hua could always

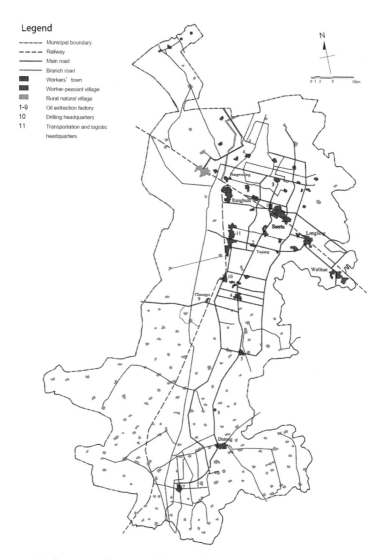

Legend

- Municipal boundary
-- Railway
— Main road
— Branch road
▓ Workers' town
▓ Worker-peasant village
▒ Rural natural village
1-9 Oil extraction factory
10 Drilling headquarters
11 Transportation and logistic
   headquarters

MAP 7 Settlements in Daqing in the 1980s (based on the Daqing Agricultural Land Resource Map produced by the Daqing Agricultural Zoning Office), 1987. Original map by the Daqing Agricultural Zoning Office, redrawn by the author.

depend. When Hua and Song returned from cadre school, Old Huang had just been discharged from the Palace of Heaven, where he had been held in custody for six months due to his rebellious past and overseas connections. Despite the serious charges he faced, Old Huang did physical exercises every day in his small cell and never succumbed to the political and physical pressures. When the two families first met after several years of separation, Old Huang was still a strong man. Neither of the couples shed any tears, nor did they complain about their situations. Old Huang's wife kept their house as tidy as always. Chen Ruihe, formally "Master Chen," had married a doctor in Ranghulu Hospital and they already had two children. Their house was like a maze, filled with blueprints, drafts, and books. But now Master Chen spent his time reading something new: cookbooks. The former design maniac had become fixated on meeting his family's needs for nourishment.

The Institute was to restore its Division of Master Planning, and Hua and Song were informed that one of them would be assigned to work there. Neither the leaders nor Song expected that Hua would react so strongly against such an assignment. She saw urban planning, their major by training, as the main source of their past frustrations. It was like a healed wound was about to be torn open again. "The job of planning is too political, so I wanted to keep a good distance from it," she later recalled. She insisted that they both be assigned to work in the Division of Civil Engineering. But this was not a matter of personal choice. It was an order. One of them would be required to work in planning. There was no way for them to rebel against the organization. Song too did not want to work as a planner anymore, but he was more practical. At home he tried to persuade Hua to accept reality.

With escalating frustration and anger, Hua said some words that she would live to regret for the rest of her life: "What kind of man are you who cannot resist some pressure? Have you ever been a true rebel? I would rather get a divorce than see my man submit to the organization!"

That was the first time external pressures had created tensions in their relationship. Song did not say anything, but he left Hua to calm down on her own. After several days, with mixed feelings Hua reported to the Division of Master Planning so that Song could remain in the Division of Civil Engineering. She insisted that a talented man like Song should build a career in architecture and engineering that was more solid than planning. As for herself, she had already abandoned all hope of becoming a respected city planner in the mining district. Actually she doubted if she could move further on her career path at all. Her mixed feelings also stemmed from the fact that she was pregnant with their second child, and she had doubts whether motherhood was the right role for her too. In the early 1970s, the state began to disseminate propaganda about the benefits of family planning, using the slogan "Three is too many, one is not enough—two is perfect." The average fertility rate for urban women dropped rapidly, from five children in the 1950s to two in the 1970s. In order to provide companionship for Xiaohua, and with a secret desire that this time she would give birth to a boy, Hua and Song made the decision to keep the baby. Pregnancy also helped Hua to delay her return to the planning job for a few more months.

Construction of the oil transport pipeline from Daqing to the port of Qinhuangdao began on August 3, 1970. It was openly referred to as the "83" Project. Song was assigned to work on the engineering team for the project. The team followed along the route of the pipeline construction, from Daqing to Jilin, Changchun, and finally Qinhuangdao in Hebei province. News spread that the Ministry of the Petroleum Industry would establish a Bureau of Pipelines near Qinhuangdao. Hoping this would be a good chance for the family to leave Daqing and live in a city, Hua fully supported Song's new job. Over the course of the next four years, Song was very rarely at home. Hua saw him once every two or three months. Thus the daily burden of coping with all the family responsibilities fell heavily on Hua's shoulders.

But their eight years in Daqing had trained them well. They had been transformed from hot-blooded young rebels to resourceful parents. Due to her work shifts in the school canteen, Hua learned to cook. She was able to make good handmade noodles, and she could shred potatoes as fine as a professional chef. She also learned to tailor clothes and make shoes. And she was already an adequate carpenter. She competently tended the home furnace and stove. At the time, eggs were the most available source of nutrients for families due to the strict state rationing. Song was always able to bring home eggs purchased from the village black markets. Because such transactions were illegal, during railway checks Song used to put the eggs in a bucket and cover them up with his clothing as camouflage. But this was too obvious for the security patrols. Once Song was apprehended right before the train was to depart from the station. When the security patrols tried to pull his bucket off the train, the eggs fell to the ground and broke. All the witnesses burst out with sighs at the waste. From then on, Song began to carry the eggs in a suitcase. He carefully wrapped them with newspapers and built solid structures out of paper inside the suitcase to protect them. Thereafter he was able to bring home many more eggs and they were never broken. Many frequent travelers on the train eagerly copied this practice. "Finally I found a good way to use my professional knowledge of structural mechanics," he once said, half-mocking and half-bragging in front of Hua.

When Hua's second daughter was born, the baby was named Yan, which refers to the wild geese that migrate south in the spring. How anxious they were to return to the south! After fifty-six days of maternity leave, Hua reported back to the Division of Master Planning. Although she did not have any household help, she chose not to send Yan to the daycare center during the first few months. Her office and their home were in the same compound. She would return home to nurse Yan several times during her work hours. After putting the baby to sleep, she would carefully put her in her bed, surrounded by quilts and pillows, and then lock the house and leave. Sometimes when she returned, she would discover that Yan's little face was covered with tears. The tears burned a deep hole in her mother's heart, but Hua believed that the daycare centers in Daqing were full of germs and viruses. They lacked ventilation, and the waste and sewage disposal systems were inadequate. Infectious diseases often spread through the centers. Additionally, there were no nurses at the centers; care was provided by the dependents based on their own limited rural experiences.

As winter approached, Hua once again suffered from depression. The frequent stresses, cold, and a sleeping disorder eventually led to serious asthma. She was on the brink of collapse. Near the end of 1971, Hua and Song submitted their first petition to leave Daqing.

* * *

The Great Leap Outward

Despite the strong objections of the radicals, Deng Xiaoping steadfastly carried out the 4-3 Plan. In January 1974, the State Planning Commission proposed the Ten-Year National Economic Development Plan Outline for 1976–1985. Due to improved diplomatic relations with the United States and Western Europe, the national defense industry no longer received top priority. State planners continued to push for large-scale imports of technology and equipment for the chemical and metallurgical industries, again advocating the goal of "catching up with the United States and Great Britain." Initial deliberation of the plan began in 1975. In January, Yu Qiuli was promoted to vice premier while retaining his position on the State Planning Commission.

On Chinese New Year's Day in February 1975, a movie called *Pioneers* (Chuang ye) was screened to the public. It was inspired by the story of the Daqing oil campaign. Iron Man Wang Jinxi and the petroleum leaders were the heroes of the movie. The next day, Minister of Culture Yu Huiyong received an urgent phone call and was summoned to Jiang Qing's office. Due to the intervention of Madame Mao, the screening was called to a sudden halt. The Office of Political Research (Zhengzhi yan-jiushi), Deng Xiaoping's think-tank under the direction of Hu Qiaomu, tracked down the author of *Pioneers,* Zhang Tianmin, and helped Zhang appeal to Mao Zedong. On July 25, 1975, Mao instructed that the screening be resumed.[24]

However, Deng's victory was only temporary. In November 1975, the Ten-Year National Economic Development Plan Outline for 1976–1985 was submitted to a National Planning Conference for discussion. After criticizing the plan, the radicals denounced Deng's role as a possible successor to Mao. In November 1975, Yu Qiuli left Beijing for Guangzhou on sick leave. In April 1976, Deng Xiaoping was purged for a second time. But to the radicals' surprise, Mao chose Hua Guofeng instead of Wang Hongwen or Zhang Chunqiao to assume Deng's position. Despite the criticism, Hua Guofeng continued implementation of the plan, placing an emphasis on heavy industrial development with foreign assistance. Before long, in October 1976, the Gang of Four was arrested, and Yu Qiuli returned to Beijing to work under the leadership of Hua Guofeng.

A HUMBLE CONFERENCE SHED

In 1976 Daqing's crude oil production set a new record: 50.3 million metric tons. At the same time, Daqing enjoyed its position as a top national model. Because Hua Guofeng's only claim to legitimacy as chairman of the Party was Mao's blessing, he tried to ensure Mao's continuing significance. When Mao died in 1976, a mausoleum was erected in Tiananmen Square, enshrined with the symbolic slogan "The Chairman is forever with us." A joint editorial, entitled "Study the Documents Well and Grasp the Key Link," published on February 7, 1977, in *People's Daily*, the journal *Hongqi* (Red Flag), and *Jiefangjun bao* (People's Liberation Army Daily), established a formula to set Mao Zedong Thought in concrete: "We will resolutely uphold whatever policy decisions Chairman Mao made, and unswervingly follow whatever instructions Chairman Mao gave." Hua Guofeng elevated the Dazhai and Daqing models to an even higher level. In 1977, a national industrial conference, "In Industry, Learn from Daqing," was held in Beijing and Daqing. There Hua announced that China would realize the "Four Modernizations" by the year 2000, that is, the modernization of industry, of agriculture, of national defense, and of science and technology. He quoted Mao's words from 1949: "If we do not exceed the United States in fifty or sixty years, we should kick ourselves off of this planet."[25] State media stated that although the struggle had been acute during the Cultural Revolution, the oil workers had put Maoist Thought in command. Self-reliance was still stressed, but there was greater emphasis on the role of technology.

The national conference brought huge crowds to Daqing. A stadium, shown in Figure 6.5, was built to accommodate the grand event. Although it was a multifunctional stadium, it was given a downgraded name of "conference shed" (*da hui peng*), representing its down-to-earth spirit and frugal nature. Other public buildings in Daqing were similarly named. For example, the movie theater was called the "central meeting room" (*zhongxin huiyishi*), and hotels were called "reception stations" (*jiedai zhan*). Decoration and ornament were strictly forbidden. Song Zhenming, the second generation of Daqing leaders, required that these public buildings be constructed in an "authentic *gandalei* style," having a "country feeling on the outside but being modern on the inside." The other Daqing leader, Zhang Hongchi, who had been promoted from a grass-roots model worker, suggested building a "big hay shed" (*da cao peng*) for the stadium. But neither mud bricks nor hay could support such large-scale structures. Finally, the building was constructed with prefabricated slabs, absent any decorations or paintings. The stadium stood on a barren field without landscaping. There were no elaborate entrances, no gardens, and no flower beds. Even the placement of several green plants inside the

FIGURE 6.5 Daqing celebrating the collapse of the "Gang of Four" in front of Iron Man Memorial Hall, the only architecture design in which Song was involved in Daqing, 1976. Source: Daqing geming weiyuanhui, *Daqing*.

stadium aroused some arguments among the leaders. The idea of erecting a modest flag pole in front of the building was prohibited by Song Zhenming.[26] Construction was completed at Daqing speed within 150 days.

Tens of thousands of people visited Daqing in 1977. *Gandalei* housing continued to represent the Daqing spirit, but the level of frugality in Daqing became a subject of debate. When one of the central leaders stayed in the guestroom of Compound No. 2 and found hardwood floors, he commented, "It seems Daqing is not as frugal as I thought." When Song Zhenming heard this comment, he murmured to himself, "We are not shepherds. We cannot always live with the blue sky as a roof and the green plains as a carpet."[27]

Following this interpretation of the *gandalei* spirit, it seemed that people in Daqing who had lived in such "temporary housing" for nearly twenty years had no hope of upgrading to better living conditions.

*   *   *

Both Hua's and Song's families were worried about little Yan and her struggling mother in Daqing. In 1972, Song's older sister sent one of her daughters, fourteen-year-old Peizhen, to help Hua with babysitting (fig. 6.6). Young Peizhen's presence released Hua temporarily from physical and psychological pressures. After Nixon visited Beijing in February, China National Radio began broadcasting English-language classes, and there was a national wave to study English. The Design Institute also offered off-hour English classes, provided by a woman from the intelligence office. Hua eagerly diverted her attention to the study of English.

Hua's colleagues in the office tried to cheer her up. Three cadres, who formally worked in the State Surveying and Mapping Bureau, had spent half their lives along the border. Already in their forties, they were often afflicted with occupational diseases, such as arthritis or stomach illnesses. The Daqing Design Institute accepted these mapping experts who could no longer endure field work. They joked that they were being "recycled." Though they were downtrodden, they were devoted to their work and maintained their sense of humor. Young colleagues introduced the hobby of practicing calligraphy to the office. Copying the masterpieces of well-known calligraphers also helped to distract Hua and calm her down. But Hua did not pay as much attention to her work as before. After she lost

FIGURE 6.6 Song and Hua standing in front of their home, built of brick, with their second daughter, Yan, and niece Peizhen, at the Design Institute, Ranghulu, 1973. Photo courtesy of Zha Binhua and Yang Ruisong.

faith in urban-rural integrated patterns, drawing and mapping became just a mechanical exercise.

Yan was becoming an adorable little girl. Song liked to show her off proudly to his colleagues and old friends during his precious time at home. After Peizhen left, Yan was sent to the daycare center. Their first daughter, Xiaohua, was already of school age. She returned from Nanjing to live with Hua and Song and attended school in Ranghulu. The neighbors helped Hua to build an advanced two-story hen coop in their yard. Raising chickens greatly contributed to the health and nutrition of many families at the time. Little Yan was responsible for picking up the eggs in the coop whenever the hens proudly announced that there were new eggs.

In 1974, construction of a pipeline linking Shengli Oil Field to the Shanghai Refinery, one of the major projects in the 4-3 Plan, was put on the agenda. A design institute for the oil pipeline was to be established in Langfang, Hebei province, a city located between Tianjin and Beijing. One year later, some good news finally arrived. The former head of the Fourth Division was named a vice director of the institute, and Hua heard that both she and Song were included on the list of people to be transferred. The official transfer order was delayed for a year until conflicts were settled at the state level, but on one of the last days of 1975, a Liberation truck finally came to carry the family of four and their belongings away from Daqing. They thus began their long journey back to the urban world.

*   *   *

BUILD TEN MORE DAQINGS!

Hua Guofeng combined the Maoist rhetoric of full mass mobilization, that is, "continuing the revolution," with ambitious goals for economic growth, and he proposed the slogan "Another Great Leap." Good news came from China's industrial front: total oil production exceeded 100 million metric tons in 1977. China ranked eighth in the world in terms of crude oil production. If growth were to continue at this rate, China would soon surpass Nigeria, Iraq, Kuwait, and Venezuela and become the world's fourth largest oil producer.[28] This booming prospect dazzled both China's leaders and the outside world. In October 1977, George H. W. Bush, head of the U.S. Liaison Office in Beijing, wrote a report suggesting that Washington look to China as a possible source of oil.[29]

In March 1978 Yu Qiuli's comrade-in-arms Kang Shi'en was promoted to vice premier, director of the State Economic Commission, and vice director of the State Planning Commission. The younger generation of Daqing leaders, such as Tang Ke and Song Zhenming, were also promoted to be in charge of key state energy and industrial sectors. In the spring of 1978, Gu Mu led the first government ministerial-level economic delegation to tour Western Europe. They received a warm welcome from the developed, capitalist world, and many countries were willing to offer them favorable low-interest loans.

In the energy sector there were extensive exchanges of visits between China and the United States and China and Japan in 1977 and 1978. The most significant efforts were the joint-venture agreements with foreign oil companies to survey, explore, and develop China's offshore potential.[30] Shortly thereafter the United States and the People's Republic of China issued a joint communiqué announcing the establishment of diplomatic relations as of January 1, 1979.

Based on the Ten-Year Plan, China embarked on ambitious economic goals. "Build more than ten Daqing-style enterprises" was the slogan for Chinese industry. State investment would total about 60 billion yuan, exceeding the total amount of investment during the previous twenty-eight years. The plan required US$18 billion in imports, most of which would be paid for from greater exports of crude oil.[31] In many respects, except for the extensive foreign imports, the strategy did not depart too far from the Maoist development policy: high rates of saving; a priority on heavy industry, such as metallurgy and machine building, and a focus on the petrochemical industry; a general neglect of the agricultural sector as well as education and science; and a "production first, livelihood second" strategy as well as a campaign style of mobilization and management. The protocols signed with Japan and Western countries involved bartering oil and coal for plants and technology. Later, the agreements introduced a large number of low-interest foreign loans and the employment of foreign experts.

However, this "large-scale, foreign, and capital-intensive" plan faced criticism from two groups: veteran cadres, mainly in the State Council, who were in charge of planning before the "planning revolution," and a younger group of liberal economists who supported reform. The two groups would later be differentiated based on their visions of China's future, but they were joined for a time by their common opposition to one faction among the leadership. Veteran cadres, such as Chen Yun, Bo Yibo, and Li Xiannian, called for an overall balance in economic development instead of an emphasis on heavy industrial growth at the expense of attention to people's livelihoods. Among this group, Chen Yun played an important role in opposing the ambitious ten-year plan. Chen had a long-standing suspicion of Maoist-style rapid economic development. He was the only one who had stood up to oppose the Great Leap Forward policies, earning him great prestige among the central leadership. Instead of another Great Leap, the veteran planners advocated a policy of "readjustment, reform, correction, and improvement" during the post-Mao transition period.[32] Chen suggested that "living, clothing, and eating" (i.e., agriculture and light industry) should be development priorities. Such priorities had been rejected by Mao during the Great Leap Forward as well as later, during the Third Front campaign. Major projects in the plan, such as the Shanghai Baoshan Steel Plant and the new refinery project for Daqing, faced pressure to be reexamined and halted. The veteran planners questioned whether foreign direct investment was an appropriate solution for China's development problems, and they worried that the considerable spending on heavy industry would lead to a large state deficit.[33]

Deng Xiaoping was undoubtedly a key figure in these shifting forces. Formerly a supporter and architect of the Ten-Year Plan, he had not been opposed to rapid industrial development or foreign assistance. However, his position shifted to oppose the vision promoted by Hua Guofeng. Helped by Hu Yaobang, Deng criticized the current policies from an ideological point of view. A theoretical debate on the "criterion of truth" was initiated to target the "whatever" faction that was associated with Chairman Hua and his clique. Questioning the policies of the Great Leap and the Daqing model, the Office of Political Research invited several liberal economists, including Ma Hong, Xue Muqiao, Yu Guangyuan, and Feng Lanrui, to reform the Marxist political economy so as to serve as a new guide for national economic development policies.

In September 1978, Vice Premier Deng toured the northeast. In Daqing he stated that local workers had contributed greatly to the country but had sacrificed too much of their personal lives. He is reported to have said, "It is time for Daqing to 'build a beautiful oil city.'" *Daqing*

Zhan Bao (later renamed *Daqing Daily*) did not release any news about Deng's visit. Many work-unit leaders filed petitions to build modern, multistory housing for their staff and workers, but the petitions were rejected by the high-level leaders. The Party leader of Daqing Oil Field, Chen Liemin, insisted that the single-story *gandalei* housing style would dominate Daqing's landscape "forever": "I will never in my life move into a *loufang* [multistory house]!" The administrative head of Daqing Oil Field, Wang Sumin, who had a serious disagreement with Chen Liemin during a meeting about the petitions, was downgraded to a position as a drilling engineer and repatriated to the southwestern hinterlands.[34]

In November 1978, a CCP Central Work Conference was held to prepare for the forthcoming Third Plenum of the CCP's Eleventh Congress. Hua Guofeng tried to limit the discussions to the national economic plan and socialist modernization. However, influenced by Chen Yun's speeches, many conference delegates criticized Hua's second Great Leap, calling it a "Great Leap Outward," and proposed a reexamination of the fabricated charges against the veteran leaders during the Cultural Revolution. Following the Third Plenum of the Eleventh Party Congress, Chen Yun and Deng Xiaoping became members of the Standing Committee of the Politburo.

THE CONDITION OF THE CHINESE WORKING CLASS

In early 1978 the Office of Political Research, led by Yu Guangyuan, conducted a survey of living conditions among Chinese workers. The survey report, revealing that poor living conditions had seriously influenced labor productivity, was circulated to the central leaders. According to data from the Ministry of Building Construction, average living space per person had dropped from 4.5 square meters in 1952 to 3.6 square meters in 1978. In 182 Chinese cities, 35.8 percent of the urban households were in urgent need of housing.[35] After twenty years of the "production first" strategy, the cities were suffering greatly from a lack of state investments. Urban infrastructure was on the brink of collapse after so many years of overuse without proper maintenance.

In 1979, the *People's Daily*, under the direction of Hu Yaobang, head of the Propaganda Department, initiated a discussion about "the purpose of socialist production." On October 20, 1979, a commentator's article, appearing on the front page of the paper, was titled "Truly Clarify the Purpose of Socialist Production." The article was clearly targeting the "Great Leap Outward" plan, criticizing that (1) the starting point of national economic planning was based on certain heavy industrial products and not on the consumption needs of the population; (2) capital accumulation was overemphasized in terms of redistribution, in sharp contrast to ignorance about consumption; (3) in the field of basic construction, there was an imbalance between "productive" and "nonproductive" construction; and (4) there was too much investment in heavy industry and insufficient investment in agriculture and light industry. The article challenged the ideology of "production first, livelihood second," arguing that this ideology had negatively affected the productivity of China's working class, and thus it should no longer be promoted as a national model. Production should be the means, not the ends, of socialist development. The ultimate aim of socialist production was to meet the people's consumption needs, not to increase production. During the following month, the *People's Daily* published articles by Yu Guangyuan and many others supporting such criticisms. In the field of philosophy, rising humanist concerns were voiced, criticizing the treatment of people as a means to achieving state goals rather than as an end in themselves.[36]

The petroleum leaders reacted strongly to such criticisms. From November 1979 to January 1980, the *Daqing Zhanbao*, the *North China Oil Paper* (Huabei shiyou bao), and the *Petroleum Industry Newsletter* (Shiyou gongye jianbao) all published numerous articles in response to the *People's Daily* commentator's article. This was the first time in the history of the PRC that a local or industrial newspaper had dared to challenge the Party's central newspaper. In two articles published on November 17 and November 19, 1979, and written by the Investigation and Research Office of the Ministry of the Petroleum Industry, the local newspapers responded that in the new age "production first, livelihood second" was still applicable. One article was titled "Less Empty Talk, More Solid Work" (Shaoshuo konghua, duogan shishi) and the other "Improve the People's Livelihood on the Basis of Developing Production." The article in *Daqing Zhanbao* was broadcast nationwide on China National Radio on December 5 and 6, 1979.[37]

In January 1980 Hua Guofeng stepped in to stop further publication of such articles, and within several weeks, the media were silenced. One month later, at the Fifth Plenum of the CCP's Eleventh Congress, Hu Yaobang was elected general secretary of the Central Committee of the CCP, and Hu and Zhao Ziyang also joined the Standing Committee of the Politburo. In September, Zhao Ziyang formally replaced Hua Guofeng as premier. Daqing's temporary success ended with Hua's loss of central power, and Hua's role as chairman of the Party was much diminished. In June, the *People's Daily* reopened the discussion on the purpose of socialist production. In December, a national conference on the topic, initiated by Yu Guangyuan, was convened in Beijing. By the end of 1979, despite the great pressure for rapid growth, the Ministry of the Petroleum Industry could promise only that oil production in 1980 would be at the same level as that in 1979. Contracts for crude oil exports could not be met, and the goal of "building ten more Daqings" was no longer on the agenda.

The Sinking of the Oil Rig

On July 22, 1980, backed by the Secretariat of the CCP Central Committee, the *People's Daily* charged the petroleum group with covering up the sinking of an oil rig, Bohai No. 2, during a storm in November 1979. The disaster led to the loss of seventy-two lives. The petroleum leaders were accused of negligence at the time of the storm and then of refusing to disclose the disaster.

On August 26, 1980, Minister of the Petroleum Industry Song Zhenming wrote a self-criticism that appeared in all the major newspapers and was relieved of his position. Kang Shi'en was also relieved of his position as vice premier and was reprimanded. Yu Qiuli was shuffled out of the State Planning Commission and replaced by Yao Yilin, whose opinions were similar to those held by Chen Yun. "Readjustment" replaced the "Great Leap Outward" as the development goal for 1979 and 1980. *Loufang* as modern urban symbols began to appear in Daqing Oil Field.

Since the 1980s, Daqing has faded from the national scene as a socialist model. Large-scale housing construction has resumed in all Chinese cities. In 1979 alone, the total constructed area of urban housing reached 62.56 million square meters, setting a record since 1949. Midrise planned residential districts have gradually replaced low-rise self-built mud or brick houses as urban farming and chicken coops in the cities have gradually disappeared. Nevertheless, a pro–small-town development policy has been sustained.

The Third National Urban Planning Work Conference held in Beijing in 1978 declared that the principle of planning was to "control the size of the large cities and develop more small cities." The 1984 Urban Planning Bylaw and the 1990 Urban Planning Act further confirmed the pro–small-city principle. Small and medium-size cities enjoyed fewer population controls and faster land-use growth than other cities.

In 1980 the Daqing Oil District was elevated to city status. In 1981, the newly established Daqing Urban Planning Bureau began to draft the city's first master plan (1981–2000) as Daqing's nonagricultural population already exceeded 490,000 people. The plan, completed in 1984, proposed the goal of developing Daqing into "a new industrial city" by the year 2000 and carefully defined Daqing's development strategy as "relative dispersion with several modest concentrations" (*xiang dui fen san, shi dang ji zhong*). As a result, the new settlements became much more concentrated. The three existing towns, thirty-four central villages, and 260 settlement points were restructured into six workers' towns, twenty-four central villages, and twenty-seven resident villages. The scale of the central village was increased from a population of six thousand to a population of twenty thousand, and the resident villages, with much greater densities and better services, replaced the settlement points.[38] Low-rise mud housing in Daqing had been gradually replaced by middle-rise concrete-and-brick housing since 1984.

Five years later, in 1989, Daqing municipality revised its master plan. The 1989 plan was much more centralized compared to the 1981 plan. It clearly articulated the goal of building an oil city centered in Saertu, Dongfeng (literally East Wind), and Longfeng. This plan represents Daqing's official farewell to its former decentralized model, and in 1990 it was awarded first prize among the Heilongjiang Province Science and Technology Awards.

By 1994 Daqing's urban population exceeded 1 million. In the 2000 master plan of Daqing City, Saertu was no longer the city center, nor was it still an urban settlement. The central belt-shaped area had given way to oil production. The ensuing urban development mainly took place in East Town, which is composed of the former Dongfeng Village, Long-feng, and West Town, which is composed of the former Ranghulu and Chengfeng Villages. East Town serves as the municipal administrative center, whereas West Town is the headquarters for Daqing oil produc-tion. According to the 2000 master plan, residential houses built within the boundaries of the oil field were to be abandoned and the residents were to be gradually relocated to new towns.[39]

EPILOGUE

After leaving Daqing, Hua and her family lived in Langfang, Hebei province for a few years. It was a small town between Beijing and Tianjin where the Bureau of Oil Pipeline, under the Ministry of Petroleum Industry, was located. Under the Daqing spirit, their living conditions were similar to those in Daqing. A single-story brick house was standard. After the Great Tangshan Earthquake in July 1976, they had to stay in a temporary hut for a year, which reminded them of the old days on the collective farm.

The true turning point came in 1980. Unleased housing demand started the second wave of urban booms in PRC history. Ironically, the resumption of the urban planning profession became the means of Hua and Song's long desired return to urban society. With the restoration of planning administrations in major Chinese cities, Hua and Song were able to join the newly established Nanjing City Planning Bureau at the end of 1981. The second half of their professional careers finally corresponded to a great demand for city building. However, Hua uncompromisingly resigned her position three years later and turned to an architecture design institute in Nanjing. She retired in 2002 as an architect.

* * *

After three decades of extensive urban construction, the physical landscape influenced by the Daqing model is scarcely visible today. Many of the settlement points, built either along remote production borders or under Third Front mountains, have been abandoned. Daqing's name is seldom mentioned nowadays. The northeast, the land with rich natural resources, the most important heavy industry base for Japan's colonial empire and then the young socialist republic, has now become China's rust belt.

At a time when China has achieved unprecedented growth while accumulating more and more unsolved problems, this book has attempted to trace the original formation of the socialist state and its urban policies. The metamorphosis of Daqing's physical landscape marked an unusual episode for socialist China and epitomized the major threats and changes experienced by the Chinese state and society since the 1950s. In twentieth-century China, no family could escape the larger story of the structural changes occurring. By the beginning of the second half of the century, the lives and life choices of the common people had become much more intertwined with the fate and choices of the state.

In 1949 less than 10 percent of the national population was urban in mainland China, and many Chinese cities could hardly be considered modern. However, there was an even greater disparity between urban and rural areas. Large swaths of rural land remained in their original condition, if not worse, and rural residents struggled to maintain their very low living standards. The new People's Republic of China faced major challenges in feeding, clothing, and providing decent housing and health care for the massive, densely settled population, which was increasing by 100 million people every seven years.[1] Both state and society were seeking to come up with a revolutionary path to modernization. A centrally planned economy was embraced as an advanced system that would help China make ends meet and eventually achieve greater national wealth and power. The Soviet method of rapid heavy industrialization, focusing on the large cities and the more developed areas, excluded the masses of rural people and resulted in catastrophic outcomes. Periodic famines greatly harmed early development efforts. Beginning in the mid-1950s, China began to significantly cut the costs of urban construction to remedy the scarcity of resources. This eventually gave birth to the Daqing model, which lowered urban construction standards to the level of rural standards. In the 1960s living conditions in Daqing were grim, but conditions in the vast countryside were even worse. The goals of state measures to curb urbanization and limit urban consumption were to economize on the costs of industrialization. There were constant struggles in balancing the investment of resources between agriculture and industry and between the cities and the countryside. The pursuit of egalitarianism between town and country served as a means to an end, not an end in itself.

The effectiveness of the Daqing model lies in its resiliency in continuously expanding production despite many hardships and scarcities, thus greatly relying on individual behavior. Because almost all expansion was channeled back into additional production, the burden of coping was left to each family. The problems encountered by families represented much more than their individual difficulties. Conditions in the cities were better than those in the country, but the hardships of life were equally felt. The savings on urban construction caused a serious deterioration in urban living standards and public infrastructure. Housing was in short supply. There was insufficient running water, gas, coal, and heat. Commuting was largely dependent on either walking or bicycles. Extra work hours were followed by extra hours of domestic drudgery that were necessary for family life. A shortage of doctors and medicine meant that diseases lingered longer and spread wider. But above all, the shortage of food was the most serious threat. The principle of "integration of industry and agriculture, integration of workers and peasants, integration of town and countryside" was carried out down to the family level, between husbands and wives: industrial workers shared food rations with their peasant wives, and women engaged in farming in order to supplement the nutritional needs of their undernourished husbands and children.

With the introduction of the Daqing model, the late 1960s and the 1970s saw a continuous diffusion of the concentrated urban growth that had been achieved during the First Five-Year Plan period. The investment concentrated in the north was diverted to the south. Industries along the coast were moved inland. Population growth in the large cities was strictly controlled, even leading at times to negative growth. From 1949 to 1957, the cities ranking at the top in terms of population growth were Baotou in Inner Mongolia; Taiyuan, Changzhi, and Datong in Shanxi; and Qiqihar, Fushun, Jiamusi, Jilin, Shenyang, and Harbin in the northeast. But from 1965 to 1978, the fastest-growing cities were Panzhihua, Xiangfan, Guilin, and Zhuzhou in the southwest and Yan'an, Wulumuqi, and Xining in the west. The only rapidly growing "city" in the northeast was Daqing. However, growth in all of these cities was not as rapid as it had been in the 1950s.

The 1960s and 1970s witnessed the emergence of numerous mining districts and factory complexes that statistically were not large enough to be counted as cities and whose populations were engaged in more than just mining and manufacturing. This dispersed pattern of development created a diffused physical landscape throughout the country, with a much lower population density and a greater extension. The decentralized model was also favored because the country faced the threat of war; under this model it would be more difficult for the enemy in the air to distinguish urban from rural areas, industry from agriculture, and the centers from the peripheries. There were attempts to make the regions self-sufficient and independent regardless of any air strikes.

Because the decades between the 1964 and the 1982 censuses remain a "demographic mystery," scholars lack an accurate knowledge of the national population distribution between those years.[2] Nevertheless, based on available data in the two censuses, the population residing in small-town clusters—whose nonagricultural populations were not large enough to reach municipal status—grew much faster than the population residing in the cities. Furthermore, almost half of the added population in the urban areas, that is, 21 million in eighteen years, was registered as urban "agricultural households."[3] This was common for families whose members had different registration statuses. Very often it was *nan gong nü nong*, nonagriculturally registered husbands and agriculturally registered wives, and the children's status followed their mother's. These agricultural households in the cities, small towns, and nonagricultural units served as temporary workers and resumed peasant status when they were no longer needed. The existence of a flexible labor force and worker-peasant employment ambiguities was crucial for sustainable industrial production growth. It served as a human resource hub for the country's modernization drive, absorbing pressures and providing needed support. It is a measure that has lasted and functions even today.

As for the state, the decentralization of space was accompanied by a decentralization of power and a deterioration of central control capabilities. Management from above was much more difficult due to the widely dispersed distribution of resources, including capital, material, and human resources. Power was further eroded by the anarchist state of communications and transportation caused by the Cultural Revolution. Both intentionally and unintentionally, the central functions of planning controls were diverted to regional and local levels. If China's planned economy in the 1950s was already crude and incomplete compared to the Soviet model, it had become even more fragmented by the 1970s. The state planning machine under the leadership of Yu Qiuli lost its monopoly control over many key resources, and its daily functions were limited to crisis management, supplying basic energy, and maintaining key nationwide transportation networks. There had been several attempts to resume stronger central controls through traditional political measures or ambitious capital investment plans, but it was not until the early 1980s that a more influential central institution was reestablished through the introduction of market reforms and China's new joint adventure with global capitals.

This book has presented rich details at the state and local levels, and from political, socioeconomic, spatial, and individual perspectives, that illustrate and interpret those complex historic moments in the nation. The period during which Daqing rose up as a national model is probably one of the most controversial periods of the PRC's history in terms of historic interpretation. Entering the reform and opening-up era, the official narrative of its immediate past has been reconstructed to meet the needs of changing political conditions: those of the ultraleftists, the cult of personality and "the feudal residual" that led to the PRC's "lost decade(s)," and the end of the 1970s, when the national economy and society were facing a crisis. On the other hand, there are always scholars questioning this overly simplistic image and who see the Revolution and the Reform as a continuing process.[4] The legacy of the past, or to be more precise, the continuation before and after the Reform, can be seen in many ways, politically, economically, socially, and spatially. For example, in terms of food provisions, the 1970s marked a crucial period for the later takeoff of Chinese agriculture. Beginning from the Great Leap Forward in the late 1950s, large-scale irrigation projects were carried out by laborers on collective farms and urban youth who had been sent to the countryside. These irrigated areas grew rapidly until the late 1970s.[5] The initial success of heavy industry provided Chinese agriculture with modern technology and equipment. During the 1970s, millions of pumps were installed to provide water to the dry North China Plain, where there was rich soil and abundant sunshine. Mechanical power, replacing human and animal power, spread throughout the countryside.[6] Due to the efforts of the Petroleum Group in particular, the 4-3 Plan in 1973 initiated large-scale imports of synthetic ammonia and urea factories. A strong domestic fertilizer industry was gradually established, and by the late 1970s a cheap and steady fertilizer supply was available. Traditional organic fertilizer, which is labor-intensive to use and unpleasant to handle, thus became less relevant in the countryside. In 1973 Chinese scientists successfully developed high-yield hybrid rice. As during the first two decades of socialism, China built an extensive seed production and distribution system across the central, provincial, county, commune, and brigade levels and was able to quickly disseminate new generations of seeds to millions of peasants. The completion of the technological revolution, the establishment of a strong domestic fertilizer industry, and hard-core improvements in irrigation infrastructure all occurred in the 1970s. In 1973 and 1974, due to a modest surplus, China was able to export rice to the outside world. Over the following ten years, Chinese agricultural production enjoyed ongoing growth. After the rural reforms in the late 1970s, per capita agriculture soared, reaching a peak in 1984. By the early 1990s, China's total grain yields had tripled compared with 1952, and in 1993 food rationing was abolished. The availability of food was no longer the most serious challenge facing the country. The dramatic improvements in Chinese agriculture are often interpreted as an outcome of the rural reforms in the 1980s. But despite the disruptions of the Cultural Revolution, the continuing efforts made during the 1960s and the 1970s deserve more credit.[7]

This book has fulfilled the scholarly task of reconstructing the social and political experience of the Maoist past to be genuinely comprehensive, dynamic, and subtle. The narrative depicts socialism as a revolutionary ideology under the noble dream of equality and equity and as a system of socioeconomic rules, taking dynamic forms when implemented by men and women, those with enormous power and resources, together with those who had less power and resources. Through the city-building process, I have investigated the politics between party leaders and elite ministerial cadres and examined state institutions' diverse interests, conflicts, tensions, functions, and dysfunctions. This examination has disclosed both the great abilities and the limitations of a state in controlling society and resources. It recorded the newborn PRC with its young revolutionary generation entering middle age. There are sincere leftist revolutionaries who are at the same time calculating politicians. There are changing social ideals and growing realism responding to the numerous campaigns. My research discovered both strong ideological beliefs and decorative political rhetoric, both nobility of soul and humanity of body.

Last but not least is the unspoken element in the book: the land. Through historic efforts to achieve a higher standard of living, there is a changing landscape with diminishing resources. This is especially true in Daqing's case, and for China applying the Daqing model in general. China has been the most populous nation on earth for thousands of years. The tension between the population and the land is always there. China is used to maintaining a very high labor input in the land. Land utilization had approached a maximum and been extended to China's full geographic range long before its modern era. The dramatic rise of the population and its pressure on land resources had led to tragically high death tolls from rebellions, wars, and natural catastrophes. Past generations very often forgot to see the connections. Nowadays, it is almost needless to say that the past model of development, including the excessive exploitation of natural resources, has had profound negative environmental effects. These have begun to affect the lives of every Chinese person. While we are striving for a better future, we must be aware that there is very limited open space left.

Notes

Preface

1. According to Jianshe bu, *Zhongguo chengshi jianshe tongji nianjian 2014*, the total built area of Chinese cities was 7,438 square kilometers in 1981 and 49,772 square kilometers in 2014.

2. See, for example, Paul A. Cohen, "Reflections on a Watershed Date: The 1949 Divide in Chinese History," in Wasserstrom, *Twentieth-Century China*.

Introduction

1. Yao Mingli, "Daqing de guoqu xianzai yu weilai," 43.
2. Yuan Mu and Rongkang Fan, "Daqing Jingshen Daqing Ren."
3. Spence, *The Search for Modern China*, 629.

Chapter 1. The Discovery of Daqing

1. Fuller and Clapp, *The Science of Petroleum*, 139.

2. Gilliam, "The Standard Oil Company in China." In 1911 the U.S. Supreme Court ruled that Standard Oil, one of the world's first and largest international corporations, was an illegal monopoly. As a result, in exchange for the European market, Standard Oil conceded a considerable share of its East Asian market to the Royal Dutch-Shell Company. See also Mohr, *The Oil War*, 61–62.

3. Among the most popular imported commodities, kerosene was called *yangyou* (foreign oil) by the Chinese people, together with the "foreign cloth" and "foreign fire" (i.e., matches) entering the Chinese market.

4. "Chiling danshui ting wenwu, suishi mi cha, yu you buxiao min ren si wa mei-tan, liji qiangbi, yi du gouchuan yangren de biduan" 饬令淡水厅文武随时密查，遇有不肖民人私挖煤炭，立即枪毙，以杜勾串洋人的弊端 (Danshuiting Is Ordered That It Can Investigate and at Any Time Cases of Unscrupulous People Who Dig for Coal Can Be

Immediately Shot), *Siguo xin dang Yingguo an* 四国新档英国案 (Four Countries New Files, British Cases), vol. 2, p. 29, in *Jiawu zhanqian zhi Taiwan meiwu* 甲午战前之台湾 煤务 (cited in "Pre-1894 Coal Industry in Taiwan"), 18.

5. *Qingshi gao, shihuo zhi*, 16; Sun Yutang, *Zhongguo jindai gongye shi ziliao*, vol. 1, pt. 2, p. 582; see also Wu, *Empires of Coal*, chap. 5.

6. Williams to Bryan, October 21, 1913, in *Records of Department of the State Relating to Internal Affairs of China, 1910–1929*, 893.51/1477, U.S. National Archives, Washington, DC.

7. Reinsch to Secretary of State, February 16, 1914, 893.6363/1, U.S. National Archives, Washington, DC.

8. Kirby, "Engineers and the State in Modern China."

9. *China Year Book 1936*, 32.

10. Kirby, *Germany and Republican China*, 78.

11. See Weng Wenhao, *Weng Wenhao wencun*.

12. Zheng Youkui et al., *Jiu Zhongguo de ziyuan weiyuanhui*.

13. Ibid.

14. On oil in Xinjiang as a source of contention and cooperation between China and the USSR, see Whiting and Sheng, *Sinkiang*.

15. This was to become part of the first Sino-Soviet joint-venture petroleum company that was established in 1950.

16. Mao Zedong, "Report to the Second Plenary Session of the Seventh Central Committee of the Communist Party of China," March 5, 1949, in *Selected Works*, vol. 4, pp. 361–375.

17. Zheng Youkui et al., *Jiu Zhongguo de ziyuan weiyuanhui*.

18. "Jiben jianshe gongzuo chengxu zanxing banfa" 基本建设工作程序暂行办法 (Temporary Instructions on Procedures for Basic Construction Work), in Sun Yueqi, *Zhongguo Guomindang geming weiyuanhui*.

19. Chen Yu, a senior communist member who organized the Guangzhou–Hong Kong workers' strike in 1925, was the first and only minister of the Ministry of the Fuel Industry, from 1949 to 1955. He was born in a village in Bao'an county, Guangdong province, and served as Party secretary and governor of Guangdong province beginning in 1957.

20. Chen Zhengren (alternative name, Chen Lin), whose "revolutionary career" was based on his experiences in Jiangxi province, was its first minister, with Zhou Rongxi, Wan Li, and Liu Xiufeng as vice ministers.

21. The Chinese use the idiom *renshan renhai* 人山人海 to describe the vast crowds of people present in modern-day China.

22. *Dangdai Zhongguo de dizhi shiye*, 35.

23. National Statistical Bureau, *Zhongguo guding zichan touzi tongji ziliao*; *Dangdai Zhongguo de dizhi shiye*.

24. Cheng, *China's Petroleum Industry*, 4.

25. *Shiyou shiren zai Daqing youtian jishi*.

26. Wen Houwen et al., *Kang Shi'en zhuan*.

27. Dong Zhikai and Wu Jiang, *Xin Zhongguo gongye de dian jishi*.

28. Liu Guoguang et al., *Zhongguo shige wunian jihua yanjiu baogao*.

29. Cheng, *China's Petroleum Industry*, 1.

30. China State Council, *First Five-Year Plan, 1953–1957*, and *Proposal of the Second Five-Year Plan*, presented to the CCP Eighth National Congress, in *Zhongguo shige wunian jihua yanjiu baogao*, 52–113.

31. Chen Zhengxiang, *Zhongguo de shiyou*, 11–12.

32. Yu Qiuli, *Yu Qiuli huiyilu*, 510–512.

33. Ibid., 527.

34. Yergin, *The Prize*, 351–367.

35. Wildcat wells are oil wells drilled in areas not known to be oil fields.

36. Wen Houwen et al., *Kang Shi'en zhuan*, 106.

Chapter 2. Production First, Livelihood Second

1. Yu Qiuli, *Yu Qiuli huiyilu*, 596.

2. Wen Houwen et al., *Kang Shi'en zhuan*.

3. Tamanoi, *Crossed Histories*, 5; Ho, *Studies on the Population of China*, 162.

4. Young, *Japan's Total Empire*.

5. Ibid.

6. Dong Zhikai, *1949–1952 xin Zhongguo jingji fenxi*, 27, 41.

7. Wen Houwen et al., *Kang Shi'en zhuan*, 88.

8. Ibid.

9. Yu Qiuli, *Yu Qiuli huiyilu*, 610.

10. Ibid., 886.

11. Daqing Railway Gazette Office, *Daqing tielu zhi*, 9.

12. Quoted in Yu Qiuli, *Yu Qiuli huiyilu*, 887.

13. Ibid.

14. Based on a Sino-Soviet agreement signed by Mao and Stalin, most Russians were repatriated to their home country in 1952.

15. Yu Qiuli, *Yu Qiuli huiyilu*, 578.

16. For more on Sun Jingwen, see Xu Zhen and Li Weichen, "Sun Jingwen," 329–380.

17. Yu Qiuli, *Yu Qiuli huiyilu*.

18. Ibid., 675; Bo Yibo, *Ruogan zhongda juece yu shijian de huigu*, 885.

19. Wen Houwen et al., *Kang Shi'en zhuan*, 132.

20. Yu Qiuli, *Yu Qiuli huiyilu*, 677.

21. In the oil field, the term "dependent" referred to the spouses of the oil workers or staff members who did not hold permanent jobs in the system and were registered as "agricultural households." Dependents were primarily rural women, either illiterate or with limited education.

22. Chen Zhengxiang, *Zhongguo de shiyou*, 184–185.

Chapter 3. Breakthrough on a Narrow Front

1. Cao Hongtao and Chu Chuanheng, *Dangdai Zhongguo de chengshi jianshe*.

2. Once the major capital construction projects were finalized in the First Five-Year Plan, the location of these projects became the priority of the State Council. The loca-

tion of the major projects was decided upon by the Central Finance and Economics Commission and, later, by the State Planning Commission. The work team that determined the location was usually composed of about one hundred cadres, led by a vice premier, and included representatives from the ministries, Soviet consultants, and the local governments. The ministers of Railways, Public Health, Water Resources, Energy, Public Security, Culture, and Urban Construction were standing members, together with the related industrial administrative sectors.

　　3. State Statistical Bureau, *China Statistical Yearbook, 1983.*

　　4. Many of the Soviet-assisted projects were initially located in the northeast and the northwest, where the Soviets maintained considerable influence, and along the coastal areas, where the traditional industrial cities were located. China's state leaders at first highly respected the preferences of the Soviets in the location of major projects. For example, although Zhou Enlai on numerous occasions had proposed that the first auto plant be located on the outskirts of Beijing, it was ultimately located in Changchun in the northeast. See Mok, "China's Motor Cities"; Cao Hongtao and Chu Chuanheng, *Dangdai Zhongguo de chengshi jianshe,* 37.

　　5. For example, to name but a few, Balinikov in Beijing and Shanghai; Muyin (穆欣) in Shanghai, Shenyang, Hangzhou, Guangzhou, and Shijiazhuang; and Palatin (巴拉金) in Wuhan, Jilin, Baotou, Zhengzhou, and Guangzhou.

　　6. Cao Hongtao and Chu Chuanheng, *Dangdai Zhongguo de chengshi jianshe*; Huang Li, "Zhongguo xiandai chengshi guihua lishi yanjiu."

　　7. *Dangdai Zhongguo de jiben jianshe,* 26.

　　8. Kornai, *Economics of Shortage.*

　　9. *Dangdai Zhongguo de jiben jianshe,* 35.

　　10. "Movement of the dead" refers to the relocation of graveyards because of the construction. Xi'an Lanzhou chengshi jianshe qingkuang ji ji dian yijian, "Chengshi jianshe ju Xi'an xiaozu."

　　11. *Zhongguo shige wunian jihua yanjiu baogao* (Research Report on Ten Chinese Five-Year Plans), 96.

　　12. For example, see the reforms passed at the Third Plenum of the Eighth Party Congress, "Regulations on Improving the Industrial Management System (Draft)," "Regulations on Improving the Commercial System (Draft)," "Regulations on Improving the Financial System and the Division of Financial Administrative Power between the Center and the Localities (Draft)," all published by the State Council on November 8, 1957, China Central Archives.

　　13. Jin Chongji, *Zhou Enlai zhuan,* 26–69.

　　14. Bo Yibo, *Ruogan zhongda juece yu shijian de huigu,* 552.

　　15. Ibid., 575.

　　16. Liu Shaoqi, "Report on the Work of the Central Committee," 28.

　　17. For example, see Wang Huabing, "Women dui dongbei mou chang zhuzhaiqu guihua sheji de jiancha"; Niu Ming, "Liang Sicheng xiansheng shi ruhe wai qu jianzhu yishu he mi zu xingshi de"; Wang Ying, "Guan yu xingshi zhuyi fugu zhuyi jianzhu sixiang de jiancha."

　　18. The instructions state, "Nonproductive construction is a part of basic construction, but it is not the main part. Production-related construction is the main component

and the material structure of state socialist industrialization. Non-productive architecture on its own does not create value. It should serve production. Therefore, lowering its standards will not hinder production but rather it will save money for developing production." See "Jianjue jiangdi fei shengchan xing jianshe biaozhun."

19. Li Fuchun, "Li xing jieyue."

20. Dong Zhikai and Wu Jiang, *Xin Zhongguo gongye de dian jishi*, 292–296; Huang Li, "Zhongguo xiandai chengshi guihua lishi yanjiu," 57–58.

21. Guojia jianshe weiyuanhui chengshi jianshe bu chengshi gongzuo zu, "Xi'an shi gongye ji wenjiao jianshe yu chengshi ge xiang fuwu shiye fazhan peihe wenti diaocha yanjiu huibao tigang."

22. *Dangdai Zhongguo de chengsh jianshe*, 68.

23. Yu Qiuli, *Yu Qiuli huiyilu*, 706.

24. Qin Zhijie, "Cong fensan dao jizhong," 353.

25. One of Deng's negative comments was "This is not a big campaign [*hui zhan* 会战]; this is a big mess [*hun zhan* 混战]!" From interviews with former Daqing headquarters staff, conducted in September 2007 in Daqing.

26. Quoted in Yu Qiuli, *Yu Qiuli huiyilu*, 691.

27. Ibid.

28. Andashi shiwei, "Guanyu muqian chengshi gongzuo de jige zhuyao wenti de baogao."

29. Recalling this period, a designer who had worked in the Daqing headquarters commented, "Yu Qiuli brought his old warlord work style to Daqing. No one dared to speak up when he was angry." From an interview conducted in November 2007 in Daqing.

30. A *mu* is the traditional Chinese measure for farmland. One *mu* equals about one-sixth of an acre.

31. Quoted in Qin Zhijie, "Cong fensan dao jizhong," 354.

32. Ibid.

33. Daqing Oil Field Design Institute, "Gandalei fangwu de sheji yu shigong."

Chapter 4. Celebrating Daqing

1. One year later, China successfully built a nuclear bomb. See Lewis and Xue, *China Builds the Bomb*.

2. Lei Li, *Lishi fengyun zhong de Yu Qiuli*.

3. Wen Houwen et al., *Kang Shi'en zhuan*, 225–227.

4. Mao Zedong, "Guanyu jiaoyu geming de tanhua" 关于教育革命的谈话 (Speech on the Revolution in Education), February 13, 1964, in *Jianguo yilai Mao Zedong wengao*, vol. 11, pp. 22–24.

5. Ibid.

6. Lei Li, *Lishi fengyun zhong de Yu Qiuli*, 15.

7. Quoted in Song Liansheng, *Gongye xue Daqing shimo*, 176.

8. Hu Qiaomu, *Hu Qiaomu huiyi Mao Zedong*, 15.

9. Liu Guoguang et al., *Zhongguo shige wunian jihua yanjiu baogao*, 259.

10. "Liushi niandai sanxian jianshe juece wenxian xuanzai."

11. Bo Yibo, *Ruogan zhongda juece yu shijian de huigu.*

12. Quoted in Liu Guoguang et al., *Zhongguo shige wunian jihua yanjiu baogao*, 269.

13. See Burr and Richelson, "Whether 'to Strangle the Baby in the Cradle.'"

14. Fang Weizhong and Jin Chongji, *Li Fuchun zhuan*, 639.

15. Lei Li, *Lishi fengyun zhong de Yu Qiuli*, 17.

16. Ibid.

17. It was argued that too many resources were concentrated in the northeast and Inner Mongolia due to the Soviet influence.

18. It was Zhou who summarized Mao's instructions with these three phrases.

19. Quoted in Lei Li, *Lishi fengyun zhong de Yu Qiuli*, 20.

20. In 1965, gross agricultural output had increased 8.3 percent and that of industry had increased 26.4 percent. The high growth rate was maintained until the end of 1966, when Mao launched the Cultural Revolution.

21. *Chengzhen juzhuqu guihua shili*, 2.

22. *Zhanbao* (战报) (Battlefield Newsletter), December 10, 1964, p. 2.

23. *Dui Daqing jingyan de zhengzhi jingjixue kaocha*, 322.

24. Barefoot doctors were farmers who received basic medical training and worked in rural villages. The policy was promoted during the Mao period, with the purpose of providing health care in rural areas where urban-trained doctors would not settle. The barefoot doctors promoted basic hygiene, preventative health care, and family planning, and they treated common illnesses. The name comes from the habit of southern farmers who would often work barefoot in the fields.

25. "Daqing funü zhi" bianzuan weiyuanhui, *Daqing funü zhi*.

26. This occurred at the same time that Ranghulu's plan for a three-story headquarters was abandoned.

27. *Daqing Shizhi*, 81.

28. Dong Zhikai and Wu Jiang, *Xin Zhongguo gong ye de dian ji shi.*

29. Liu Xiufeng died in 1971 during the Cultural Revolution. See Meng Guangshui et al., "Liu Xiufeng."

30. Feng Lei and Wang Shouchang, "'Chang qian qu' you meiyou shezhi de biyao?"

31. *Dangdai Zhongguo de chengshi jianshe*, 98.

32. State Planning Commission comment on urban construction in Beijing. Ibid., 87–90.

Chapter 5. Living in an Urban-Rural Heterotopia

1. Li Jing, *Li Jing riji.*

2. Yuan Mu and Fan Rongkang, "Daqing jingshen, Daqing ren."

3. Li Jing, *Li Jing riji*, 125.

4. From interviews with former oil school teachers, conducted in September 2007 in Daqing.

5. Daqing weiyuanhui, Zhengzhi bu, *Zhongguo gongren jieji de xianfeng zhanshi.*

6. Quoted in Song Liansheng, *Gongye xue Daqing shimo*, 80.

7. Based on a suggestion by Sun Jingwen, vice minister of the petroleum industry, the slogan was later changed to "Charge when conditions allow, and create conditions when they are unavailable!"

8. The Great Leap Forward represented an important period during China's women's emancipation movement. According to the journal *Labor*, "in 1958, 55 million women were emancipated from household work." Well-known slogans, such as "Women hold up half the sky," "There is no difference between men and women in this new age," "We can do anything, and anything we do, we can do it well," and "Everyone is busy, and no one is left idle in the family," became popular during this period. From 1957 to 1960, the number of female staff in state-owned enterprises and institutions more than tripled, from 3.3 million to 10 million. See Jin Yihong, "Tie guniang zai si kao."

9. "Daqing funü zhi" bianzuan weiyuanhui, *Daqing funü zhi*.

10. Gongren ribao bianjibu, *Daqing jiashu de geming mofan*.

11. Sun Weishi was the adopted daughter of Zhou Enlai and Deng Yingchao. Her father, Sun Bingwen, had been a close colleague and friend of Zhou at the Huangpu Military Academy; he was killed in Shanghai in 1927. In 1937, Zhou located Sun Weishi in Shanghai and adopted her. She lived with Zhou and Deng in Xibaipo, the Party base in Shanxi, then in Moscow and in Beijing until she married. From 1939 to 1946 she was educated at the Communist University of the Toilers of the East and at the National Theatre Institute in Moscow, where Lin Biao got to know her. She served as Mao's translator in Moscow in 1949. For stories about Sun Weishi, see Wang Mingxia and Xuan Gong, "Zhou Enlai yi nü Sun Weishi de kanke rensheng."

12. Sun Weishi, "Daqing tongxin," *Hongqi* 12 (1965): 41–49.

13. Wang Mingxia and Xuan Gong, "Zhou Enlai yi nü Sun Weishi de kanke rensheng."

14. During this period, an "intellectual" in China generally referred to someone with a higher education, such as a college degree, or even a high school education, as most Chinese were still poorly educated. Intellectuals were not limited to educated elites as the term is now widely understood.

15. *Dui Daqing jingyan de zhengzhi jingjixue kaocha*, 322.

16. Daqing Campaign Work Committee, "Guanyu genghao de guanche dang dui jishu ganbu de zhengce jinyibu jiaqiang dui jishu gongzuo lingdao de jueding."

17. According to Mao, the majority of intellectuals could be classified as "petit bourgeoisie," though he agreed that there existed a distinction between intellectuals who served the landlord and bourgeois classes and those who served the workers and peasants. Mao absolutely belonged to the latter group. Whether in his early works or the later movements that he promoted, Mao demonstrated an ambiguous attitude toward intellectuals but high respect for laborers and the working classes.

18. Mao Tsetung, "Yenan Forum on Literature and Art," 73.

19. The Daqing Campaign Work Committee under the Ministry of the Petroleum Industry replaced the headquarters of the Songliao campaign as the leading organ in Daqing in 1962.

20. From interviews with former oil workers and cadres, conducted in 2007 and 2008 in Daqing.

21. *Daqing huizhan shixuan*.

22. Zhou Enlai, "Zhengfu gongzuo baogao."

23. Yu Qiuli, *Yu Qiuli huiyilu*, 642–643.

24. Ibid., 642.

25. Ibid.

26. Mao Zedong, *Mao Zedong sixiang wan sui*, 642–643.

27. "Chedi suqing Zhongguo Heluxiaofu jiqi dai li ren zai Daqing kuangqu jianshe shang fan mai de hei huo"; "Gongye zhanxian de xianyan hongqi."

28. Daqing gongren pipan zu, "Fan Daqing, kan hongqi."

29. Wen Houwen et al., *Kang Shi'en zhuan*, 263.

30. MacFarquhar and Schoenhals, *Mao's Last Revolution*, 191; Lei Li, *Lishi fengyun zhong de Yu Qiuli*, 95–99.

31. Lei Li, *Lishi fengyun zhong de Yu Qiuli*, 104.

32. Wen Houwen et al., *Kang Shi'en zhuan*.

33. The information in this section is mostly from interviews with former Daqing headquarters staff who wish to retain their anonymity. The interviews were conducted in 2007 and 2008 in Daqing.

34. Red Guard United Team, "Maizang Zhongguo de heluxiaofu guchui de nuli zhuyi," *Zhanbao*, June 10, 1967, 2.

35. MacFarquhar and Schoenhals, *Mao's Last Revolution*, 135.

36. "Daqing hongqi yong fang guangmang."

37. "Oil Sabotage Aggravated by Transport Chaos."

38. It was reported in 1967 that workers had returned their bonuses to the government as an act of "rejecting bribes by the revisionists."

39. Wen Houwen et al., *Kang Shi'en zhuan*, 263.

Chapter 6. Challenging the Daqing Model

1. Chen Donglin, "Wenge qijian guomin jingji zhuangkuang yanjiu shuping."

2. Wen Houwen et al., *Kang Shi'en zhuan*, 293.

3. Iriye, "Chinese-Japanese Relations."

4. Lieberthal and Oksenberg, *Policy Making in China*.

5. Liu Guoguang et al., *Zhongguo shige wunian jihua yanjiu baogao*, 304.

6. Yokoi, "Plant and Technology."

7. Yu Qiuli, "Zhongliu di zhu, li huan kuang lan," 42–63.

8. Chen Donglin, "Qishi niandai qianqi de Zhongguo di erci dui wai yinjin gaochao."

9. Quoted in Spence, *The Search for Modern China*, 607.

10. Chen Zhengxiang, *Zhongguo de shiyou*; Lieberthal and Oksenberg, *Policy Making in China*.

11. Giles, "Liquid Asset."

12. Lieberthal and Oksenberg, *Policy Making in China*, 194.

13. Iriye, "Chinese-Japanese Relations."

14. Chen Zhengxiang, *Zhongguo de shiyou*, 204.

15. During this incident, the ultraleftists, in particular Jiang Qing, expressed criticism of the State Council and the Ministry of Transportation's policy of shipbuilding and ship purchases.

16. Wen Houwen et al., *Kang Shi'en zhuan*, 321–330.

17. Guojia tongji ju, Renkou tongji si, *Zhongguo renkou tongji nianjian*.

18. Liu Guoguang et al., *Zhongguo shige wunian jihua yanjiu baogao*, 300.

19. "Bombard the Headquarters: My Big-Character Poster" was a short document written by Mao on August 5, 1966.

20. The most serious of the Sino-Soviet border clashes—which brought the two communist-ruled countries to the brink of war—occurred in March 1969 in the vicinity of Zhenbao Island on the Ussuri River, also known as Damanskii Island.

21. *Dangdai Zhongguo de chengshi jianshe*, 102.

22. Ibid., 204.

23. Qin Zhijie, "Cong fensan dao jizhong."

24. Lei Li, *Lishi fengyun zhong de Yu Qiuli*, 147–156; Wen Houwen et al., *Kang Shi'en zhuan*, 324–327; Yu Guangyuan, *Wo yi Deng Xiaoping*, 27.

25. Liu Guoguang et al., *Zhongguo shige wunian jihua yanjiu baogao*, 405.

26. Based on interviews.

27. Ibid.

28. Chen Zhengxiang, *Zhongguo de shiyou*, 41.

29. October 3, 1977, Crest 15-Year Program Archive, CIA-RDP99- 00498R000 100050063-0, National Archives at College Park, MA.

30. Lee, *China and Japan*; Francisco, "Petroleum Politics."

31. Bo Yibo, *Ruogan zhongda juece yu shijian de huigu*.

32. "Communiqué of the Third Plenum of the Central Committee," December 1978. *Beijing Review*, October 10, 2008, http://www.bjreview.com.cn/special/third_plenum _17thcpc/txt/2008-10/10/content_156226.htm, accessed December 8, 2015.

33. Xiong Lianghua, *Hongse zhanggui Chen Yun*; Zhao Ziyang, *Prisoner of the State*, 102.

34. From interviews with former Daqing headquarters staff, conducted in 2007 and 2008 in Daqing.

35. Cao Hongtao and Chu Chuanheng, *Dangdai Zhongguo de chengshi jianshe*.

36. Wang Ruoshui, *Hu Yaobang xia tai de beijing*; Li Honglin, *Si zhong zhuyi zai Zhongguo*.

37. See the various articles in *Daqing Zhanbao* in November and December 1978, such as "Shaoshuo konghua, duogan shishi" (Less Empty Talk, More Solid Work), November 17, 1978; "Zhi neng zai fazhan shengchan de jichu shang ganshan shenghuo" (We Can Only Improve Our Livelihood by Developing Production), November 19, 1978; "Gao sihua bixue xian shengchan hou shenghuo" (Production First and Livelihood Second Is Necessary for the Four Modernizations), November 21, 1978, and Zheng Xuansong, "Xian gai lou zai na you, haishi xian na you zai gai lou?" (Multistory Housing First or Oil Production First?), December 6, 1978.

38. Heilongjiang Planning Institute, "Daqing Master Plan (1981–2000)."

39. Heilongjiang Planning Institute, "Daqing Master Plan (2000–2020)."

Epilogue

1. The population increase slowed down during the late 1980s.

2. Chan and Xu, "Urban Population Growth and Urbanization."

3. The estimation is based on the data from Guojia tongji ju, Renkou tongji si, *Zhong-guo renkou tongji nianjian.*

4. For example, Shue, *The Reach of the State.*

5. The growth of irrigated areas began to stagnate with the dissolution of collectives in the countryside. See Naughton, *The Chinese Economy,* 258–260.

6. Small tractors, which were primarily produced by collective enterprises, proved to be more suited to the Chinese situation. Plants producing large tractors, such as that in Luoyang, were established during the First Five-Year Plan, but wide application of mechanical power to the Chinese rural economy occurred much more recently, when the large-scale operations required large tractors and harvester combines.

7. See McMillan et al., "The Impact of China's Economic Reforms"; Huang and Rozelle, "Technological Change."

Bibliography

Unpublished Sources

Andashi shiwei 安达市市委 (Party Committee of Anda City). "Guanyu muqian cheng-shi gongzuo de jige zhuyao wenti de baogao" 关于目前城市工作的几个主要问题的报告 (Report on Several Important Issues regarding Contemporary Urban Work). Octo-ber 1962. Archives of the China Urban Planning and Design Institute, Beijing.

Daqing Agricultural Zoning Office 大庆农业区划办公室. "Daqing Tudi Ziyuan Tuji" 大庆土地资源图集 (Collection of Daqing Agricultural Land Resource Maps). 1987.

Daqing huizhan shixuan 大庆会战诗选 (Selected Poems of Daqing Campaign). Edited by Daqing Campaign Working Committee, 1974. Daqing Archives.

Daqing Railway Gazette Office 大庆铁路修志办公室, ed. Daqing tielu zhi 1897–1984 大庆铁路志, 1897–1984 (Gazetteer of Daqing Railway 1897–1984). 1985. Daqing Mu-nicipal Archives.

Daqing Shiyou Guanliju Caiyou Er Chang 大庆石油管理局采油二厂 (Daqing No. 2 Oil Exaction Factory). "Daqing Caiyou Er Chang: 1964–1989" 大庆采油二厂:1964–1989 (Daqing No. 2 Oil Exaction Factory, Photo Album). Daqing Municipal Archives.

Guojia jianshe weiyuanhui chengshi jianshe bu chengshi gongzuo zu 国家建设委员会城市建设部城市工作组 (National Urban Construction Department of the State Construc-tion Commission, Urban Working Team). "Xi'an shi gongye ji wenjiao jianshe yu chengshi ge xiang fuwu shiye fazhan peihe wenti diaocha yanjiu huibao tigang" 西安市工业及文教建设与城市各项服务事业发展配合问题调查研究汇报提纲 (Survey and Re-search Report Outline of the Xi'an Industrial and Cultural and Educational Construction and Urban Development and Services). 1957. Archives of China Urban Planning and Design Institute, Beijing.

Guojia Jiwei Chengsh Guihua Yanjiuyuan 国家计委城市规划研究院 (Urban Planning and Research Institute, State Planning Commission). "Anda shi chengsh guihua ziliao" 安达市城市规划资料辑要 (Urban Planning Materials of Anda City). 1960. Archives of China Urban Planning and Design Institute, Beijing.

———. "Guanyu Anda shi chengsh jianshe wenti de wenjian" 关于安达市城市建设问题的文件 (Documents regarding Urban Construction in Anda City). October 1962. Archives of China Urban Planning and Design Institute, Beijing.

Heilongjiang Planning Institute 黑龙江省城市规划勘测设计研究院. "Daqing City Master Plan (1981–2000)." 1981. Harbin.

———. "Daqing City Master Plan (2000–2020)." 2000. Harbin.

Huang Li 黄立. "Zhongguo Xiandai Chengshi Guihua Lishi Yanjiu 1949–1965" 中国现代城市规划历史研究：1949–1965 (Historic Research on China Contemporary Urban Planning). PhD dissertation, Wuhan Technology University, 2006.

Xi'an Lanzhou chengshi jianshe qingkuang ji ji dian yijian 西安、兰州城市建设情况及几点意见 (Opinions of the Xi'an and Lanzhou Urban Construction on the Situation). "Chengshi jianshe ju Xi'an xiaozu" 城市建设局西安小组 (The X'ian work team, Bureau of Urban Construction). September 12, 1954, no. 75-1-3. Archives of China Urban Planning and Design Institute, Beijing.

Published Sources

Bernstein, Thomas. *Up to the Mountain and Down to the Village*. New Haven, CT: Yale University Press, 1977.

Bernstein, Thomas, and Hua-Yu Li, eds. *China Learns from the Soviet Union, 1949–Present*. Lanham, MD: Lexington Books, 2010.

Black, Brian. *Petrolia: The Landscape of America's First Oil Boom*. Baltimore: Johns Hopkins University Press, 2000.

Bo Yibo 薄一波. *Ruogan zhongda juece yu shijian de huigui* 若干重大决策与事件的回顾 (Reflections on Certain Important Policies and Experiences). Beijing: Zhonggong zhongyang dang xiao chubanshe, 1991–1993.

Brown, Jeremy. *City versus Countryside in Mao's China: Negotiating the Divide*. New York: Cambridge University Press, 2012.

Buck, David. "Changes in Chinese Urban Planning since 1976." *Third World Planning Review*, no. 6 (1984): 5–20.

———. "Directions in Chinese Urban Planning." *Urbanism Past and Present*, no. 1 (1975–1976): 24–35.

Burr, William, and Jeffrey Richelson. "Whether 'to Strangle the Baby in the Cradle': The United States and the Chinese Nuclear Weapons Programs, 1960–64." *International Security* 25, no. 3 (2000–2001): 54–99.

Cao Hongtao 曹洪涛 and Chu Chuanheng 储传亨, eds. *Dangdai Zhongguo de chengshi jianshe* 当代中国的城市建设 (Contemporary China's Urban Construction). Beijing: Zhongguo shehui kexue chubanshe, 1990.

Cell, Charles P. "The Urban-Rural Contradiction in the Maoist Era: The Pattern of Deurbanization in China." *Comparative Urban Research* 7, no. 3 (1980): 28–69.

Chan, Kam Wing. *Cities with Invisible Walls: Reinterpreting Urbanization in Post-1949 China*. Hong Kong: Oxford University Press, 1994.

Chan, Kam Wing, and Xu Xueqiang. "Urban Population Growth and Urbanization in China since 1949: Reconstructing a Baseline." *China Quarterly*, no. 104 (December 1985): 583–613.

Chan, Leslie W. *The Taching Oilfield: A Maoist Model for Economic Development.* Edited by S. T. Leong. Contemporary China Paper, vol. 8. Canberra: Australian National University Press, 1974.

"Chedi suqing Zhongguo Heluxiaofu jiqi dai li ren zai Daqing kuangqu jianshe shang fan mai de hei huo" 彻底肃清中国赫鲁晓夫及其代理人在大庆矿区建设上贩卖的黑货 (Thoroughly Clear the Smuggled Goods Which Are Being Sold by the Chinese Khrushchev and His Agents Working on Construction in the Daqing Mining District). *Zhanbao* 战报 (Battlefield Newsletter), September 2, 1967.

Chen Donglin 陈东林. "Qishi niandai qianqi de Zhongguo di erci dui wai yinjin gaochao" 七十年代起的中国第二次对外引进高潮 (The Second High Tide of Foreign Imports in the Early 1970s). *Zhonggong dangshi yaniiu* 中共党史研究 (Research on Chinese Communist Party History), no. 2 (1996): 77–82.

———. "Wenge qijian guomin jingji zhuangkuang yanjiu shuping" 文化大革命时期国民经济状况研究述评 (The National Economy in the Cultural Revolution). *Dangdai Zhongguo shi yan jiu* 当代中国史研究 (Research on Contemporary China History), no. 2 (2008): 63–72, 127.

Chen Zhengxiang 陈正祥. *Zhongguo de shiyou* 中国的石油 (Oil in China). Hong Kong: Tiandi tushu youxian gongsi, 1979.

Cheng Chu-yuan. *China's Petroleum Industry: Output Growth and Export Potential.* New York: Praeger, 1976.

Chengzhen juzhuqu guihua shili 城镇居住区规划实例 (Models of Urban Residential District Planning). Beijing: Zhonggong jianzh gongye chubanshe, 1979.

China Academy of Urban Planning 中国城市规划学会, ed. *Wu Shi Nian Hui Mou: Xin Zhongguo De Chengshi Guihua* 五十年回眸：新中国的城市规划 (Fifty Years of Memory: New China's Urban Planning). Beijing: Shang wu yin shu guan, 1999.

China National Statistics Bureau 中国国家统计局. *Zhongguo Tongji Nianjian* 中国统计年鉴 (China Statistical Yearbook). Hong Kong: Hong Kong jing ji dao bao she, 1985.

China Year Book 1936. Shanghai: North China Daily News and Herald, 1936.

Cochran, Sherman. *Encountering Chinese Networks: Western, Japanese, and Chinese Corporations in China, 1880–1937.* Berkeley: University of California Press, 2000.

Cohen, Paul A. *Discovering History in China: American Historical Writing on the Recent Chinese Past.* New York: Columbia University Press, 1984.

Dangdai Zhongguo de chengshi jianshe 当代中国的城市建设 (Contemporary China's Urban Construction). Beijing: Zhongguo shehui kexue chubanshe, 1990.

Dangdai Zhongguo de dizhi shiye 当代中国的地质事业 (Contemporary China's Geology Industry). Beijing: Dangdai zhongguo chubanshe, 1999.

Dangdai Zhongguo de jiben jianshe 当代中国的基本建设 (Capital Construction in Contemporary China). Beijing: Zhongguo shehui kexue chubanshe, 1989.

"Daqing funü zhi" bianzuan weiyuanhui 大庆妇女志编纂委员会, ed. *Daqing funü zhi* 大庆妇女志 (Gazetteer of Daqing Women). Beijing: Fangzhi chubanshe, 1995.

Daqing geming weiyuanhui 大庆革命委员会 (Daqing Revolutionary Committee), ed. *Daqing* 大庆 (Photo Album). Shanghai: Shanghai renmin chubanshe, 1977.

Daqing huizhan gongwei 大庆会战工委 (Daqing Campaign Work Committee). "Guanyu genghao de guanche dang dui jishu ganbu de zhengce jinyibu jiaqiang dui jishu gongzuo lingdao de jueding" 关于更好的贯彻党对技术干部的政策进一步加强对技术工作领导

的决定 (Decision about Further Reinforcing the Leadership of Technical Work and Implementing the Party's Policies for Technical Cadres). *Zhanbao* 战报 (Battlefield Newsletter), August 10, 1962.

Daqing geming weiyuanhui 大庆革命委员会 (Daqing Revolutionary Committee). ed. *Daqing* 大庆 (Photo Album). Shanghai: Renmin chubanshe, 1977.

Daqing gongren pipan zu 大庆工人批判组 (Daqing Workers' Criticizing Team). "Fan Daqing, kan hongqi: Mudi shi cuan dang duoquan" 反大庆 砍红旗 目的是篡党夺权 (The Purpose of Opposing Daqing and Cutting the Red Flag Is to Usurp State Power and Replace the Party). *Renmin ribao* 人民日报 (*People's Daily*), December 23, 1976.

"Daqing hongqi yong fang guangmang" 大庆红旗放光芒 (The Red Flag of Daqing Shines Forever). *Zhanbao* 战报 (Daqing Battlefield Newsletter), June 1, 1968.

Daqing Oil Field Design Institute. "Gandalei fangwu de sheji yu shigong" 干打垒房屋的设计与施工 (The Design and Building of *Gandalei* Houses). *Jianzhu xuebao* 建筑学报 (Architectural Journal), nos. 4–5 (1966): 30–32.

Daqing Shizhi 大庆市志 (Historic Records of Daqing City). Nanjing: Nanjing chubanshe, 1988.

Daqing weiyuanhui, Zhengzhi bu 大庆委员会，政治部 (Daqing CCP Committee, Political Department). *Zhongguo gongren jieji de xianfeng zhanshi: Tieren Wang Jinxi* 中国工人阶级的先锋战士：铁人王进喜 (The Pioneer Warrior of the Chinese Working Class: Iron Man Wang Jinxi). Beijing: Renmin meishu chubanshe, 1977.

Davis, Deborah S., Richard Kraus, Barry Naughton, and Elizabeth J. Perry, eds. *Urban Spaces in Contemporary China: The Potential for Autonomy and Community in Post-Mao China.* New York: Woodrow Wilson Center Press and Cambridge University Press, 1995.

Dong Zhikai 董志凯. *1949–1952 Nin Zhongguo Jingji Feixi* 1949–1952 年中国经济分析 (Analysis of Chinese Economy: 1949–1952). Beijing: Zhongguo shehui kexue chubanshe, 1996.

Dong Zhikai 董志凯 and Wu Jiang 吴江. *Xin Zhongguo gongye de dian jishi: 156 xiang jianshe yanjiu, 1950–2000* 新中国工业的奠基石: 156 项建设研究，1950–2000 (Industry Cornerstone of New China). Guangzhou: Guangdong jingji chubanshe, 2004.

Dui Daqing jingyan de zhengzhi jingjixue kaocha 对大庆经验的政治经济学考察 (A Political Economy Examination of the Experience of the Daqing Model). Beijing: Renmin chubanshe, 1979.

Editorial. "Jian Jue Jiangdi Fei Shengchan Xing Jianshe Biaozhun" 坚决降低非生产性建设标准 (Steadfastly Decreasing the Standard in Non-Production-Related Construction). *People's Daily*, 1955.

Elvin, Mark, and William Skinner, eds. *The Chinese Cities between Two Worlds.* Stanford: Stanford University Press, 1974.

Fang Weizhong 房维中 and Jin Chongji 金冲及, eds. *Li Fuchun zhuan* 李富春传 (Li Fuchun: A Biography). Beijing: Zhongyang wenxian chubanshe, 2001.

Feng Lei 冯磊 and Wang Shouchang 王寿昌. "'Chang qian qu' you meiyou shezhi de biyao?" 厂前区"有没有设置的必要? (Is It Necessary to Establish an "Entrance Square"?). *Renmin ribao* 人民日报 (*People's Daily*), December 7, 1964.

Francisco, Ellennor Grace M. "Petroleum Politics: China and Its National Oil Companies." Master's thesis, Centre international de formation européene, Institut européene, June 2013.

Friedman, Edward, Paul G. Pickowicz, Mark Selden, with Kay Ann Johnson, eds. *Chinese Village, Socialist State.* New Haven, CT: Yale University Press, 1991.

Fuller, M. L., and F. G. Clapp. *The Science of Petroleum.* Vol. 1. London, 1938.

Giles, William E. "Liquid Asset: China's City of Taching Abounds with Ducks, Hogs, and Also Oil." *Wall Street Journal,* July 7, 1975.

Gilliam, James Thomas. "The Standard Oil Company in China, 1863–1933." PhD dissertation, Ohio State University, 1987.

Goldman, Merle, and Roderick MacFarquhar, eds. *The Paradox of China's Post-Mao Reforms.* Cambridge, MA: Harvard University Press, 1999.

Gongren ribao bianjibu 工人日报编辑部 (Editorial Office of the *Worker's Daily*). *Daqing jiashu de geming mofan: Xue Guifang* 大庆家属的革命模范：薛桂芳 (The Revolutionary Model of Daqing Dependents: Xue Guifang). Beijing: Gongren chubanshe, 1966.

"Gongye zhanxian de xianyan hongqi" 工业战线的鲜艳红旗 (Bright Red Banner on the Industrial Front). In *Daqing you tian daibiao zai quanguo gongye xue Daqing huiyi shang de fa yan huibian* 大庆油田代表在全国工业学大庆会议上的发言汇编 (Collection of Speeches by the Daqing Representatives at the National Conference "In Industry, Learn from Daqing"). Beijing: Renmin chubanshe, 1977.

Guojia tongji ju, Renkou tongji si 国家统计局，人口统计司 (National Statistical Bureau, Population Census Department). *Zhongguo renkou tongji nianjian* 中国人口统计年鉴 (China Population Statistics Yearbook). Beijing: Zhongguo zhanwang chubanshe, 1988.

Harvey, David. "From Space to Place and Back Again: Reflections on the Condition of Postmodernity." In *Mapping the Futures,* edited by Jon Bird, Barry Curtis, Tim Putnam, George Robertson, and Lisa Tickner, 3–29. London: Routledge, 1993.

Hershatter, Gail. *The Gender of Memory: Rural Women and China's Collective Past.* Berkeley: University of California Press, 2011.

Ho Ping-ti. *Studies on the Population of China, 1368–1953.* Cambridge, MA: Harvard University Press, 1959.

Hu Feng 胡风. *Hu Feng Wen Ji* 胡风文集 (Works of Hu Feng). Hong Kong: Li sheng shu dian, 1955.

Hu Qiaomu 胡乔木. *Hu Qiaomu huiyi Mao Zedong* 胡乔木回忆毛泽东 (Hu Qiaomu's Recollections about Mao Zedong). Beijing: Renmin chubanshe, 1994.

Hu Xiangyao 胡象尧. "Daqing Kuangqu De Sheji Geming Hua" 大庆矿区的建设过程是设计人员思想革命化的过程 (The Construction of Daqing Mining District Is the Process of Daqing Designer's Revolutionization). *Jian zhu xue bao* 建筑学报 (Architectural Journal), nos. 4–5 (1966): 28–29.

Hu Xiaojing 胡晓菁. "Guanyu Daqing Youtian De Faxian Zhi Zheng" 关于大庆油田的发现之争 (The Debate on the Discovery of Daqing Oil Field). *Kexue Wenhua Pinglun* 科学文化评论 (Science and Culture Review) 3, no. 2 (2006): 66–84.

Hua Lanhong. *Chong Jian Zhongguo: Chengshi Guihua San Shi Nian 1949–1979* (Reconstruct China: Urban Planning in the Thirty Years). Beijing: SDX Joint Publishing, 2006.

Huang Jiamo 黄嘉谟. Jiwu Zhanqian zhi Taiwan Meiwu 甲午战前之台湾煤务 (Pre-1894 Coal Industry in Taiwan). Taiwan: Zhongyang yanjiuyuan, jindaishi yanjiusuo, 1961.

Huang Jikun and Scott Rozelle. "Technological Change: Rediscovering the Engine of Productivity in China's Rural Economy." *Journal of Development Economics* 49, no. 2 (1996): 337–369.

Hutchings, Graham. *Modern China: A Guide to a Century of Change,* Cambridge, MA: Harvard University Press, 2003.

Ip Hung-yok. *Intellectuals in Revolutionary China, 1921–1949: Leaders, Heroes and Sophisticates.* New York: Routledge, 2005.

Iriye, Akira. "Chinese-Japanese Relations, 1945–90." *China Quarterly*, no. 124 (1990): 624–638.

Ivens, Joris, Marceline Loridan-Ivens, and Jean Bigiaoui, directors. *How Yukong Moved the Mountains.* Documentary. 1976.

Jeffrey, Nick. "Administrative/Political Structure for Planning." *Architecture Design* 43, no. 3 (1974): 144–149.

Jiang Weihong 姜维泓 and Zhiqiang Jin 金志强. "Women Yao Xiandai Jian Zhu" 我们要现代建筑 (We Want Modern Architecture). *Jian zhu xue bao* 建筑学报 (Architectural Journal), no. 6 (1956): 56.

"Jianjue jiangdi fei shengchan xing jianshe biaozhun" 坚决降低非生产性建筑的标准 (Steadfastly Lower the Standards in Nonproductive Construction). *People's Daily*, June 19, 1955.

Jianshe bu 建设部 (Ministry of Construction), ed. *Zhongguo chengshi jianshe tongji nianjian 2014* 中国城市建设统计年鉴 2014 (Statistical Yearbook of China Urban Cosntruction). Beijing: Jianzhu gongye chubanshe, 2015.

Jianzhu Gongchengbu Jianzhu Kexue Yanjiuyuan 建筑工程部建筑科学研究院 (Science Academy of Building, Ministry of Building Construction), ed. *Jian Zhu Shi Nian* 建筑十年 (Ten Years of Architecture). Beijing: Jian zhu gong ye chubanshe, 1959.

Jin Chongji 金冲及, ed. *Zhou Enlai zhuan (1949–1976)* 周恩来传, 1898–1949 (Biography of Zhou Enlai [1949–1976]). Beijing: Zhongyang wenxian chubanshe, 1998.

Jin Yihong 金一虹. "Tie guniang zai si kao: Zhongguo wenhua da geming qijian de shehui xingbie yu laodong" 铁姑娘再思考: 中国文化大革命期间的社会性别与劳动 (Iron Girls Revisited: Social Gender and Labor in the Cultural Revolution). *Shehuixue yanjiu* 社会学研究 (Sociology Research), no. 1 (2006): 169–193.

Kirby, William. "Engineers and the State in Modern China." In *Prospects for the Professions in China,* edited by William P. Alford, William Kirby, and Kenneth Winston. New York: Routledge, 2010.

———. *Germany and Republican China.* Stanford: Stanford University Press, 1984.

Kirkby, Richard. "China's Strategy for Development." *Architecture Design* 43, no. 3 (1974): 139–143.

———. *Urbanisation in China: Town and Country in a Developing Economy 1949–2000.* London: Croom Helm, 1985.

Kojima Reiitsu. *Urbanization and Urban Problems in China.* Tokyo: Institute of Developing Economies, 1987.

Kornai, János. *Economics of Shortage.* New York: Elsevier, 1980.

Lee, Chae-Jin. *China and Japan: New Economic Diplomacy.* Stanford, CA: Hoover Institute Press, 1984.

Lefebvre, Henri. *Writings on Cities.* Malden, MA: Blackwell, 1996.

Lei Li 雷厉. *Lishi fenyun zhong de Yu Qiuli* 历史风云中的余秋里 (Yu Qiuli during Historic Events). Beijing: Zhongyang wenxian chubanshe, 2007.

Leung, C. K., and Norton Ginsburg. "China: Urbanization and National Development." In *Department of Geography Research Paper.* Chicago: University of Chicago, 1980.

Lewis, John Wilson, and Litai Xue. *China Builds the Bomb.* Stanford: Stanford University Press, 1988.

Li Changrong et al., eds. *Daqing Funiu Zhi* 大庆妇女志 (The Gazette of Daqing Women). Beijing: Fangzhi chubanshe, 1995.

Li Dongzhang 李懂章, ed. *Er Hao Yuan De Gushi* 二号院的故事 (The Stories of No. 2 Compound). Harbin: Heilongjiang renmin chubanshe, 2006.

Li Fuchun 李富春. "Li xing jieyue, wei wancheng shehuizhuyi jianshe er fen dou: Li Fuchun fu zongli baogao zhaiyao" 厉行节约，为完成社会主义建设而奋斗：李富春副总理报告摘要 (Taking Economic Measures, Fighting for the Fulfillment of Socialist Construction. Abstract of Vice Premier's Report). *People's Daily*, June 21, 1955.

Li Honglin 李洪林. *Si zhong zhuyi zai Zhongguo* 四种主义在中国 (Four Isms in China). Beijing: Shenghuo, Dushu, Xinzhi san lian shu dian, 1988.

Li Jing 李敬. *Li Jing Riji: Daqing Youtian 1960–1966* 李敬日记：大庆油田 1960–1966 (Dairy of Li Jing: Daqing Oil Field 1960–1966). 3 vols. Beijing: Xinhua chubanshe, 2001.

Li Rui 李锐. *Da Yue Jin Qin Li Ji* 大跃进亲历记 (My Personal Experience of the Great Leap Forward). Shanghai: Shanghai yuan dong chubanshe, 1996.

Liang Sicheng 梁思成. "Wo Wei Shen Me Zhe Yang Ai Women De Dang" 我为什么这样爱我们的党 (Why I Loved Our Party So Much). *People's Daily*, July 14, 1957.

Lieberthal, Kenneth, Joyce Kallgren, Roderick MacFarquhar, and Frederic Wakeman Jr., eds. *Perspectives on Modern China: Four Anniversaries.* Armonk, NY: M. E. Sharpe, 1991.

Lieberthal, Kenneth, and Michel Oksenberg. *Policy Making in China: Leaders, Structures, and Processes.* Princeton, NJ: Princeton University Press, 1988.

Lin, Yutang. *My Country and My People.* London: William Heinemann Ltd., 1936.

Ling, H. C. *The Petroleum Industry of the People's Republic of China.* Stanford, CA: Hoover Institution Press, 1975.

Liu Guoguang 刘国光, Zhuoyuan Zhang, Zhikai Dong, and Li Wu, eds. *Zhongguo shige wunian jihua yanjiu baogao* 中国十个五年计划研究报告 (Research Reports on China's Ten Five-Year Plans). Beijing: Renmin chubanshe, 2006.

Liu Shaoqi. "Report on the Work of the Central Committee of the Communist Party of China to the Second Session of the Eighth National Congress." May 5, 1958. In

Second Session of the Eighth National Congress of the Communist Party of China. Peking: Foreign Languages Press, 1958.

"Liushi niandai sanxian jianshe juece wenxian xuanzai, 8.1964–11.1965" 六十年代三线建设决策文献选载, 8.1964–11.1965 (Selected Documents on Decisions on the Third-Front Construction). *Dang de wenxian* 党的文献 (Party Documents), no. 3 (1995): 33–48.

Lu Dingyi 陆定一, ed. *Ma En Lie Si Lun Gongchan Zhuyi Shehui* 马恩列斯论共产主义社会 (Marx, Engels, Lenin and Stalin: Theories of Communist Society). Beijing: Renmin chubanshe, 1958.

Lu Duanfang. *Remaking Chinese Urban Form: Modernity, Scarcity and Space, 1949–2000.* London: Routledge, 2006.

Lü Xiaobo and Elizabeth J. Perry, eds. *Danwei: The Changing Chinese Workplace in Historical and Comparative Perspective.* Armonk, NY: M. E. Sharpe, 1997.

Luard, D. E. T. "The Urban Communes." *China Quarterly* 29 (July–September 1960): 74–79.

Ma, Laurence J. C. "Anti-Urbanism in China." In *Association of American Geographers*, 1976.

———. *Cities and City Planning in the People's Republic of China: An Annotated Bibliography.* Washington, DC: U.S. Department of Housing and Urban Development, Office of Policy Development and Research, 1980.

Ma, Laurence J. C., and Edward Hanten, eds. *Urban Development in Modern China.* Boulder, CO: Westview Press, 1981.

MacFarquhar, Roderick, and Michael Schoenhals. *Mao's Last Revolution.* Cambridge, MA: Belknap Press of Harvard University Press, 2006.

Mackin, Anne. *Americans and Their Land: The House Built on Abundance.* Ann Arbor: University of Michigan Press, 2006.

Mao Tsetung. "Yenan Forum on Literature and Art" (May 1942). In *Selected Works of Mao Tsetung*, vol. 3. Peking: Foreign Languages Press, 1965.

Mao Zedong 毛泽东. *Jianguo yilai Mao Zedong wengao* 建国以来毛泽东文稿 (Mao Zedong's Manuscripts since the Foundation of the PRC). Vol. 7. Beijing: Zhongyang wenxian chubanshe, 1987.

———. *Jianguo yilai Mao Zedong wengao* 建国以来毛泽东文稿 (Mao Zedong's Manuscripts since the Foundation of the PRC). Vol. 11 (1964.1–1965.12). Beijing: Zhongyang wenxian chubanshe, 1996.

———. *Mao Zedong sixiang wan sui* 毛泽东思想万岁 (Long Live Mao Zedong Thought). Beijing: N.p., 1969.

———. *Mao Zedong Zaoqi Wengao* 毛泽东早期文稿 *1912.6–1920.11* (Mao Zedong's Early Manuscripts). Changsha: Hunan chubanshe, 1995.

———. "Report on the Second Plenum of the Seventh China Communist Party Congress." In *Mao Zedong Xuanji* 毛泽东选集 (Selected Works of Mao Zedong). Vol. 4. Beijing: Renmin chubanshe, 1991.

———. *The Secret Speeches of Chairman Mao: From the Hundred Flowers to the Great Leap Forward.* Edited by Roderick MacFarquhar, Timothy Cheek, and Eugene Wu. Harvard Contemporary China Series. Cambridge, MA: Council on East Asian Studies, Harvard University, 1989.

———. *Selected Works of Mao Zedong*. Beijing: Foreign Languages Press, 1975.

McMillan, John, John Whalley, and Zhu Lijing. "The Impact of China's Economic Reforms on Agricultural Productivity Growth." *Journal of Political Economy* 97, no. 4 (1989): 781–807.

Meng Guangshui, Liu Yukui, and Li Xuejun. "Liu Xiufeng." In *Zhonggong dangshi renwu zhuan* 中共党史人物传 (Biographies of CCP Leaders), edited by Qi Wang and Zhiling Chen. Vol. 70. Beijing: Zhongyang wenxian chubanshe, 2000.

Mohr, Anton. *The Oil War*. New York: Harcourt Brace, 1926.

Mok Chung-Yuk. "China's Motor Cities: Industrialization and Urban Development under State Socialism, 1948–90." PhD dissertation, University of Michigan, 1994.

Munro, Donald J. *The Concept of Man in Contemporary China*. Ann Arbor: University of Michigan Press, 1977.

Murphey, Rhoads. "Aspects of Urbanization in Contemporary China: A Revolutionary Model." *The Association of American Geographers* 7 (1975): 165–168.

———. *The Fading of the Maoist Vision: City and Countryside in China's Development*. New York: Methuen, 1980.

National Statistical Bureau 国家统计局. *Zhongguo guding zichan touzi tongji ziliao* 中国固定资产投资资料 (Statistical Data on Contemporary China's Fixed Assets Investment). Beijing: Zhongguo tongji chubanshe, 1986.

Naughton, Barry. *The Chinese Economy: Transitions and Growth*. Cambridge, MA: MIT Press, 2007.

Ni, Ernest. "Distribution of Urban and Rural Population of Mainland China: 1953 and 1958." In *International Population Reports Series*. Washington, DC: U.S. Department of Commerce, 1960.

Niu Ming 牛明. "Liang Sicheng xiansheng shi ruhe wai qu jianzhu yishu he mi zu xingshi de" 梁思成先生如何歪曲建筑艺术和民族形式的 (How Has Mr. Liang Sicheng Distorted Architecture and National Style). *Jian zhu xue bao* (Architectural Journal), no. 2 (1955): 1–9.

"Oil Sabotage Aggravated by Transport Chaos." *China Notes*, no. 253 (February 29) 1968: 5.

Orleans, Leo A. "The Recent Growth of China's Population." *Geographical Review* 49, no. 1 (1959): 43–57.

Pye, Lucian W. *The Spirit of Chinese Politics*. Cambridge, MA: Harvard University Press, 1968.

Qian Bocheng 钱伯城. "Cong Mao Zedong Zhuan Jiang Qi" 从毛泽东传讲起 (Thoughts from the Biography of Mao Zedong). *Wan xiang* 万象, no. 5 (2004): 22–25.

Qin Zhijie 秦志杰. "Cong fensan dao jizhong" 从分散到集中 (From Dispersion to Aggregation). In *Wushinian huimou: Xin Zhongguo de chengshi guihua* 五十年回眸：新中国的城市规划 (Fifty Years Review: City Planning in New China), edited by China Academy of Urban Planning. Beijing: Shangwu yinshuguan, 1999.

Qingshi gao, shihuo zhi (wu) 清史稿 · 食货志[五] (The History of Food Products during the Qing Dynasty, pt. 5).

Salaff, Janet. "The Urban Communes and Anti-City Experiment in Communist China." *China Quarterly* 29 (January–March 1967): 82–110.

Shabad, Theodore. "The Population of China's Cities." *Geographical Review* 49, no. 1 (1959): 38–41.

Shaw, Yu-ming, ed. *Power and Policy in the PRC*. Boulder, CO: Westview Press, 1985.

Shi Mingzheng. "Secondary Sources in Chinese Urban History: A Topical Bibliography." *Journal of Urban History* (November 2000): 114–124.

Shiyou shiren zai Daqing youtian jishi 石油师人在大庆油田纪事 (The Petroleum Army in Daqing Oil Field). Beijing: Shiyou gongye chubanshe, 1997.

Shue, Vivienne. *The Reach of the State: Sketches of the Chinese Body Politic*. Stanford: Stanford University Press, 1988.

Sichuan Sheng Panzhihua Shi Zhi Bianzuan Weiyuanhui (Editing Committee of Sichuan Panzhihua History). *Panzhihua Shi Zhi* (History of Panzhihua). Chengdu: Sichuan kexue jishu chubanshe, 1995.

Solinger, Dorothy. *From Lathes to Looms: China's Industrial Policy in Comparative Perspective, 1979–1982*. Stanford: Stanford University Press, 1991.

———. "The Place of Central City in China's Economic Reform: From Hierarchy to Network." *City & Society*, no. 5 (1991): 23–39.

Solomon, Richard H. *Mao's Revolution and the Chinese Political Culture*. Berkeley: University of California Press, 1971.

Song Liansheng 宋连生. *Gongye xue Daqing shimo* 工业学大庆始末 (From the Beginning to the End of Industry Learning from Daqing). Wuhan: Hubei renmin chubanshe, 2005.

———. *Nong Ye Xue Dazhai Shimo* 农业学大寨始末 (In Agriculture Learn from Dazhai). Wuhan: Hubei renmin chubanshe, 2005.

Spence, Jonathan. *The Search for Modern China*. 2nd ed. New York: Norton, 1999.

State Statistical Bureau, compiler. *China Statistical Yearbook, 1983*. Hong Kong: Economic Information Agency, 1983.

Steiner, Arthur. "Chinese Communist Urban Policy." *American Political Science Review* 44, no. 1 (1950): 47–63.

Sun Sheng Han. "Controlled Urbanization in China." PhD dissertation, Simon Fraser University, 1995.

Sun Weishi 孙维世. *Chu Sheng De Tai Yang* 初升的太阳 (Rising Sun). Tianjin: Hebei renmin chubanshe, 1966.

———. "Daqing tongxin" 大庆通信 (Correspondence from Daqing). *Hong qi* 红旗 (Red Flag), no. 12 (1965): 41–49.

Sun Yutang 孙毓棠. *Zhongguo jindai gongye shi ziliao* 中国近代工业史资料 (Materials on the History of Industry in Modern China). Taibei: Wenhai chubanshe, 1979.

Tamanoi, Mariko Asano, ed. *Crossed Histories: Manchuria in the Age of Empire*. Honolulu: Association for Asian Studies and University of Hawaii Press, 2005.

Tang Wing-Sheng. "Urbanisation in China: A Review of Its Causal Mechanisms and Spatial Relations." *Progress in Planning* 48, no. 1 (1997): 1–65.

Ullman, Morris B. "Cities of Mainland China: 1953 and 1957." In *International Population Reports*. Washington, DC: U.S. Department of Commerce, 1961.

Walder, Andrew W. *Communist Neo-Traditionalism: Work and Authority in Chinese Industry*. Berkeley: University of California Press, 1984.

———, ed. *The Waning of the Communist State: Economic Origins of Political Decline in China and Hungary*. Berkeley: University of California Press, 1995.

Wang Donglin 汪东林. *1949 nian yihou de Liang Shuming* 1949 年以后的梁漱溟 (Liang Shuming after 1949). Beijing: Dang dai Zhongguo chubanshe, 2007.

Wang Huabing 王华彬. "Women dui dongbei mou chang zhuzhaiqu guihua sheji de jiancha" 我们对东北某厂居住区规划设计工作的检查 (Design Critic on the Planning of a Residential District in a Factory of the Northeast). *Jian zhu xue bao* 建筑学报 (Architectural Journal), no. 2 (1955): 20–23.

Wang Jun 王军. *Cheng Ji* 城记 (The Story of a City). Beijing: Shenghuo dushu xinzhi san lian shu dian, 2003.

Wang Mingxia 王明霞 and Xuan Gong 炫公. "Zhou Enlai yi nü Sun Weishi de kanke rensheng" 周恩来义女孙维世的坎坷人生 (The Tough Life of Zhou Enlai's Goddaughter Sun Weishi). *Dang shi zong lan* (Overview of Party History), no. 5 (2008): 24–29.

Wang Ruoshui 王若水. *Hu Yaobang xia tai de beijing: Rendao zhuyi zai Zhongguo de mingyun* 胡耀邦下台的背后：人道主義在中國的命運 (The Background of Hu Yaobang's Stepped Down: The Fate of Humanism in China). Hong Kong: Ming jing chubanshe, 1997.

Wang Shuoke 王硕克 and Jingqi Cheng 程敬琪. "Ju Min Dian Fen Bu Guihua De Yanjiu" 居民点分布规划的研究 (Research on the Distribution of Settlement Points). *Jian zhu xue bao* 建筑学报 (Architectural Journal), no. 1 (1959): 10–14.

Wang Ying 王鹰. "Guan yu xingshi zhuyi fugu zhuyi jianzhu sixiang de jiancha" 关于形式主义复古主义建筑思想的检查 (Criticism toward Formalism and Reactionism in Architecture). *Jian zhu xue bao* 建筑学报 (Architectural Journal), no. 2 (1955): 9–14.

Wasserstrom, Jeffrey N., ed. *Twentieth-Century China: New Approaches*. London: Routledge, 2003.

Wen Houwen 温厚文 et al., eds. *Kang Shi'en zhuan* 康世恩传 (Kang Shi'en: A Biography). Beijing: Dangdai Zhongguo chubanshe, 1998.

Weng Wenhao 翁文灏. *Weng Wenhao wencun: Kexue yu gongyehua* 翁文灏文存：科学与工业 (The Writings of Weng Wenhao: Science and Industrialization). Beijing: Zhonghua shuju, 2009.

Whiting, Allen, and Shih-tsai Sheng. *Sinkiang: Pawn or Pivot*. East Lansing: Michigan State University Press, 1958.

Whyte, Martin King, ed. *One Country, Two Societies: Rural-Urban Inequality in Contemporary China*. Cambridge, MA: Harvard University Press, 2010.

Wu, Shellen Xiao. *Empires of Coal: Fueling China's Entry into the Modern World Order, 1860–1920*. Stanford: Stanford University Press, 2015.

Xia Fei 霞飞. "Mao Zedong zai shangge shiji liushi niandai de yi ge zhongda zhanlue juece" 毛泽东在上个世纪六十年代的一个重大战略决策 (Mao Zedong's Important Strategic Decisions in the 1960s). *Dang shi zong heng* (Party History), no. 1 (2008): 42–45.

Xie Jiarong. "Mining Resources in the Northeast and My Opinions." *Science* 31, no. 11 (1949): 405–430.

Xie Yichun and Frank J. Costa. "Urban Planning in Socialist China: Theory and Practice." *Cities* 10, no. 2 (1993): 103–114.

Xiong Lianghua 熊亮华. *Hongse zhanggui Chen Yun* 红色掌柜陈云 (Red Manager Chen Yun). Wuhan: Hubei renmin chubanshe, 2005.

Xu Zhen 徐振 and Li Weichen 李维諶. "Sun Jingwen" 孙敬文. In *Zhonggong Dang Shi Ren Wu Zhuan* 中共党史人物传 (Biographies of CCP Leaders), edited by Qi Wang and Zhiling Chen. Vol. 75. Beijing: Zhongyang wenxian chubanshe, 2000.

Yan Zixiang 闫子祥. "Zhongguo Jianzhu Xuehui Di Si Jie Huiyi Shang De Jianghua" 中国建筑学会第四届代表大会及学术会议总结发言 (Speech on the 4th Conference of China Architect Society). *Jian zhu xue bao* 建筑学报 (Architectural Journal), nos. 4–5 (1966): 21–23.

Yang Dali. *Calamity and Reform in China: State, Rural Society, and Institutional Change since the Great Leap Famine.* Stanford: Stanford University Press, 1996.

Yao Mingli 姚明理. "Daqing De Guoqu Xianzai Yu Weilai" 大庆的过去现在与未来 (The Past, Present, and Future of Daqing). *Zhongguo shiyou* 中国石油 (China Oil) 2, no. 1 (1985): 43.

Ye Weili with Ma Xiaodong. *Growing Up in the People's Republic: Conversations between Two Daughters of China's Revolution.* New York: Palgrave Macmillan, 2005.

Yeh, Anthony Gar-on, ed. *Reference Materials on Urban Development and Planning in China.* Working Paper No. 44. Hong Kong: University of Hong Kong, Centre of Urban Planning and Environmental Management, 1989.

Yergin, Daniel. *The Prize: The Epic Quest for Oil, Money and Power.* New York: Free Press, 2008.

Yokoi, Yoichi. "Plant and Technology: Contracts and the Changing Pattern of Economic Interdependence between China and Japan." *China Quarterly*, no. 124 (December 1990): 694–714.

Young, Louise. *Japan's Total Empire: Manchuria and the Culture of Wartime Imperialism.* Berkeley: University of California Press, 1999.

Yu Guangyuan 于光远. *Wo yi Deng Xiaoping* 我忆鄧小平 (My Memories of Deng Xiaoping). Hong Kong: Shidai guoji chuban yu xian gong si, 2005.

Yu Qiuli 余秋里. *Yu Qiuli huiyilu* 余秋里回忆录 (The Memoir of Yu Qiuli). Beijing: Jiefangjun chubanshe, 1996.

———. "Zhongliu di zhu, li huan kuang lan" 中流砥柱，力换狂澜 (The Tower of Strength Who Stops the Rot). In *Women de Zhou zongli* 我們的周总理 (Our Premier Zhou), edited by "Wo men de Zhou zong li" bian ji zu. Beijing: Zhongyang Wenxian chubanshe, 1990.

Yuan Mu 袁木 and Fan Rongkang 范荣康. "Daqing Jingshen Daqing Ren" 大庆精神, 大庆人 (Daqing Spirit, Daqing People). *People's Daily*, April 20, 1964.

"Zai Di San Jie Quanguo Renmin Daibiao Dahui Di Yi Ci Huiyi Shang Zhou Enlai Zuo Zhengfu Gongzuo Baogao" 在第三届全国人民代表大会第一次会议上的周恩来政府工作报告 (Zhou Enlai's Government Work Report on the First Session of the Third People's Congress). *People's Daily*, December 31, 1964.

Zha Binhua 查滨华. "Jiehe Gongnong, Gaibian Sixiang" 结合工农，改变思想 (Integrating with Workers and Peasants to Change Thoughts). *Jian zhu xue bao* 建筑学报 (Architectural Journal), nos. 4–5 (1966): 33–34.

Zhao Ziyang. *Prisoner of the State: The Secret Journal of Zhao Ziyang*. New York: Simon and Schuster, 2009.

Zheng Youkui 郑友揆, Cheng Linsun 程麟荪, and Zhang Chuanhong 张传洪. *Jiu Zhongguo de ziyuan weiyuanhui (1932–1949): Shishi yu pingjia* 旧中国的资源委员会 [1932–1949]：史实与评价 (The National Resources Commission of Old China [1932–1949]: Facts and Comments). Shanghai: Shanghai shehui kexueyuan chubanshe, 1991.

Zhongguo gongchandang Daqing weiyuanhui zheng zhi bu 中国共产党大庆委员会政治部 (Daqing CCP Committee, Department of Politics). *Zhongguo Gongren Jieji De Xianfeng Zhanshi: Tieren Wang Jinxi* 中国工人阶级的先锋战士：铁人王进喜 (The Pioneer Warrior of Chinese Working Class: Iron Man Wang Jinxi). Beijing: Renmin meishu chubanshe, 1977.

Zhou Buyi 周卜颐. "Cong Beijing Ji Zuo Xin Jianzhu De Fenxi Tan Wo Guo De Jianzhu Chuangzuo" 从北京几座新建筑的分析谈我国的建筑创作 (Analysis of Our Architecture Production Based on Several New Buildings in Beijing). *Jian zhu xue bao* 建筑学报 (Architectural Journal), no. 3 (1957): 41–50.

Index

Page numbers for maps and figures are in italics.

Harvard-Yenching Institute Monograph Series

(titles now in print)